TEACHER'S GUIDE

Connected Mathematics 2

Data Distributions

Describing Variability and Comparing Groups

Glenda Lappan
James T. Fey
William M. Fitzgerald
Susan N. Friel
Elizabeth Difanis Phillips

 PEARSON

Boston, Massachusetts · Glenview, Illinois · Shoreview, Minnesota · Upper Saddle River, New Jersey

Connected Mathematics™ was developed at Michigan State University with financial support from the Michigan State University Office of the Provost, Computing and Technology, and the College of Natural Science.

 This material is based upon work supported by the National Science Foundation under Grant No. MDR 9150217 and Grant No. ESI 9986372. Opinions expressed are those of the authors and not necessarily those of the Foundation.

The Michigan State University authors and administration have agreed that all MSU royalties arising from this publication will be devoted to purposes supported by the Department of Mathematics and the MSU Mathematics Enrichment Fund.

Acknowledgments appear on page 224, which constitutes an extension of this copyright page.
Acknowledgments for the student pages appear on student page 105, which constitutes an extension of this copyright page.

13-digit ISBN 978-0-13-366200-9
10-digit ISBN 0-13-366200-4
1 2 3 4 5 6 7 8 9 10   11 10 09 08

Authors of Connected Mathematics

(from left to right) Glenda Lappan, Betty Phillips, Susan Friel, Bill Fitzgerald, Jim Fey

Glenda Lappan is a University Distinguished Professor in the Department of Mathematics at Michigan State University. Her research and development interests are in the connected areas of students' learning of mathematics and mathematics teachers' professional growth and change related to the development and enactment of K–12 curriculum materials.

James T. Fey is a Professor of Curriculum and Instruction and Mathematics at the University of Maryland. His consistent professional interest has been development and research focused on curriculum materials that engage middle and high school students in problem-based collaborative investigations of mathematical ideas and their applications.

William M. Fitzgerald (*Deceased*) was a Professor in the Department of Mathematics at Michigan State University. His early research was on the use of concrete materials in supporting student learning and led to the development of teaching materials for laboratory environments. Later he helped develop a teaching model to support student experimentation with mathematics.

Susan N. Friel is a Professor of Mathematics Education in the School of Education at the University of North Carolina at Chapel Hill. Her research interests focus on statistics education for middle-grade students and, more broadly, on teachers' professional development and growth in teaching mathematics K–8.

Elizabeth Difanis Phillips is a Senior Academic Specialist in the Mathematics Department of Michigan State University. She is interested in teaching and learning mathematics for both teachers and students. These interests have led to curriculum and professional development projects at the middle school and high school levels, as well as projects related to the teaching and learning of algebra across the grades.

CMP2 Development Staff

Teacher Collaborator in Residence
Yvonne Grant
Michigan State University

Production and Field Site Manager
Lisa Keller
Michigan State University

Administrative Assistant
Judith Martus Miller
Michigan State University

Technical and Editorial Support
Brin Keller, Peter Lappan, Jim Laser,
Michael Masterson, Stacey Miceli

Assessment Team
June Bailey and Debra Sobko (Apollo Middle School, Rochester, New York), George Bright (University of North Carolina, Greensboro), Gwen Ranzau Campbell (Sunrise Park Middle School, White Bear Lake, Minnesota), Holly DeRosia, Kathy Dole, and Teri Keusch (Portland Middle School, Portland, Michigan), Mary Beth Schmitt (Traverse City East Junior High School, Traverse City, Michigan), Genni Steele (Central Middle School, White Bear Lake, Minnesota), Jacqueline Stewart (Okemos, Michigan), Elizabeth Tye (Magnolia Junior High School, Magnolia, Arkansas)

Development Assistants
At Lansing Community College *Undergraduate Assistant:* James Brinegar

At Michigan State University *Graduate Assistants:* Dawn Berk, Emily Bouck, Bulent Buyukbozkirli, Kuo-Liang Chang, Christopher Danielson, Srinivasa Dharmavaram, Deb Johanning, Wesley Kretzschmar, Kelly Rivette, Sarah Sword, Tat Ming Sze, Marie Turini, Jeffrey Wanko; *Undergraduate Assistants:* Daniel Briggs, Jeffrey Chapin, Jade Corsé, Elisha Hardy, Alisha Harold, Elizabeth Keusch, Julia Letoutchaia, Karen Loeffler, Brian Oliver, Carl Oliver, Evonne Pedawi, Lauren Rebrovich

At the University of Maryland *Graduate Assistants:* Kim Harris Bethea, Kara Karch

At the University of North Carolina (Chapel Hill) *Graduate Assistants:* Mark Ellis, Trista Stearns; *Undergraduate Assistant:* Daniel Smith

Advisory Board for CMP2

Thomas Banchoff
Professor of Mathematics
Brown University
Providence, Rhode Island

Anne Bartel
Mathematics Coordinator
Minneapolis Public Schools
Minneapolis, Minnesota

Hyman Bass
Professor of Mathematics
University of Michigan
Ann Arbor, Michigan

Joan Ferrini-Mundy
Associate Dean of the College of
Natural Science; Professor
Michigan State University
East Lansing, Michigan

James Hiebert
Professor
University of Delaware
Newark, Delaware

Susan Hudson Hull
Charles A. Dana Center
University of Texas
Austin, Texas

Michele Luke
Mathematics Curriculum
Coordinator
West Junior High
Minnetonka, Minnesota

Kay McClain
Assistant Professor of
Mathematics Education
Vanderbilt University
Nashville, Tennessee

Edward Silver
Professor; Chair of Educational
Studies
University of Michigan
Ann Arbor, Michigan

Judith Sowder
Professor Emerita
San Diego State University
San Diego, California

Lisa Usher
Mathematics Resource Teacher
California Academy of
Mathematics and Science
San Pedro, California

Field Test Sites for CMP2

During the development of the revised edition of *Connected Mathematics* (CMP2), more than 100 classroom teachers have field-tested materials at 49 school sites in 12 states and the District of Columbia. This classroom testing occurred over three academic years (2001 through 2004), allowing careful study of the effectiveness of each of the 24 units that comprise the program. A special thanks to the students and teachers at these pilot schools.

Arkansas

Magnolia Public Schools
Kittena Bell*, Judith Trowell*; *Central Elementary School:* Maxine Broom, Betty Eddy, Tiffany Fallin, Bonnie Flurry, Carolyn Monk, Elizabeth Tye; *Magnolia Junior High School:* Monique Bryan, Ginger Cook, David Graham, Shelby Lamkin

Colorado

Boulder Public Schools
Nevin Platt Middle School: Judith Koenig

St. Vrain Valley School District, Longmont
Westview Middle School: Colleen Beyer, Kitty Canupp, Ellie Decker*, Peggy McCarthy, Tanya deNobrega, Cindy Payne, Ericka Pilon, Andrew Roberts

District of Columbia
Capitol Hill Day School: Ann Lawrence

Georgia

University of Georgia, Athens
Brad Findell

Madison Public Schools
Morgan County Middle School: Renee Burgdorf, Lynn Harris, Nancy Kurtz, Carolyn Stewart

Maine

Falmouth Public Schools
Falmouth Middle School: Donna Erikson, Joyce Hebert, Paula Hodgkins, Rick Hogan, David Legere, Cynthia Martin, Barbara Stiles, Shawn Towle*

Michigan

Portland Public Schools
Portland Middle School: Mark Braun, Holly DeRosia, Kathy Dole*, Angie Foote, Teri Keusch, Tammi Wardwell

Traverse City Area Public Schools
Bertha Vos Elementary: Kristin Sak; *Central Grade School:* Michelle Clark; Jody Meyers; *Eastern Elementary:* Karrie Tufts; *Interlochen Elementary:* Mary McGee-Cullen; *Long Lake Elementary:* Julie Faulkner*, Charlie Maxbauer, Katherine Sleder; *Norris Elementary:* Hope Slanaker; *Oak Park Elementary:* Jessica Steed; *Traverse Heights Elementary:* Jennifer Wolfert; *Westwoods Elementary:* Nancy Conn; *Old Mission Peninsula School:* Deb Larimer; *Traverse City East Junior High:* Ivanka Berkshire, Ruthanne Kladder, Jan Palkowski, Jane Peterson, Mary Beth Schmitt; *Traverse City West Junior High:* Dan Fouch*, Ray Fouch

Sturgis Public Schools
Sturgis Middle School: Ellen Eisele

Minnesota

Burnsville School District 191
Hidden Valley Elementary: Stephanie Cin, Jane McDevitt

Hopkins School District 270
Alice Smith Elementary: Sandra Cowing, Kathleen Gustafson, Martha Mason, Scott Stillman; *Eisenhower Elementary:* Chad Bellig, Patrick Berger, Nancy Glades, Kye Johnson, Shane Wasserman, Victoria Wilson; *Gatewood Elementary:* Sarah Ham, Julie Kloos, Janine Pung, Larry Wade; *Glen Lake Elementary:* Jacqueline Cramer, Kathy Hering, Cecelia Morris,

Robb Trenda; *Katherine Curren Elementary:* Diane Bancroft, Sue DeWit, John Wilson; *L. H. Tanglen Elementary:* Kevin Athmann, Lisa Becker, Mary LaBelle, Kathy Rezac, Roberta Severson; *Meadowbrook Elementary:* Jan Gauger, Hildy Shank, Jessica Zimmerman; *North Junior High:* Laurel Hahn, Kristin Lee, Jodi Markuson, Bruce Mestemacher, Laurel Miller, Bonnie Rinker, Jeannine Salzer, Sarah Shafer, Cam Stottler; *West Junior High:* Alicia Beebe, Kristie Earl, Nobu Fujii, Pam Georgetti, Susan Gilbert, Regina Nelson Johnson, Debra Lindstrom, Michele Luke*, Jon Sorensen

Minneapolis School District 1
Ann Sullivan K–8 School: Bronwyn Collins; Anne Bartel* (Curriculum and Instruction Office)

Wayzata School District 284
Central Middle School: Sarajane Myers, Dan Nielsen, Tanya Ravnholdt

White Bear Lake School District 624
Central Middle School: Amy Jorgenson, Michelle Reich, Brenda Sammon

New York

New York City Public Schools
IS 89: Yelena Aynbinder, Chi-Man Ng, Nina Rapaport, Joel Spengler, Phyllis Tam*, Brent Wyso; *Wagner Middle School:* Jason Appel, Intissar Fernandez, Yee Gee Get, Richard Goldstein, Irving Marcus, Sue Norton, Bernadita Owens, Jennifer Rehn*, Kevin Yuhas

---

* indicates a Field Test Site Coordinator

Ohio

Talawanda School District, Oxford
Talawanda Middle School: Teresa Abrams, Larry Brock, Heather Brosey, Julie Churchman, Monna Even, Karen Fitch, Bob George, Amanda Klee, Pat Meade, Sandy Montgomery, Barbara Sherman, Lauren Steidl

Miami University
Jeffrey Wanko*

Springfield Public Schools
Rockway School: Jim Mamer

Pennsylvania

Pittsburgh Public Schools
Kenneth Labuskes, Marianne O'Connor, Mary Lynn Raith*; *Arthur J. Rooney Middle School:* David Hairston, Stamatina Mousetis, Alfredo Zangaro; *Frick International Studies Academy:* Suzanne Berry, Janet Falkowski, Constance Finseth, Romika Hodge, Frank Machi; *Reizenstein Middle School:* Jeff Baldwin, James Brautigam, Lorena Burnett, Glen Cobbett, Michael Jordan, Margaret Lazur, Tamar McPherson, Melissa Munnell, Holly Neely, Ingrid Reed, Dennis Reft

Texas

Austin Independent School District
Bedichek Middle School: Lisa Brown, Jennifer Glasscock, Vicki Massey

El Paso Independent School District
Cordova Middle School: Armando Aguirre, Anneliesa Durkes, Sylvia Guzman, Pat Holguin*, William Holguin, Nancy Nava, Laura Orozco, Michelle Peña, Roberta Rosen, Patsy Smith, Jeremy Wolf

Plano Independent School District
Patt Henry, James Wohlgehagen*; *Frankford Middle School:* Mandy Baker, Cheryl Butsch, Amy Dudley, Betsy Eshelman, Janet Greene, Cort Haynes, Kathy Letchworth, Kay Marshall, Kelly McCants, Amy Reck, Judy Scott, Syndy Snyder, Lisa Wang; *Wilson Middle School:* Darcie Bane, Amanda Bedenko, Whitney Evans, Tonelli Hatley, Sarah (Becky) Higgs, Kelly Johnston, Rebecca McElligott, Kay Neuse, Cheri Slocum, Kelli Straight

Washington

Evergreen School District
Shahala Middle School: Nicole Abrahamsen, Terry Coon*, Carey Doyle, Sheryl Drechsler, George Gemma, Gina Helland, Amy Hilario, Darla Lidyard, Sean McCarthy, Tilly Meyer, Willow Nuewelt, Todd Parsons, Brian Pederson, Stan Posey, Shawn Scott, Craig Sjoberg, Lynette Sundstrom, Charles Switzer, Luke Youngblood

Wisconsin

Beaver Dam Unified School District
Beaver Dam Middle School: Jim Braemer, Jeanne Frick, Jessica Greatens, Barbara Link, Dennis McCormick, Karen Michels, Nancy Nichols*, Nancy Palm, Shelly Stelsel, Susan Wiggins

---

* indicates a Field Test Site Coordinator

Reviews of CMP to Guide Development of CMP2

Before writing for CMP2 began or field tests were conducted, the first edition of *Connected Mathematics* was submitted to the mathematics faculties of school districts from many parts of the country and to 80 individual reviewers for extensive comments.

School District Survey Reviews of CMP

Arizona
Madison School District #38 (Phoenix)

Arkansas
Cabot School District, Little Rock School District, Magnolia School District

California
Los Angeles Unified School District

Colorado
St. Vrain Valley School District (Longmont)

Florida
Leon County Schools (Tallahassee)

Illinois
School District #21 (Wheeling)

Indiana
Joseph L. Block Junior High (East Chicago)

Kentucky
Fayette County Public Schools (Lexington)

Maine
Selection of Schools

Massachusetts
Selection of Schools

Michigan
Sparta Area Schools

Minnesota
Hopkins School District

Texas
Austin Independent School District, The El Paso Collaborative for Academic Excellence, Plano Independent School District

Wisconsin
Platteville Middle School

Individual Reviewers of CMP

Arkansas
Deborah Cramer; Robby Frizzell (*Taylor*); Lowell Lynde (*University of Arkansas, Monticello*); Leigh Manzer (*Norfork*); Lynne Roberts (*Emerson High School, Emerson*); Tony Timms (*Cabot Public Schools*); Judith Trowell (*Arkansas Department of Higher Education*)

California
José Alcantar (*Gilroy*); Eugenie Belcher (*Gilroy*); Marian Pasternack (*Lowman M. S. T. Center, North Hollywood*); Susana Pezoa (*San Jose*); Todd Rabusin (*Hollister*); Margaret Siegfried (*Ocala Middle School, San Jose*); Polly Underwood (*Ocala Middle School, San Jose*)

Colorado
Janeane Golliher (*St. Vrain Valley School District, Longmont*); Judith Koenig (*Nevin Platt Middle School, Boulder*)

Florida
Paige Loggins (*Swift Creek Middle School, Tallahassee*)

Illinois
Jan Robinson (*School District #21, Wheeling*)

Indiana
Frances Jackson (*Joseph L. Block Junior High, East Chicago*)

Kentucky
Natalee Feese (*Fayette County Public Schools, Lexington*)

Maine
Betsy Berry (*Maine Math & Science Alliance, Augusta*)

Maryland
Joseph Gagnon (*University of Maryland, College Park*); Paula Maccini (*University of Maryland, College Park*)

Massachusetts
George Cobb (*Mt. Holyoke College, South Hadley*); Cliff Kanold (*University of Massachusetts, Amherst*)

Michigan
Mary Bouck (*Farwell Area Schools*); Carol Dorer (*Slauson Middle School, Ann Arbor*); Carrie Heaney (*Forsythe Middle School, Ann Arbor*); Ellen Hopkins (*Clague Middle School, Ann Arbor*); Teri Keusch (*Portland Middle School, Portland*); Valerie Mills (*Oakland Schools, Waterford*); Mary Beth Schmitt (*Traverse City East Junior High, Traverse City*); Jack Smith (*Michigan State University, East Lansing*); Rebecca Spencer (*Sparta Middle School, Sparta*); Ann Marie Nicoll Turner (*Tappan Middle School, Ann Arbor*); Scott Turner (*Scarlett Middle School, Ann Arbor*)

Minnesota
Margarita Alvarez (*Olson Middle School, Minneapolis*); Jane Amundson (*Nicollet Junior High, Burnsville*); Anne Bartel (*Minneapolis Public Schools*); Gwen Ranzau Campbell (*Sunrise Park Middle School, White Bear Lake*); Stephanie Cin (*Hidden Valley Elementary, Burnsville*); Joan Garfield (*University of Minnesota, Minneapolis*); Gretchen Hall (*Richfield Middle School, Richfield*); Jennifer Larson (*Olson Middle School, Minneapolis*); Michele Luke (*West Junior High, Minnetonka*); Jeni Meyer (*Richfield Junior High, Richfield*); Judy Pfingsten (*Inver Grove Heights Middle School, Inver Grove Heights*); Sarah Shafer (*North Junior High, Minnetonka*); Genni Steele (*Central Middle School, White Bear Lake*); Victoria Wilson (*Eisenhower Elementary, Hopkins*); Paul Zorn (*St. Olaf College, Northfield*)

New York
Debra Altenau-Bartolino (*Greenwich Village Middle School, New York*); Doug Clements (*University of Buffalo*); Francis Curcio (*New York University, New York*); Christine Dorosh (*Clinton School for Writers, Brooklyn*); Jennifer Rehn (*East Side Middle School, New York*); Phyllis Tam (*IS 89 Lab School, New York*); Marie Turini (*Louis Armstrong Middle School, New York*); Lucy West (*Community School District 2, New York*); Monica Witt (*Simon Baruch Intermediate School 104, New York*)

Pennsylvania
Robert Aglietti (*Pittsburgh*); Sharon Mihalich (*Freeport*); Jennifer Plumb (*South Hills Middle School, Pittsburgh*); Mary Lynn Raith (*Pittsburgh Public Schools*)

Texas
Michelle Bittick (*Austin Independent School District*); Margaret Cregg (*Plano Independent School District*); Sheila Cunningham (*Klein Independent School District*); Judy Hill (*Austin Independent School District*); Patricia Holguin (*El Paso Independent School District*); Bonnie McNemar (*Arlington*); Kay Neuse (*Plano Independent School District*); Joyce Polanco (*Austin Independent School District*); Marge Ramirez (*University of Texas at El Paso*); Pat Rossman (*Baker Campus, Austin*); Cindy Schimek (*Houston*); Cynthia Schneider (*Charles A. Dana Center, University of Texas at Austin*); Uri Treisman (*Charles A. Dana Center, University of Texas at Austin*); Jacqueline Weilmuenster (*Grapevine-Colleyville Independent School District*); LuAnn Weynand (*San Antonio*); Carmen Whitman (*Austin Independent School District*); James Wohlgehagen (*Plano Independent School District*)

Washington
Ramesh Gangolli (*University of Washington, Seattle*)

Wisconsin
Susan Lamon (*Marquette University, Hales Corner*); Steve Reinhart (*retired, Chippewa Falls Middle School, Eau Claire*)

Data Distributions
Describing Variability and Comparing Groups

The Student Edition pages for the Unit Opener follow page 18.

Data Distributions
Describing Variability and Comparing Groups

Goals of the Unit

- Apply the process of statistical investigation to pose questions, to identify ways data are collected, and to determine strategies for analyzing data in order to answer the questions posed

- Recognize that variability occurs whenever data are collected

- Describe the variability in the distribution of a given data set

- Identify sources of variability, including natural variability and variability that results from errors in measurement

- Determine whether to use the mean or median to describe a distribution

- Use the shape of a distribution to estimate the location of the mean and the median

- Use a variety of representations, including tables, bar graphs, and line plots, to display distributions

- Understand and use counts or percents to report frequencies of occurrence of data

- Compare the distributions of data sets using their centers (mean, median, and mode), variability (outliers and range), and shape (clusters and gaps)

- Decide if a difference among data values or summary measures matters

- Develop and use strategies to compare data sets to solve problems

Developing Students' Mathematical Habits

The overall goal of *Connected Mathematics* is to help students develop sound mathematical habits. Through their work in this and other data units, students learn important questions to ask themselves about any situation involving data analysis, such as:

- *Is there anything surprising about the data and their distribution?*

- *Where do the data cluster in the distribution?*

- *How can I use the mean or median and range to help me understand and describe a data distribution?*

- *What strategies can I use to compare two different data sets?*

Mathematics of the Unit

Pearson Prentice Hall Professional Development

Overview

This unit is a new unit for CMP2. It has four investigations that focus students' attention on distributions of data, variability, measures of center, and comparing data sets. The big ideas of the unit are addressed in more detail in the Mathematics Background.

Exploring statistics as a process of data investigation involves a set of four interrelated components:

- Posing the question: formulating the key question(s) to explore and deciding what data to collect to address the question(s)

- Collecting the data: deciding how to collect the data as well as actually collecting it

- Analyzing the data: organizing, representing, summarizing, and describing the data and looking for patterns in the data

- Interpreting the results: predicting, comparing, and identifying relationships and using the results from the analyses to make decisions about the original question(s)

This dynamic process often involves moving back and forth among the four interconnected components—for example, collecting the data and, after some analysis, deciding to refine the question and gather additional data.

In many of the problems, data are provided. We assume students have had prior experience collecting data as part of statistical investigations. If they have not, we encourage you to have your class collect their own data for some of the problems. The problems can be applied either to the data provided or to data collected by students.

Even if your students have already had experience collecting data, they may be interested in investigating data about their class. Students' interest is often enhanced if they have the opportunity to use the process of data investigation to explore questions that are of interest to them. Keep in mind that collecting data is time consuming, so carefully choose the problems for which you will have students generate data.

Problems in contexts are used to help students informally reason about the mathematics of the unit. The problems are deliberately sequenced to provide scaffolding for more challenging problems. Contexts, representations, and describing variability help students develop statistical reasoning.

Summary of Investigations

Investigation 1
Making Sense of Variability

The first investigation engages students in looking at the variability in data distributions using a variety of contexts involving different kinds of data. Students focus on finding ways to describe distributions. They begin by examining the distribution of colors found in M&M™ candies; there is a consistent pattern that was established by the company making the candies. To what extent is this pattern evident when one bag or many bags are opened and colors counted? Next, students look at numbers of immigrants coming to the United States. They look at two ways to report frequencies: as counts and as percents, or relative frequencies. Finally, students consider measurement error in data. They do this in the context of measuring head sizes to discover what size caps to order.

Investigation 2
Making Sense of Measures of Center

This investigation deepens students' understanding of the three measures of center, their use, and their relationships to shapes of distributions. The mean is reviewed and modeled both as an "equal share" and as a "balance point" in a distribution. The occurrence of repeated values in distributions is examined, and its impact on determining the mode and the location of the median is explored. Students consider a variety of contexts, each represented visually with a graph, and make decisions about the best way to respond to questions using measures of center. Finally, students investigate how changing data values in a distribution—and, consequently, the shape of the distribution—impacts the location of the mean or the median.

Investigation 3

Comparing Distributions: Equal Numbers of Data Values

Students compare data sets with equal numbers of data values. This permits comparisons of frequencies reported using counts. Students explore the data from a computer reaction time game used by a middle-grades class. The data for each person are "scores" (time in seconds to respond) in five trials. Students develop ways to compare individuals and then a group of 40 students. Eventually, they are asked to use these data to make recommendations to a video game designer about the time she needs to give students to react to objects that appear on the screen in her video game.

Investigation 4

Comparing Distributions: Unequal Numbers of Data Values

Students explore comparing data sets with unequal numbers of data values. They use relative frequencies expressed as percents rather than counts. The context is a data set of 150 roller coasters—100 steel coasters and 50 wood coasters. The question involves comparing which coasters are faster, steel or wood. Once that is determined, students look at what other attributes might influence speed, and then they do some informal work with covariation and the use of scatter plots.

Mathematics Background

In *Data Distributions,* several big ideas about statistics are explored. The sections that follow highlight these important ideas. On the next page is a concept map that provides some insights into the overall relationships among these and other important concepts.

The Process of Statistical Investigation (Doing Meaningful Statistics)

This process involves four parts: pose a question, collect the data, analyze the data, and interpret the analysis in light of the question. When completed, students need to communicate the results.

Students need to think about the process of statistical investigation whether they are collecting their own data or are using data provided for them. When students are involved in a problem in which

they do their own data collection, following through with the process of statistical investigation is a natural part of the task. When students are analyzing a data set they have not collected, it is important to help them first understand the data. You can do this by having students ask themselves the same kinds of questions they would ask if they were carrying out the data collection process themselves. Questions such as these are helpful:

- *What question was asked that resulted in these data being collected?*
- *How do you think the data were collected?*
- *Why are these data represented using this kind of presentation?*
- *What are ways to describe the data distribution?*

In *Data Distributions,* there are several data sets that are provided for your use. The benefit of using provided data is that you know the content that can be developed by using these data sets. However, if you have time, many of the tasks in *Data Distributions* lend themselves to having your students collect their own data, e.g., counting colors of M&M candies in small bags of M&Ms, collecting data about the numbers of grams of sugar in different cereals on different shelves in the local supermarket, and trying out a reaction time game. Students can analyze their own data for some of the problems in this unit in addition to analyzing the data provided.

Distinguishing Different Types of Data

Attributes and Values

To avoid any confusion with prior algebra work, in *Data Distributions* we refer to attributes (rather than variables) and the values associated with those attributes. An *attribute* is a name for a particular characteristic of a person, place, or thing about which data is being collected. For example, we can have the attribute of "red" to characterize a color of some M&M candies or the attribute of "Fastest Time" to characterize the fastest time taken in five trials reported from a computer reaction time game. *Values* are the data that occur for each individual case of an attribute—that is, the number of red candies recorded for the attribute "red" from one bag of M&M candies or the time in seconds recorded for the attribute "Fastest Time" for one student who played the computer reaction time game.

Doing Meaningful Statistics—Central Statistical Ideas for *Data Distributions*

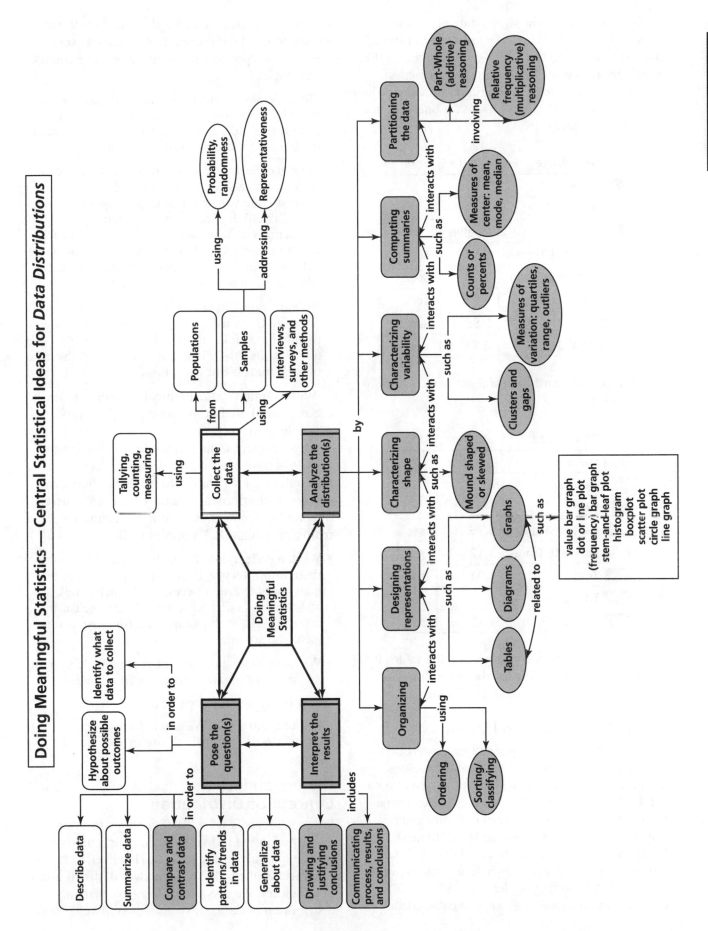

The data card below shows data about one student, Diana. There are a number of different attribute names on the left that are related to the times reported in playing a computer reaction time game five times. On the right, there is a value for each of these attributes. Diana is one case in a data set of 40 cases.

Attribute	Value	Unit
Name	Diana	
Gender	F	
Age	twelve	
Fastest Time	0.59	sec
Slowest Time	1.08	sec
Trial 1	1.02	sec
Trial 2	0.83	sec
Trial 3	0.73	sec

A second data card for a student named Andrew is also shown.

Attribute	Value	Unit
Name	Andrew	
Gender	M	
Age	eleven	
Fastest Time	0.76	sec
Slowest Time	1.12	sec
Trial 1	1.01	sec
Trial 2	0.8	sec
Trial 3	1.12	sec

Each case has the same attributes; the values for the attributes will be different because each case shown in a data card is about a different student.

Categorical or Numerical Values

Questions in real life often result in answers that involve one of two general kinds of data values: categorical or numerical. Knowing the type of data values that an attribute has helps us to determine the most appropriate measures of center and displays to use. Students learned to distinguish between categorical and numerical data in *Data About Us*. This unit provides a finer distinction for numerical data, having students focus on both counting and measuring as ways to collect data.

Counted data also are called discrete data. When we use counted data (discrete data values), there are no values possible between consecutive counts; for example:

- We can collect data about family size and organize them by using frequencies of how many families have zero children, one child, two children, and so on, but 1.5 children do not exist in reality.

- We can collect data about responses to a question such as, "On a scale of 1 to 5 with 1 as 'low interest,' rate your interest in participating in the school's field day" and organize them by using frequencies of how many people indicated each of the ratings 1, 2, 3, 4, or 5. In this case, responses between 4 or 5 are not possible because of the stipulation on what choices can be made.

- We can collect data about pulse rates and organize them using frequencies of how many people have pulse rates in the intervals of 60–69 beats, 70–79 beats, and so on. A pulse rate of 65.5 beats is not an option.

With counted data, the mean or median may be decimal numbers but the actual data are reported as whole numbers.

Measurement data also are called continuous data. When we use measurements (or continuous data values), it is possible to measure "between" any two measurements we may have. Of course, the measurement tools we use determine the reality of doing this. Examples include:

- We can collect data about height and organize them into intervals by using frequencies of how many people are between 40–44 inches tall, 45–49 inches tall, and so on. We can measure more exactly to the nearest half-inch, quarter-inch, and so on.

- We can collect data about time spent sleeping in one day and organize them by frequencies of how many people slept 7 hours, $7\frac{1}{2}$ hours, 8 hours, and so on. We can measure more exactly to the nearest minute or second.

Understanding the Concept of Distribution

When students work with data, they are often interested in the individual cases, particularly if the data are about themselves. However, statisticians like to look at the overall distribution of a data set. We use graphs to help clarify a distribution of data. Distributions (unlike individual cases) have properties such as measures of central tendency (i.e., mean, median, mode), or variability (e.g., outliers, range), or shape (e.g., clumps, gaps).

There appear to be several general ways students think about data:

- At the beginning level, students often may focus only on each data value (e.g., each student's own fastest reaction time). They may not see that a group of cases may be related (e.g., several fastest reaction times cluster around 0.7–0.9 seconds). However, when looking at outliers, a focus on individual data values is necessary. For example, how might we interpret a single reaction time of 2.4 seconds if median times in five trials for each of 40 students are ≤ 1.4 seconds?

- A next level is to pay attention to subsets of data values that may be the same or similar (i.e., a category or a cluster). For example, if students are using numerical data, they might notice a cluster in the interval of 0.85 and 0.9 seconds for fastest reaction times.

- A final level involves viewing all the data values as an "object" or distribution (Figure 1). Students look for features of the distribution that are not features of any of the individual data values (e.g., shape or clusters). In looking at the distribution of the fastest reaction times, we can see that much of the data are less than 1 second. The distribution is somewhat flat in shape, with data that vary from a little less than 0.6 second to almost 1.2 seconds.

Exploring the Concept of Variability

What Variability Is and Why It's Important

When we look at distributions, we often are interested in the measures of center—what's typical (i.e., mean, mode, median). However, any measure of center alone can be misleading. We need to consider the variability of the distribution. Generally, students' earlier work with data analysis has emphasized describing what is typical about a distribution of data. During the middle grades, there is a shift toward consideration of variability; students are better prepared mathematically and developmentally to consider this concept. Describing variability includes looking at measures of center, range, at where data cluster or where there are gaps in a distribution, at the presence of outliers, and at the shape of the distribution.

Variability refers to the similarities and differences we find among data values in a distribution. There are various causes for variability. In *Data Distributions* students encounter both variability that comes from measurement errors and the natural variability that occurs when studying individual cases in a sample or population. Using statistics and data analysis is all about describing areas of stability (or consistency) in the natural variability that occurs in a distribution. One way to think about variability and stability is to consider addressing the following questions about any set of data with which students are working:

Suppose we are analyzing the distribution of the fastest reaction times for 40 students when they use their dominant hands. (Figure 1)

- If data from a different group of 40 seventh-grade students (who had not played the reaction time game before) were collected, would we expect the distribution of these new data to be the same as or different from the distribution of data for the original 40 students?

- If we expect the distribution to be different, how different and in what ways would it be different? (This question addresses differences among data values, shapes of distributions, locations of data values, and so on.)

- What might we expect to be the same about the two distributions? (This question addresses the use of measures of center, variability, descriptions of shapes of distributions, and so on.)

Figure 1   **Fastest Reaction Times for 40 Students (Dominant Hand)**

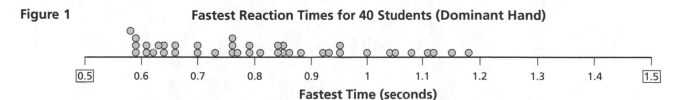

Fastest Time (seconds)

• Several questions highlight interesting aspects of variability. What does a distribution look like? How much do the data points vary from each other? How consistent are the data? What are possible reasons why there is variability in the data?

A distribution's shape is most obvious when we look at a graph—line plot, bar graph, or histogram—of the data. There is a relationship between the shape of a distribution and the locations of the mean and the median. At a gross level, there are distributions in which the mean and median are located close together and there are distributions in which the mean and median are located farther apart. Three different examples of data about the amount of sugar per serving in different cereals are shown below (Figure 2). The shape of the data influences these locations. For graphs A and B, the data are either clustered together or evenly distributed without obvious peaks or clusters. For graph C, the "skewness" of the distribution (a cluster at one end with data values spread out on the other) affects the computation of the mean so that both statistics are not in similar locations.

Making Sense of a Data Set Using Different Strategies for Data Reduction

Statisticians use the term *data reduction* to describe what they do when they use representations or statistics during the analysis part of the process of statistical investigation.

Using Standard Graphical Representations
Some often-used representations in the K–12 curriculum that are addressed in *Data Distributions* are shown on the next page.

Line plot Each case is represented as an "X" (or a dot) positioned over a labeled number line.

Line Plot With X's: Measures of Jasmine's Head

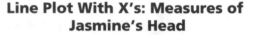
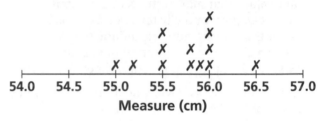

Figure 2

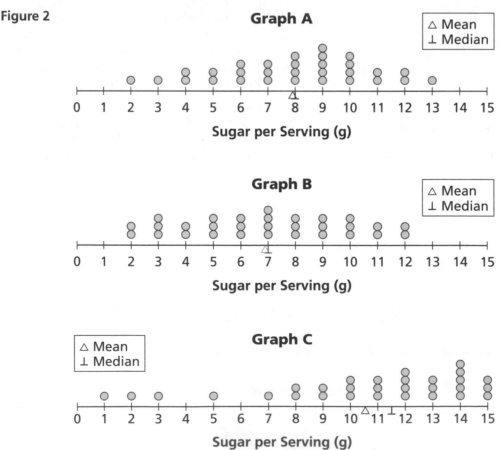

Line Plot With Dots: Measures of Jasmine's Head

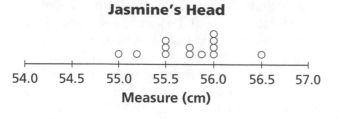

Measure (cm)

Value bar graph Each case is represented by a separate bar whose relative length corresponds to the magnitude or value of that case.

Ordered Value Bar Graph: Measures of Jasmine's Head

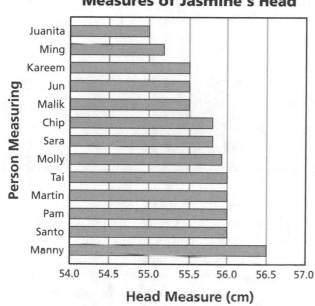

Person Measuring

Juanita, Ming, Kareem, Jun, Malik, Chip, Sara, Molly, Tai, Martin, Pam, Santo, Manny

Head Measure (cm)

Frequency bar graph A bar's height is not the value of an individual case but rather the number (frequency) of cases that all have that value.

Bag 1

9% Green, 24% Yellow, 7% Orange, 7% Blue, 33% Brown, 21% Red

Percent / **Color**

Scatter plot The relationship between two different attributes is explored by plotting values of two numeric attributes on a Cartesian coordinate system.

Relationship Between Maximum Height and Top Speed for 150 Roller Coasters

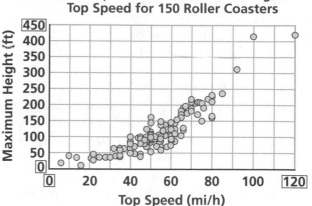

Maximum Height (ft) / **Top Speed (mi/h)**

Reading Standard Graphs

As a central component of data analysis, graphs deserve special attention. In a study of graph comprehension to assess the understanding of students in grades 4 and 7 of four traditional graphs (pictographs, bar graphs, circle or pie graphs, and line graphs), three components to graph comprehension were identified that are useful here.

- *Reading the data* involves "lifting" information from a graph to answer explicit questions. For example, using the data at the left, how many students measured Jasmine's head size as 56 cm?

- *Reading between the data* includes the interpretation and integration of information presented in a graph. For example, what percent of students' measures for Jasmine's head were greater than 55.5 cm?

- *Reading beyond the data* involves extending, predicting, or inferring from data to answer implicit questions. For example, what is the head size you would recommend be used for Jasmine's head when ordering her cap?

Once students create their graphs, they use them in the interpretation phase of the data-investigation process. This is when they (and you) need to ask questions about the graphs. The first two categories of questions—reading the data and reading between the data—are basic to understanding graphs. However, it is reading beyond the data that helps students to develop higher-level thinking skills such as inference and justification.

Using Measures of Central Tendency

The three measures of central tendency have been addressed in *Data About Us*. In *Data Distributions*, the intent is to deepen understanding and to explore relationships among the three measures and shapes of distributions.

Mode is the data value or category occurring with the greatest frequency. It is ill-defined and sometimes has more than one value. It is unstable because a change in one or a few data values can lead to a change in the mode. It is not usually used for summarizing numerical data. A distribution may be unimodal, bimodal, or multimodal.

Median is the numerical value that is the midpoint of an ordered distribution. It is not influenced by extreme data values, so it is a good measure to use when working with distributions that are skewed.

Mean is the numerical value that marks the balance point of a distribution; it is influenced by all values of the distribution, including extremes and outliers. It is a good measure to use when working with distributions that are roughly symmetric.

The mean is the same thing as what is usually called the average. There are two interpretations of mean (or average) used in *Data Distributions*:

Equal share: If everyone received the same amount, what would that amount be?

Balance model: Differences from the mean "balance out" so that the sum of differences for data values below and above the mean equal 0.

Sometimes the mean or median is used to answer the question: What is a typical value that could be used to characterize these data?

Using Measures of Variability

Measures of variability establish the degree of variability of the individual data values and their deviations (or differences) from the measures of center. In *Data Distributions*, students use the range as one measure of variability; range

depends on only the minimum and maximum values. Students are encouraged to talk about where data cluster and where "gaps" appear in the data as further ways to comment on variability.

In CMP2 data units, we use minimum and maximum values as terms to specify the least and the greatest values (e.g., the minimum and maximum values are 55 cm and 56.5 cm). The range is a number found by subtracting the minimum value from the maximum value (e.g., the range of the data is 1.5 cm).

In some cases, the range may give you an idea about consistency. At other times, the data can be very consistent, but have outliers that affect the range, as in the following graph.

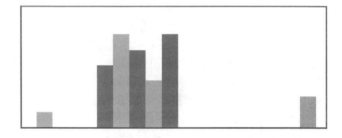

Comparing Data Sets

Statistics are useful when comparing two or more data sets. Students must sort out what it means to compare data sets with equal numbers of data values (counts can be used as frequencies) and data sets with unequal numbers of data values (percents must be used as frequencies). It appears that starting with data sets with equal numbers of data values (Investigation 3) and then moving to data sets with unequal numbers of data values (Investigation 4) more readily motivates students to move from counts to percentages to report frequencies.

Continuing to Explore the Concept of Covariation

Covariation is a way of characterizing a relationship between two (most often) numerical attributes. It means that information about values from one attribute helps us understand, explain, or predict values of the other attribute. In *Data Distributions*, students are asked to consider whether one attribute might help understand the variability in another attribute; for instance, is speed of a roller coaster related to its maximum height? Work with covariation continues to be informal and very concrete.

Big Idea	Prior Work	Future Work
Applying the process of statistical investigation to pose questions, identify ways data are collected, determine strategies for analyzing data and interpreting the analysis to answer the question posed	Collecting and organizing data in different contexts (*How Likely Is It?, Data About Us, What Do You Expect?*)	Gathering and organizing data collected from conducting experiments or playing trials of games (*Samples and Populations*)
Explaining variability in categorical and numerical data	Finding the range of a set of data (*Data About Us*)	Using endpoints, range, and shape of distribution of data to make judgments about the usefulness of the data in helping make inferences and predictions about the group to which the data pertain (*Samples and Populations*)
Explaining the difference between collecting numerical data by counting and collecting numerical data by measuring	Collecting and organizing categorical and numerical data (*Data About Us*)	Understanding that a measurement has two components, a unit of measure and a count (*Data Around Us* ©2004)
Making effective use of a variety of representations to display distributions, including tables, value bar graphs, line plots, and (frequency) bar graphs	Representing the number of proper factors of a counting number (*Prime Time*); representing data with line plots, bar graphs, coordinate graphs, and stem-and-leaf plots (*Data About Us, Accentuate the Negative, Moving Straight Ahead*)	Representing data to aid with statistical analysis (*Samples and Populations*); expanding the use of coordinate grids to include negative coordinates (*Thinking With Mathematical Models; Frogs, Fleas, and Painted Cubes; Say It With Symbols; The Shapes of Algebra; Kaleidoscopes, Hubcaps, and Mirrors*)
Understanding and deciding when to use the mean and median to describe a distribution	Finding measures of center (*Data About Us*)	Using measures of center to make inferences and predictions about events or populations (*Samples and Populations*)
Understanding and using counts or percents to report frequencies of occurrence of data	Percent defined as a ratio of "out of 100" with connections to fractions and decimals (*Bits and Pieces I, II, and III*); using counts to report frequencies (*Data About Us*)	Using percentiles to compare samples (*Samples and Populations*)
Developing and using strategies for comparing equal-sized and unequal-sized data sets to solve problems	Comparing data sets (*Data About Us*)	Making comparisons between groups of different size data sets (*Data Around Us* ©2004, *Samples and Populations*)
Describing how you can use fractions, percents, and ratios as ways to compare sets	Comparing quantities using ratios, proportions, rates, or percents (*Comparing and Scaling, What Do You Expect?*)	Comparing samples (*Samples and Populations*), comparing data sets (*Data Around Us* ©2004)

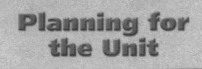

Planning for the Unit

Pacing Suggestions and Materials

Investigations and Assessments	Pacing 45–50 min. classes	Materials for Students	Materials for Teachers
1 Making Sense of Variability	$4\frac{1}{2}$ days	Labsheets 1.1 (optional), 1.2, 1ACE Exercises 8–10, 1ACE Exercise 22	Transparencies 1.1A–1.1D, 1.2A, 1.2B, 1.4A, 1.4B
Mathematical Reflections	$\frac{1}{2}$ day		
2 Making Sense of Measures of Center	6 days	Labsheet 2.1; counters (optional); ruler, half cardboard tube (paper towel tube works), several coins of the same value (optional); small stick-on notes (optional); computers with *TinkerPlots™* software (optional); Labsheet A.1 (optional)	Transparencies 2.1A, 2.1B, 2.2A–2.2C, 2.3A–2.3E, 2.4; transparency of Labsheet 2.1 (optional); stick-on notes; transparency of Labsheet A.1 (optional)
Mathematical Reflections	$\frac{1}{2}$ day		
Assessment: Check Up	$\frac{1}{2}$ day		
3 Comparing Distributions: Equal Numbers of Data Values	6 days	**All:** Computers with access to applet that measures reaction time (optional); Labsheets 3.2 (one copy for each team, optional), 3ACE Exercise 17, 3.3A–3.3K (1 set for each group of 2–3 students, optional); 3.3L (optional) **If not using software:** Labsheets 3.3M–3.3R (optional); 3.4A, 3.4B (optional) **If using software:** Computers with *TinkerPlots™* software; *Using TinkerPlots™ With CMP Problems: Students' Guide*	**All:** Transparencies 3.1A, 3.1B (optional), 3.2A, 3.2B, 3.3A, 3.3B (optional); transparency of Labsheet 3.2 (optional); transparency of Problem 3.4 (optional); chart paper and magic markers **If using software:** *Using TinkerPlots™ With CMP Problems: Teacher's Guide*
Mathematical Reflections	$\frac{1}{2}$ day		
Assessment: Partner Quiz	1 day		

Pacing Suggestions and Materials *(continued)*

Investigations and Assessments	Pacing 45–50 min. classes	Materials for Students	Materials for Teachers
4 Comparing Distributions: Unequal Numbers of Data Values	3 days	Labsheet 4ACE Exercise 17 **If not using software:** Labsheets 4.2A–4.2P (optional) **If using software:** Computers with *TinkerPlots*™ software; *Using TinkerPlots*™ *With CMP Problems: Students' Guide*; Labsheet A.1 (optional)	**All:** Transparencies 4.1A–4.1C, 4.2A–4.2D (optional) **If using software:** *Using TinkerPlots*™ *With CMP Problems: Teacher's Guide*
Mathematical Reflections	$\frac{1}{2}$ day		
Looking Back and Looking Ahead	$\frac{1}{2}$ day		
Assessment: Self Assessment	Take Home		
Assessment: Unit Test	1 day		

Total Time $24\frac{1}{2}$ days

For detailed pacing for Problems within each Investigation, see the Suggested Pacing at the beginning of each Investigation.

For pacing with block scheduling, see next page.

Materials for Use in All Investigations	
Calculators, blank transparencies and transparency markers (optional), graph paper (or gridded chart paper and magic markers), student notebooks	Blank transparencies and transparency markers (optional)

Pacing for Block Scheduling (90-minute class periods)

Investigation	Suggested Pacing	Investigation	Suggested Pacing
Investigation 1	**3 days**	**Investigation 3**	$3\frac{1}{2}$ **days**
Problem 1.1	1 day	Problem 3.1	$\frac{1}{2}$ day
Problem 1.2	$\frac{1}{2}$ day	Problem 3.2	$\frac{1}{2}$ day
Problem 1.3	$\frac{1}{2}$ day	Problem 3.3	1 day
Problem 1.4	$\frac{1}{2}$ day	Problem 3.4	1 day
Math Reflections	$\frac{1}{2}$ day	Math Reflections	$\frac{1}{2}$ day
Investigation 2	$3\frac{1}{2}$ **days**	**Investigation 4**	**2 days**
Problem 2.1	$\frac{1}{2}$ day	Problem 4.1	$\frac{1}{2}$ day
Problem 2.2	$\frac{1}{2}$ day	Problem 4.2	1 day
Problem 2.3	1 day	Math Reflections	$\frac{1}{2}$ day
Problem 2.4	1 day		
Math Reflections	$\frac{1}{2}$ day		

Vocabulary

Essential Terms Developed in This Unit	Useful Terms Referenced in This Unit	Terms Developed in Previous Units
attribute	bar graph	categorical data
counts	circle graph	line plot
distribution	counts	mean
measures	percents	median
measures of center	relative frequencies	mode
ordered value bar graph	repeated measures	numerical data
range	scales	outlier
value of an attribute	stem-and-leaf plot	scatter plot
value bar graph		
variability of a set of numerical data		

Program Resources

Go Online PHSchool.com
For: Teacher Resources
Web Code: ank-5500

Components

Use the chart below to quickly see which components are available for each Investigation.

Investigation	Labsheets	Additional Practice	Transparencies		Formal Assessment		Assessment Options	
			Problem	Summary	Check Up	Partner Quiz	Multiple-Choice	Question Bank
1	1.1, 1.2, 1ACE Exercises 8–10, 1ACE Exercise 22	✔	1.1A–1.1C, 1.2A, 1.2B, 1.4A, 1.4B				✔	✔
2	2.1, A.1	✔	2.1A, 2.1B, 2.2A–2.2C. 2.3A–2.3E, 2.4		✔		✔	✔
3	3.2, 3.3A–3.3R, 3.4A, 3.4B, 3ACE Exercise 17	✔	3.1A–3.1C, 3.1B, 3.2A, 3.2B, 3.3A, 3.3B			✔	✔	
4	4.2A–4.2P, A.1	✔	4.1A–4.1C, 4.2A–4.2D					✔
For the Unit		*ExamView* CD-ROM, Web site	LBLA		Unit Test, Notebook Check, Self Assessment		Multiple-Choice, Question Bank, *ExamView* CD-ROM	

Also Available For Use With This Unit

- Parent Guide: take-home letter for the unit
- Implementing CMP
- Spanish Assessment Resources
- Additional online and technology resources

Technology

The Use of Calculators

Connected Mathematics was developed with the belief that calculators should be available and that students should learn when their use is appropriate. For this reason, we do not designate specific problems as "calculator problems." We assume that students have access to calculators at all times, and we encourage teachers to help students learn to use calculators, estimation, mental computation, and paper and pencil computation when appropriate.

Student Interactivity CD-ROM

Includes interactive activities to enhance the learning in the Problems within Investigations.

PHSchool.com

For Students Multiple-choice practice with instant feedback, updated data sources, data sets for *TinkerPlots*™ data software.
For Teachers Professional development, curriculum support, downloadable forms, and more.

For Problem 3.1, PHSchool.com will link students to several online games that will allow students to collect their own reaction times.

See also www.math.msu.edu/cmp for more resources for both teachers and students.

ExamView® CD-ROM

Create multiple versions of practice sheets and tests for course objectives and standardized tests. Includes dynamic questions, online testing, student reports, and all test and practice items in Spanish. Also includes all items in *Assessment Resources* and *Additional Practice*.

Teacher Express™ CD-ROM

Includes a lesson planning tool, the Teacher's Guide pages, and all of the teaching resources.

LessonLab Online Courses

LessonLab offers comprehensive, facilitated professional development designed to help teachers implement CMP2 and improve student achievement. To learn more, please visit PHSchool.com/cmp2.

TinkerPlots™ Software and Access to Computers

This unit may be used with the software program *TinkerPlots* available from Key Curriculum Press. Specifically, Problems 2.4, 3.3, 3.4, and 4.2 are well suited for use with the software. They can also be completed without any software. The Teacher's Guide specifically addresses completing each of these problems with or without computer software.

If you have access to computers, having 2 or 3 students work together on a computer is ideal with enough computers so all students can work on the problems at the same time. If computers are limited, it may be that students have staggered time on computers prior to discussing a problem. Another option is that all the computer explorations are done as demonstrations.

NOTE: All ACE problems are intended for use without access to technology.

If you are using *TinkerPlots* for work with a problem, it would be nice to have ways to project the software when summarizing. As students describe strategies and/or discuss findings, the actual screen they created can be re-created. Another option is for students to print out their displays and then make transparencies of the displays that you want to have the class consider prior to summarizing the problem.

Using TinkerPlots™ With CMP Problems: Student Guide is provided for students to use as they learn how to use *TinkerPlots* in relation to doing Problems 2.4, 3.3, 3.4, and 4.2. There is an introductory section followed by three sections, each designed to accompany an investigation in *Data Distributions*.

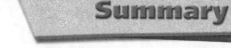

Assessment Summary

Ongoing Informal Assessment

Embedded in the Student Unit

Problems Use students' work from the Problems to informally check student understanding.

ACE exercises Use ACE exercises for homework assignments to assess student understanding.

Mathematical Reflections Have students summarize their learning at the end of each Investigation.

Looking Back and Looking Ahead At the end of the unit, use the first two sections to allow students to show what they know about the unit.

Additional Resources

Teacher's Guide Use the Check for Understanding feature of some Summaries and the probing questions that appear in the *Launch, Explore,* or *Summarize* sections of all Investigations to check student understanding.

Self Assessment

Notebook Check Students use this tool to organize and check their notebooks before giving them to their teacher. Located in *Assessment Resources*.

Self Assessment At the end of the unit, students reflect on and provide examples of what they learned. Located in *Assessment Resources*.

Formal Assessment

Choose the assessment materials that are appropriate for your students.

Assessment	For Use After	Focus	Student Work
Check Up	Invest. 2	Skills	Individual
Partner Quiz	Invest. 3	Rich problems	Pair
Unit Test	The Unit	Skills, rich problems	Individual

Additional Resources

Multiple-Choice Items Use these items for homework, review, a quiz, or add them to the Unit Test.

Question Bank Choose from these questions for homework, review, or replacements for Quiz, Check Up, or Unit Test questions.

Additional Practice Choose practice exercises for each investigation for homework, review, or formal assessments.

ExamView **CD-ROM** Create practice sheets, review quizzes, and tests with this dynamic software. Give online tests and receive student progress reports. (All test items available in Spanish.)

Spanish Assessment Resources

Includes Partner Quiz, Check Up, Unit Test, Multiple-Choice Items, Question Bank, Notebook Check, and Self Assessment. Plus, the *ExamView* CD-ROM has all test items in Spanish.

Correlation to Standardized Tests

Investigation	NAEP	Terra Nova		ITBS	SAT10	Local Test
		CAT6	CTBS			
1 Making Sense of Variability	D1a, D1b		✔	✔		
2 Making Sense of Measures of Center	D2a–c	✔	✔	✔	✔	
3 Comparing Distributions: Equal Numbers of Data Values	D2a–c		✔			
4 Comparing Distributions: Unequal Numbers of Data	D2a–c		✔			

NAEP National Assessment of Educational Progress

CAT6/Terra Nova California Achievement Test, 6th Ed.
CTBS/Terra Nova Comprehensive Test of Basic Skills

ITBS Iowa Test of Basic Skills, Form M
SAT10 Stanford Achievement Test, 10th Ed.

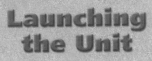

Introducing Your Students to *Data Distributions*

One way to introduce *Data Distributions* is to have a class discussion about what students think they already know about doing statistical investigations. Ask students to brainstorm vocabulary and topics. Make a list of these ideas as they say them. For example, students may say "graphs," and you may ask them to be more explicit about kinds of graphs. Students may say "average," and you may ask them to be more explicit about terms for average. Students may say "surveys," and you can ask them to be more explicit about ways they could collect data. Just record the words or concepts without elaborating on meaning in your discussion at this point, but do ask for more explicit information where appropriate.

If students don't directly mention it, ask them how they might go about conducting a statistical investigation. You can pose the question below, which sets up the situation in one of the assessments. NOTE: It is helpful to use it here to get students familiar with the data context.

- *The PTA is concerned about the backpack weights students carry and wants this class to find out how much weight middle-grades students are typically carrying. How would we go about finding this out?*

Take only a short time to brainstorm what would be involved in thinking about the design of a statistical investigation to respond to this problem. Use this to highlight the four components of a statistical investigation: pose the question, collect the data, analyze the data, and interpret and communicate the results.

Using the Unit Opener

Explain to your students that there are important and interesting questions that involve data analysis. Refer them to the three questions posed on the opening page of the student edition. You may want to discuss these questions as a class, but do not worry about finding the "correct" answers at this time. Each question is posed again in the investigations, at the time when the students have learned the mathematical concepts required to answer it. Ask your students to keep these questions in mind as they work through the investigations and to think about how they might use the ideas they are learning to help them determine the answers.

Using the Mathematical Highlights

The Mathematical Highlights page in the Student Edition provides information to students, parents, and other family members. It gives students a preview of the mathematics and some of the overarching questions that they should ask themselves while studying *Data Distributions*.

As they work through the unit, students can refer to the Mathematical Highlights page to review what they have learned and to preview what is still to come. This page also tells students' families what mathematical ideas and activities will be covered as the class works through *Data Distributions*.

Connected Mathematics 2

Data Distributions

Describing Variability and Comparing Groups

Glenda Lappan
James T. Fey
William M. Fitzgerald
Susan N. Friel
Elizabeth Difanis Phillips

PEARSON

Boston, Massachusetts · Glenview, Illinois · Shoreview, Minnesota · Upper Saddle River, New Jersey

Notes _____

_____

_____

_____

Data Distributions

Describing Variability and Comparing Groups

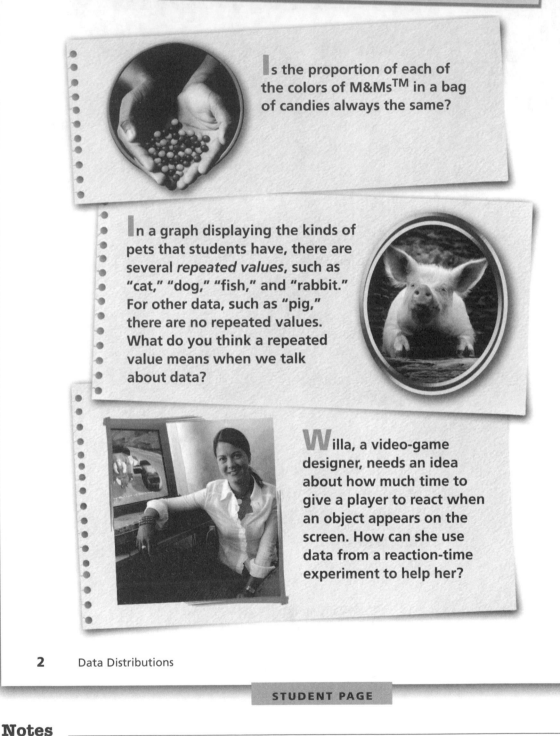

Is the proportion of each of the colors of M&Ms™ in a bag of candies always the same?

In a graph displaying the kinds of pets that students have, there are several *repeated values*, such as "cat," "dog," "fish," and "rabbit." For other data, such as "pig," there are no repeated values. What do you think a repeated value means when we talk about data?

Willa, a video-game designer, needs an idea about how much time to give a player to react when an object appears on the screen. How can she use data from a reaction-time experiment to help her?

2   Data Distributions

Notes _____

_____

_____

_____

Statistics and data analysis are used to report health risks, to summarize consumer choices for CD players, to identify the most popular movies watched over a weekend, and to indicate favorite food choices. Think for a minute about some other ways statistics and graphs are used to report information.

There are important ideas about data analysis and statistics that can help you understand, analyze, critique, and respond to various reports that you encounter. Understanding data analysis and statistics can help you decide whether information is reliable or is distorted by the graphs used to display it. The investigations in *Data Distributions* will help you use ideas about statistics and data analysis to describe the variability in a data set, to compare groups, and to make decisions as you solve problems. Think about some interesting situations that involve statistical investigations, including the three on the previous page.

Unit Opener   3

Notes

Mathematical Highlights

Describing Variability and Comparing Groups

In *Data Distributions*, you will explore important ideas related to statistics and data analysis, especially those related to describing variability and center and to making comparisons.

You will learn how to

- Apply the process of statistical investigation to pose questions, to identify ways data are collected, and to determine strategies for analyzing data in order to answer the questions posed

- Recognize that variability occurs whenever data are collected and describe the variability in the distribution of a given data set

- Identify sources of variability, including natural variability and variability that results from errors in measurement

- Determine whether to use the mean or median to describe a distribution

- Use the shape of a distribution to estimate the location of the mean and the median

- Use a variety of representations, including tables, bar graphs, and line plots, to display distributions

- Understand and use counts or percents to report frequencies of occurrence of data

- Compare the distributions of data sets using their related centers, variability, and shapes

- Decide if a difference among data values or summary measures matters

- Develop and use strategies to compare data sets to solve problems

As you work on problems in this unit, ask yourself questions about situations that involve analyzing distributions or comparing groups:

Is there anything surprising about the data and their distribution?

Where do the data cluster in the distribution?

How can I use the mean or median and range to help me understand and describe a data distribution?

What strategies can I use to compare two different data sets?

4 Data Distributions

Notes _____

_____

_____

_____

Investigation 1 | Making Sense of Variability

Mathematical and Problem-Solving Goals

- Recognize that variability occurs whenever data are collected

- Use properties of distributions to describe the variability in a given data set

- Use counts or percents to report frequencies of occurrence of data

- Use tables, line plots, value bar graphs, and bar graphs to display data distributions

- Distinguish between categorical or numerical data and between frequencies reported as counts or as percents

- Decide if a difference among data values and/or summary measures matters

- Identify sources of variability, including variability that occurs naturally in data and variability that results from errors in measurement

Summary of Problems

Problem 1.1 Variability in Categorical Data

Students examine the proportions of different colors of candies found in a bag of M&M's to describe the variability and to make predictions about a possible plan for the percentages of each color.

 Problem 1.2 Variability in Numerical Counts

Students work with counts of the numbers of immigrants to the United States over time. They consider frequencies expressed both as counts and as percents in representing these data.

 Problem 1.3 Variability in Numerical Measurements

Students use measurement data related to measuring the circumference of heads to determine cap sizes.

Problem 1.4 Two Kinds of Variability

Students continue to work with measurement data related to head sizes and distinguish between variability due to measurement error and variability that occurs naturally in measuring different people.

Mathematics Background

For background on distinguishing different types of data, understanding the concept of distribution, exploring the concept of variability, using standard graphical representations, and reading standard graphs, see pages 4–10.

	Suggested Pacing	Materials for Students	Materials for Teachers	ACE Assignments
All	5 days	Calculators; student notebooks; graph paper (or gridded chart paper and markers, or transparencies and transparency markers)		
1.1	$1\frac{1}{2}$ days	Labsheet 1.1 (optional)	Transparencies 1.1A–1.1C	1, 2, 14, 15
1.2	1 day	Labsheets 1.2, 1ACE Exercises 8–10	Transparencies 1.2A, 1.2B	8–11, 16, 17
1.3	1 day	String; metric measuring tapes or meter sticks marked with centimeters		3–7, 18
1.4	1 day	Labsheet 1ACE Exercise 22	Transparencies 1.4A, 1.4B	12, 13, 19–23
MR	$\frac{1}{2}$ day			

Goals

- Recognize that variability occurs whenever data are collected

- Use properties of distributions to describe the variability in a given data set

- Use counts or percents to report frequencies of occurrence of data

- Use bar graphs with frequencies expressed as percents to display data distributions of categorical data

In this problem, students examine the numbers of candies of each color in one or more bags of the pre–March 2004 distribution of M&M's® candies. They look at the variability that occurs in data on the colors of candies in a single bag, in each of two other single bags of candies, and finally in the total data from thirty bags of candies. They explore ways to describe the variability that they are observing.

Data Exploration Opportunity

The current M&M's candies have a different distribution than the candies made before March 2004. Data concerning numbers of each color of candies in several small bags of the pre-March 2004 M&M's candies are provided for students' use in Problem 1.1. Do *not* have students count candies in current bags of M&M's candies at this point because it may cause some confusion.

As the problem progresses (and before you do the Distribution Sort activity in Question C), you may decide to bring in a few sample small bags of the *current* M&M's candies that you can open and count colors with the students. You can make bar graphs showing the percent of each color. Students use this additional data to help decide whether the company changed the distribution when they brightened up the colors.

Launch 1.1

Use the introduction to the investigation to determine what knowledge students have about the occurrence of variability in data that they collect. In looking at each situation, focus the students' attention (1) on the kind of the data that they might collect and (2) on whether the data they collect will be more similar to or different from one another. The latter is used to point out variability that occurs within a data set.

Suggested Question Next, focus students' attention on the context of Problem 1.1.

- *You will be looking at the variability that occurs in the candy colors in a bag of M&M's candies. Think about both the variability in the numbers of each color found in one bag and the variability in the numbers of each color found between different bags of M&M's candies.* (You will come back to this question in the Summary.)

Students should be familiar with the terms *categorical data* and *numerical data* (from *Data About Us*). The scaling of the frequency axis (*y*-axis) is more apparent in this unit; in particular, attention is given to reporting frequencies as counts or as percents. Percentages are appropriate when you want to make any kinds of comparisons among data sets that do not have the same numbers of data values.

Have students read through the Did You Know? Students know about M&M's candies and probably will be "buzzing" with their own conversations about what they know about the color distributions.

Suggested Questions Since all statistical investigations begin with a question, here is the question to consider in this problem.

- *Did the Mars Company plan a specific distribution of colors of M&M's candies before and after March 2004?* (Some students may know they did but most will not recall the exact plan; if any do, ask them to remain silent at this point.)

There are several components of the process to address. Have students briefly talk about the following questions:

- *What kinds of data would help answer the question?* (counts of numbers of each color from bags of candies)

- *How might you collect such data?* (Open a bag and count; more bags will give better information.)

- *How would you analyze the data?* (Make a bar graph of counts or of percents.)

- *How would you use your analysis to help answer the question?* (Look for patterns in the data.)

Once the questions are discussed, together examine one student's work presented in the Student Edition. In particular, pay careful attention to how she chose to describe the variability in the distribution, reporting *percent* frequencies of colors in her bag of M&M's® candies.

NOTE: In *Data Distributions,* we use both value bar graphs (graphs with a bar for each data value as in Problem 1.4) and frequency bar graphs that show the frequencies of occurrence as counts or as percents of repeated data values in a distribution. In this problem, we are using a frequency bar graph with frequencies reported as percents—possibly something that students have not had a lot of experience thinking about.

Have students work in pairs. Distribute Labsheet 1.1 with the blank bar graph grids. Labsheet 1.1 is provided for students to make the actual graphs so that this part of the lesson goes more quickly and, indirectly, you can begin to address the issue of using the same scales (vertical frequency scale, same ordering of horizontal scale, and overall proportional sizing of graphs) to compare distributions using different graphs.

Explore 1.1

For Questions A–C, ask questions as you circulate to help keep students focused on the problem. You can have students do their graphs on graph paper or use Labsheet 1.1 OR have each group do their graphs on gridded chart paper so that they can be posted OR have each group do their graphs on an overhead transparency of Labsheet 1.1 so they can be displayed during the summary.

For Questions A and B, students' attention needs to be directed to the use of percents for reporting frequencies of colors because each bag has a different number of candies. Remind students that the total percentage needs to be 100%; they may find that in rounding they are at 101%. Students can discuss why this happens and if they want to "tinker" with percentages found to adjust for this error or accept the error and report total frequencies of data greater than 100%.

Question A has students focus on individual bags of M&M's; Question B reports cumulative data taken from 30 bags. Informally, students can consider the issue of sample size; a few single samples may not provide the kind of information that a greater number of samples will. Question C is intended to let students explore the pre-March 2004 and the current distributions of candies as evidenced through graphs of different samples of data to decide whether there is evidence that the company made a change in 2004.

Summarize 1.1

Use Transparencies 1.1A, 1.1B, and 1.1C to help in summarizing this problem. Transparency 1.1A provides copies of the original data and graph for Bag 1. Transparency 1.1B has the graphs for bags 1–3. Transparency 1.1C provides a copy of the graph for Question B and also, for later discussion, a copy of a graph that represents the Mars Company's planned distribution.

Begin the summary by discussing the answers to the problem. First discuss students' representations for Questions A and B, looking at scales, and so on in terms of graph construction. In particular, take some time to talk about the variability that occurs between distributions.

Suggested Questions

- *Does each bag have the same percent of each color?* (This question addresses what's different between distributions—the numbers for each color in the bags are unlikely to be the same so the percents will vary.)

- *If we were to look at data for another bag of pre–March 2004 M&M candies, what might you predict about the distribution of the numbers of each of the colors of the candies?* (This question addresses what's the same across distributions—even though the numbers of each color are different, the overall patterns in these numbers are similar.)

Then discuss the information from Questions A, B, and C. In particular, address variability by posing each of these questions:

- *Do you think we can say exactly what percent of each color the Mars Company intended? Why or why not?* (We cannot say because each bag can be somewhat different. However, the overall trends in the data help us see which colors appear more frequently and which appear less often.)

- *Do you think we can make some general statements and give some estimates about what percent of each color was intended by the Mars Company?* (We can say that there appear to be more of some colors than other colors, e.g., more of brown, red, and yellow than of green, orange, or blue; more of brown than of red or green; brown, red, and green could make up 66% to 75% of a bag of candies.)

1.1 Variability in Categorical Data

Mathematical Goals

- Recognize that variability occurs whenever data are collected
- Use properties of distributions to describe the variability in a given data set
- Use counts or percents to report frequencies of occurrence of data
- Use bar graphs with frequencies expressed as percents to display data distributions of categorical data

Launch

Use the introduction to the investigation and the Getting Ready to determine students' prior knowledge about the concept of variability in data. In Problem 1.1, you will be looking at the variability that occurs in the distribution of candy colors from a bag of M&M's®. Think about both the variability concerning the numbers of each color found in one bag and the variability concerning the numbers of each color found between different bags of M&M's. Have students read through the Did You Know? For this problem. The question is:

- *Did the Mars Company plan a specific distribution of colors of candies before and after March 2004?*

Talk through the questions about gathering and analyzing data. Together examine what one student did. In particular, spend time discussing how and why this student reported frequencies as percents rather than counts in making a bar graph. Have students work in pairs.

Materials
- Labsheet 1.1

Vocabulary
- variability
- categorical data

Explore

For Questions A–C, you can have students do their graphs on graph paper or Labsheet 1.1 OR have each group do their graphs on gridded chart paper so that they can be displayed during the summary. For Questions A and B, direct students' attention to the use of percents for reporting frequencies of colors because each bag has a different number of candies. Summarize before Question C.

Materials
- Labsheet 1.1
- Graph paper (or gridded chart paper and markers, or transparencies with grids and transparency markers)

Summarize

Use Transparencies 1.1A–1.1C to help summarize this problem. Begin the summary by first discussing students' representations for Questions A and B. Talk about the variability that occurs between distributions:

- *Does each bag have the same percent of each color?*
- *If we were to look at data about another bag of M&M's, what might you predict about the distribution of each of the colors of the candies?*

Materials
- Student notebooks
- Transparencies 1.1A–1.1C

continued on next page

continued

Finally, address variability by asking:

- *Do you think we can say exactly what percent of each color the Mars Company intends? Why/why not?*

- *Do you think we can estimate and make general statements about more or less of each color?*

ACE Assignment Guide for Problem 1.1

Differentiated Instruction
Solutions for All Learners

Core ACE 1, 2
Other ACE *Connections* 14, 15; unassigned choices from previous problems

Adapted For suggestions about adapting Exercise 2 and other ACE exercises, see the CMP *Special Needs Handbook.*
Connecting to Prior Units 14, 15: *Comparing and Scaling*

Answers to Problem 1.1

A. See Transparency 1.1B of Bags 1, 2, and 3. Answers will vary. Possible comparison statements will be similar to the original example. It does seem that the Mars Company intended that some colors occur with greater frequency.

B. See Transparency 1.1C of 30 bags and the "Theoretical" Percent of Each Color that represents the Mars Company's planned distribution. Answers will vary. Possible comparison statements will be similar to the original example. It does seem that the Mars Company intended that some colors occur with greater frequency.

C. In March 2004, the company changed the distribution of colors so that there were more green, orange, and blue candies and fewer yellow, brown, and red candies. We can see this from the graphs. Pre–March 2004 data show small numbers of green, orange, and blue candies and larger numbers of yellow, brown, and red. In the current distributions, we don't see this kind of obvious distinction. The variability among numbers of each color is less.

Variability in Numerical Counts

Goals

- Recognize that variability occurs whenever data are collected

- Use properties of distributions to describe the variability in a given data set

- Read a data table and understand how it is related to making bar graphs

- Distinguish between data as counts (numbers of European immigrants) and data as percents (percent of total immigrants to the United States who are European)

Launch 1.2

Students should be familiar with distinguishing numerical data—in this case, reported as counts of immigrants coming to the United States from Europe.

Have the students work in pairs to get familiar with both the table and Graphs 1 and 2. Transparencies 1.2A and 1.2B show the immigration data.

Suggested Questions Begin by having each pair look at the table.

- *What are the headings for each of the columns?*

- *What are the data in the columns?*

Once students have had time to make sense of the table, talk with them about it.

- *What does it mean to say that we are looking at data from a "decade?"* (looking at data from a ten-year period of time)

- *Locate the decade of 1951–60. How many immigrants came from Europe to the United States in that decade?* (1,325,727 immigrants)

- *What percent was this number of all immigrants who came to the United States in that decade?* (53%)

Ask additional such questions if students appear to be confused.

Next, have students look at Graphs 1 and 2 and decide how they show data from the table. When they have had some time, bring them back together.

Suggested Questions

- *Locate the decade of 1951–60. In Graph 1, what data are graphed in that decade?*

- *Where did these data come from?*

- *In Graph 2, what data are graphed in that decade?*

- *Where did these data come from?*

Explore 1.2

Students will need Labsheet 1.2 to use to record their answers to Question A. Comparison statements can involve comparing two different decades or several decades (e.g., before and after 1960, and so on).

As students consider Question B, have them talk about trends in terms of the *counts,* or *total numbers,* of immigrants from Europe in each decade and then in terms of the *percents* of immigrants from Europe out of *all* immigrants to the United States in any particular decade.

Summarize 1.2

Use the transparencies for Problem 1.2, and talk about how students determined their answers to Question A and the ways they made sense of how to draw the bar on the respective graph. Fill in the missing bar on each graph.

Suggested Questions Have students talk about what it means to predict a *trend.*

- *What kind of trend can we see using data represented in Graph 1?* (The numbers of people coming increased in the decades of 1820 to 1910 and decreased after that.)

- *What kind of trend can we see using data represented in Graph 2?* (The percent that Europeans were of all immigrants seems pretty high and stable from 1820 to 1910. The number of Europeans as a percent of total immigrants starts to decline after 1910).

- *Why do you suppose that there is an increase in the numbers of Europeans coming to the United States from 1820 to 1910 but there is not much change in the percent Europeans are of the total immigration during this time period? (There must have been an increase in the total numbers of immigrants coming to the U.S. during this period of time.)*

This lets students discuss what is varying in Graph 1 (counts of people) and what is varying in Graph 2 (percents that counts of European immigrants are of total counts of all immigrants coming to the United States).

Labsheet 1ACE Exercises 8–10 is provided if Exercises 8–10 are assigned.

For the Teacher If you choose to discuss the nature of immigration trends with your class, some additional information is presented below.

Before 1860 The majority of immigrants were from northern and western Europe. People left Europe for a variety of religious, political, and economic reasons. Jobless farmers during the industrial revolution sought new opportunities. New arrivals encouraged friends and family to join them.

1880 to 1920 Equal numbers of immigrants during this period were from southern and eastern Europe. (Asia and Latin America numbers begin to grow.) Most were seeking industrial employment, moving to major cities.

1920 to 1960 Starting to even out with increasing numbers from North America and Latin America, immigration rose after the war but was suppressed by quotas and the Depression. Quotas limited the number of immigrants and favored people of northern and western European heritage.

1960 to Present A larger number of immigrants came from Latin America and Asia. Prosperity in Europe decreased migration. Immigration laws eased restrictions on Asians and Latin Americans in 1965. Priority was given to people with relatives in the United States as well as to skilled workers and refugees. From 1980 to 1990, 10 percent of immigrants were from Europe, one-third from Asia, and one-half from Latin America. In 1990, new laws granted preference to immigrants bringing skills or money.

Source: Philip Martin and Elizabeth Midgley, "Immigration to the United States," *Population Bulletin* 54, 2. (Washington, DC: Population Reference Bureau, June 1999).

1.2 Variability in Numerical Counts

Mathematical Goals

- Recognize that variability occurs whenever data are collected
- Use properties of distributions to describe the variability in a given data set
- Read a data table and understand how it is related to making bar graphs
- Distinguish between data as counts (numbers of European immigrants) and data as percents (percent of total immigrants to the United States who are European)

Launch

Have the students work in pairs to get familiar with both the table and Graphs 1 and 2. Have each pair:

- *Look at the table. What are the headings for each of the columns? What are the data in the columns?*

Once students have had time to make sense of the table, talk with them about it.

- *What does it mean to say that we are looking at data from a "decade?"*
- *Locate the decade of 1951–60. How many immigrants came from Europe to the United States in that decade?*
- *What percent was this number of all immigrants who came to the United States in that decade?*

Pose another round of these questions if students appear to be confused. Next, have students look at Graphs 1 and 2 and decide how they are made to show data from the table. Bring them back together.

- *Locate the decade of 1951–60. In Graph 1, what data are graphed in that decade? Where did this data come from?*
- *In Graph 2, what data are graphed in that decade? Where did this data come from?*

Vocabulary
- numerical data

Explore

Students will need Labsheet 1.2 to record their answers to Question A. Comparison statements can involve comparing two different decades or several decades (e.g., before and after 1960, and so on). As students consider Question B, have them talk about trends in terms of the *counts*, or *total numbers*, of immigrants from Europe in each decade and then in terms of the *percents* of immigrants from Europe out of all immigrants to the United States in any particular decade.

Materials
- Calculators
- Labsheet 1.2

Talk about how students determined their answers to Question A. Fill in the missing bar on each graph. Have students talk about what it means to predict a *trend*.

- *What kind of trend can we identify using data represented in Graph 1? Using data represented in Graph 2?*

- *Why do you suppose that there is an increase in the number of Europeans coming to the United States from 1820 to 1910 but there is not much change in the percent Europeans make up of the total immigrants during this time period?*

This lets students discuss what is varying in Graph 1 (counts of people) and what is varying in Graph 2 (percents of all immigrants to the United States that are European). See the extended Summarize section for more information on immigration.

Materials
- Transparencies 1.2A, 1.2B
- Student notebooks

ACE Assignment Guide for Problem 1.2

Differentiated Instruction
Solutions for All Learners

Core ACE 8–11
Other ACE *Connections* 16, 17; unassigned choices from previous problems

Adapted For suggestions about adapting ACE exercises, see the CMP *Special Needs Handbook*.
Connecting to Prior Units 16: *Data About Us*; 17: *Comparing and Scaling, Bits and Pieces II*

Answers to Problem 1.2

A. **1. a.** 8,056,040

   b. Draw bar to just above 8,000,000 (8,500,000 would be halfway between 8,000,000 and 9,000,000).

   c. Some possibilities are: During this decade the number of immigrants from Europe was at its peak. There must have been some historical event that prompted the immigration. The number of immigrants more than doubled from the decade before.

2. a. 8,795,386

   b. ≈92%

   c. Draw bar to just above 90% (showing about 92%).

   d. Some possibilities are: the percent of the total number of immigrants stayed fairly stable from the decade before, but dropped in the decade after. (This was the second-highest percent for a decade between 1820 and 2000. There was nearly a 20% drop between the 1901–1910 decade and the next decade, etc.)

B. There are two trends that can be observed:

   1. In general, the numbers of immigrants coming from Europe increased from 1820–1910 and then declined after that.

   2. The number of Europeans as a percent of total immigrants was very high until 1911 when this percent started to decrease to an eventual low of about 10%.

1.3 Variability in Numerical Measurements

Goals

- Recognize that variability occurs whenever data are collected

- Use properties of distributions to describe the variability in a given data set

- Use line plots to display data distributions

- Decide if a difference among data values and/or summary measures matters

In this problem, students explore the results from measurement error and variability that occurs naturally when we have many values for an attribute.

Select two students, one boy and one girl. Each student in the class measures each of these student's heads and then records the data to the nearest tenth of a centimeter. Then, each student measures his or her own head size and records the data to the nearest tenth of a centimeter.

One way to do this activity is to have each student measure and cut three string lengths (use string that doesn't "stretch" easily)—one that matches the girl's head size, one that matches the boy's head size, and one that matches his or her own head size. Then they can measure these lengths using a meter stick or a metric measuring tape to the nearest tenth of a centimeter. You can also create an interesting display by taping the strings for the boy to a wall or paper with the tops even. The same representations for the girl and the same for individual members of the class will create a graphic visualization of variability.

Launch 1.3

Explain to students that they will be doing three head measurements. Two will involve each student measuring the same two students' head sizes. The third will involve measuring his or her own head size. *Refrain from discussing how to carry out these measurement tasks.* We want students to encounter variability that can be accounted for with a variety of reasons, including, "We all didn't measure head sizes the same way."

You may want students to record their data in a table on a piece of chart paper or on the blackboard or whiteboard. Some teachers have listed students' names and then added three columns, one each for the three different measurement situations.

Have students work in pairs.

Explore 1.3

Students will need the data from their classmates to complete Questions B and C. You may decide that you want to make three class line plots for Question B using chart paper. If this is so, then as the students record the data values in a class table, also have them mark "X's" on the three different line plots showing the distributions of the measures for the three different situations.

For Question C, the students complete parts (1)–(8) for each of the three distributions.

Summarize 1.3

Below are three line plots showing the three different measurement situations from a class of middle-grades students. You might expect to see results similar to these. If you do, then you will realize that there is greater variability in the measurements of head sizes for all the class than in the measurements of head size for an individual student. Below is some discussion of these three graphs written to give you ideas about the points you may want to emphasize when you look at your class data together.

In this problem, students look at the variability of the data values in relation to each other. So, for the distribution of head sizes for Sarah, many data values are the same (e.g., 56 cm) and there is little variability, while, for the head sizes of everyone in the class, there are fewer repeated measures and values are different from each other. We also want students to consider the importance of the *magnitude of the differences*. For Sarah's head sizes, the range is 2.5 centimeters; most of the measures are within one cm (18 out of 20 measures) so the magnitude of the differences is small; a cap size of 55 cm or 56 cm would work equally as well.

For Jalin, the range is also 2.5 centimeters; 16 out of the 20 head-size measures are within one centimeter's difference. Again, the *magnitude of the difference in measures when considered in the context of the problem,* ordering a fitted cap, is negligible.

However, when looking at the head sizes of all of the students in the class, the range is 6 centimeters—that is of a *magnitude that the difference would matter when thinking about cap sizes, i.e., a cap size that was 59 cm would be quite a bit larger than 53 cm.* In spite of the variability, several students (13 out of 20) are within one centimeter of each other (i.e., 54–55 cm).

Looking across the three distributions, we can see that Sarah's head size at 56 cm (mode) is unusual compared to all students' head-size measures. However, Jalin's head size seems to fall at the mode for all the students' head-size measures (54 cm).

Finally, looking at the *measures in relation to what might be a typical head size* in each situation, we can see that, in Sarah's case, there are a few data values less than the typical head size; and in Jalin's case, there are a few data values less than or greater than the typical head size (54–54.5 cm). For the class, there is greater variability among the data values in relation to a typical head size of 54–54.5 cm.

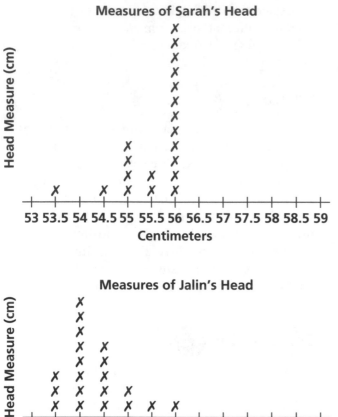

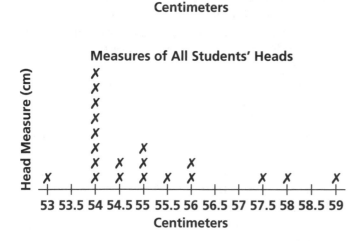

1.3 Variability in Numerical Measurements

Mathematical Goals

- Recognize that variability occurs whenever data are collected
- Use properties of distributions to describe the variability in a given data set
- Use line plots to display data distributions
- Decide if a difference among data values and/or summary measures matters

Launch

Ask students to explain what they think measurement data are and how these data might be collected. Explain to students that they will be doing three head measurements. Two will involve each student measuring the same two students' head sizes. The third will involve measuring his or her own head size. *Refrain from discussing how to carry out these measurement tasks.* We want students to encounter variability that can be accounted for with a variety of reasons, including, "We all didn't measure head sizes the same way."

You may want students to record their data in a table on a piece of chart paper or on the blackboard or whiteboard. Some teachers have listed students' names and then added three columns, one each for the three different measurement situations.

Have students work in pairs.

Explore

Students will need the data from their classmates to complete Questions B and C. You may decide that you want to make three class line plots for Question B using chart paper. If this is so, then as the students record the data values in a class table, also have them mark "X's" on the three different line plots showing the distributions of the measures for the three different situations. For Question C, the students complete parts (1)–(8) for each of the three distributions.

Materials
- Calculators
- String
- Metric measuring tapes or meter sticks (centimeters)
- Graph paper (or gridded chart paper and magic markers, or transparencies with grids and transparency markers)

Summarize

See the extended Summarize section for three line plots showing the three different measurement situations from a class of middle-grade students. You might expect to see results similar to these. If you do, then you will

Materials
- Student notebooks

continued on next page

realize that there is greater variability in the "all the class" head sizes than in the head sizes measured repeatedly for individual students.

The extended Summarize section also has some discussion of these three graphs written to give you ideas about the points you may want to emphasize when you look at your class data together, e.g., *the magnitude of the difference in measures when considered in the context of the problem in needing a head size to order a fitted cap.*

ACE Assignment Guide for Problem 1.3

Differentiated Instruction
Solutions for All Learners

Core 3–7
Other *Connections* 18; unassigned choices from previous problems

Adapted For suggestions about adapting ACE exercises, see the CMP *Special Needs Handbook*.
Connecting to Prior Units 18: *Data About Us*

Labsheet 1ACE Exercises 8–10 is provided if Exercises 8–10 are assigned.

Answers to Problem 1.3

A. data collected in class

B. data displayed in class

C. **1–8.** Answers will vary.

1.4 Two Kinds of Variability

Goals

- Recognize that variability occurs whenever data are collected
- Use properties of distributions to describe the variability in a given data set
- Use value bar graphs and line plots to display data distributions
- Decide if a difference among data values and/or summary measures matters
- Identify sources of variability, including variability that occurs naturally in data and variability that results from errors in measurement

Launch 1.4

This problem builds from work that students completed in Problem 1.3 and should actually be more of a summary activity for students.

Students can refer to their books to look at the situation about Jasmine presented in the problem. You can also show Transparency 1.4A, which matches the value bar graph in the book.

Suggested Questions Ask:

- *Data are presented about Jasmine's head size. Several different students each measured Jasmine's head size. They displayed these data in a table and a value bar graph. Describe how the table and the value bar graph are related.* (Each bar on the value bar graph matches with one of the measures on the table)

- *How is a value bar graph different from a regular (frequency) bar graph?* (The bars on a value bar graph match the individual data values; on a regular bar graph, the bars show the counts of how many times a particular data value occurred in a data set.)

- *Based on these measures for Jasmine's head size and what we did in Problem 1.3 when we measured _____'s and _____'s head sizes, what do you think measurement error means?* (Measurement error is the error made in measuring a head; we find that there is variability in the measures that were made. You can make an error by misreading the scale; by letting the thread slip; by not being

careful to measure around the same part of the head; and so on.)

Then display the next three graphs on Transparency 1.4B and have students look at the next page of their books. There are two questions to be answered:

- *How are the ordered value bar graph and the line plots related?* (The line plot with dots shows the frequency of occurrence of repeated data values; the line plot with X's is identical to the line plot with dots but made with the "X" symbol, which is easy to make when creating a plot by hand. You can point out how each value bar can be matched with a dot or an "X" on the line plots.)

- *What does each graph tell you about the distribution of these data?* (The value bar graph shows the actual length, so you immediately make a comparison of which are longer or shorter than another. The line plots tally responses and make more visible the repeated values in a set of data, etc.)

Have students work in pairs.

Explore 1.4

As students work through the problem, use this opportunity to informally assess their understandings of the investigation. The questions in this problem involve a review of the work done in Problem 1.3 and earlier in the investigation.

Summarize 1.4

For Question A, discuss the answers to parts (1)–(8). For Question B, have students display graphs. Then discuss the answers to parts (2)–(9).

Have students clarify the two kinds of variability that they have been dealing with: variability that results from measurement error (Question A) and variability that is part of the natural differences when different people are measured (Question B). We can call these *measurement variability* and *natural variability*.

There are also probably measurement errors in the class data, but the measures from head to head reflect natural variability.

Also review what it means to look at variability among data values showing head size in a distribution and what has been identified as a typical head size. For the former, we are looking at how data values differ from or are similar to each other and how spread out they are. For the latter, we are looking at how clustered or not clustered the data appear to be around a typical head size.

Labsheet 1ACE Exercise 22 is provided if Exercise 22 is assigned.

1.4 Two Kinds of Variability

PACING 1 day

Mathematical Goals

- Recognize that variability occurs whenever data are collected
- Use properties of distributions to describe the variability in a given data set
- Use value bar graphs and line plots to display data distributions
- Decide if a difference among data values and/or summary measures matters
- Identify sources of variability, including variability that occurs naturally in data and variability that results from errors in measurement

Launch

This problem builds from work that students completed in Problem 1.3 and should actually be more of a summary activity for students. You can use Transparency 1.4A, which matches the value bar graph in the book.

- *Several different students each measured Jasmine's head size and displayed these data in a table, in a value bar graph, and in a line plot. Describe how the table and the value bar graph or the line plot are related.*

- *How is a value bar graph different from a regular (frequency) bar graph?*

- *Based on these measures for Jasmine's head size and what we did in Problem 1.3 when we measured _____'s and _____'s head sizes, what do you think measurement error means?*

Display the next three graphs on Transparency 1.4B and have students look at the next page of their books. Ask:

- *How are the ordered value bar graph and the line plots related?*
- *What does each graph tell you about the distribution of these data?*

Have students work in pairs.

Materials
- Transparencies 1.4A, 1.4B

Vocabulary
- value bar graph
- variability
- ordered bar graph
- line plots

Explore

As students work through the problem, use this opportunity to informally assess their understanding of the investigation. The questions in this problem involve a review of the work done in Problem 1.3.

Materials
- Calculators
- Graph paper (or gridded chart paper and magic markers, or transparencies with grids and transparency

Summarize

Have students clarify the two kinds of variability that they have dealt with: variability from measurement error and variability from natural differences in measuring different people. Review what it means to look at variation among data values in a distribution and what has been identified as typical. For the former, we look at how data values differ from or are similar to each other and how spread out they are. For the latter, we look at how clustered or not clustered the data appear to be around the typical head size.

Materials
- Student notebooks

ACE Assignment Guide for Problem 1.4

Differentiated Instruction
Solutions for All Learners

Core ACE 12, 13
Other ACE *Connections* 19, 20; *Extensions* 21–23;
unassigned choices from previous problems

Adapted For suggestions about adapting ACE exercises, see the CMP *Special Needs Handbook*.
Connecting to Prior Units 19: *Data About Us*

Labsheet 1ACE Exercise 22 is provided if Exercise 22 is assigned.

Answers to Problem 1.4

A. 1. 55 cm and 56.5 cm.

  2. 1.5 cm

  3. The range of 1.5 cm is not very large, so the differences in measurements are small and unlikely to matter in choosing a hat size.

  4. Given the magnitude of the differences, there appear to be no outliers.

  5. The data cluster between 55.5 and 56.

  6. Given the magnitude of the differences, there are no significant gaps.

  7. Anywhere the data cluster, such as 56 cm, is appropriate.

  8. The data cluster in a small range of only 1.5 cm. Much of the data (10 out of 13 data values) are between 55.5 and 56 cm, so

while there are different measures, the variability among the measures is small.

B. 1. (Figures 1 and 2)

  2. 54 cm and 58.5 cm

  3. 4.5 cm

  4. The range of 4.5 cm is large enough, so the differences in measurements are likely to matter in choosing a cap size.

  5. The data are quite spread out, so there appear to be no easily recognized outliers.

  6. The data can be considered to cluster around 55 to 57 cm, with a number of data values also at 58 to 58.5 cm.

  7. There appear to be gaps, some with a magnitude of about 1 cm between 54 and 55 and between 57 and 58.

  8. 56.4 cm could be considered as the typical head size because it looks like it might be where the data balances. It is possible to argue that getting caps sized 55 cm, 56 cm, 57 cm, and 58 cm would fit most people comfortably.

  9. The measurements are similar because they all fall between 54.0 and 58.5 cm. The measurements are different from each other because they do not cluster and the range is big enough to matter.

Figure 1

Student Head Size

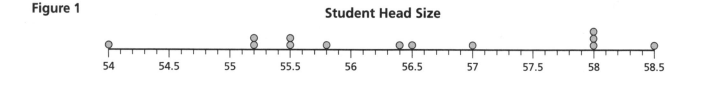

Figure 2

Head Measurements

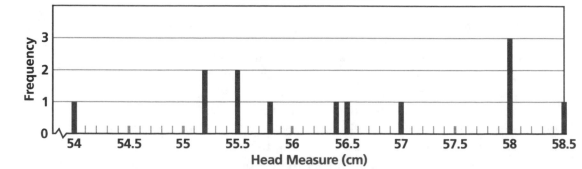

Investigation 1

Making Sense of Variability

A statistical investigation begins with a question. Decisions about what data to collect are based on the question that is asked.

When data are collected to answer a question, the data may be similar to each other, such as the number of raisins found in each of 30 different half-ounce boxes of raisins. More often, however, the data are different from each other, such as pulse rates collected from 30 different people after each person rides a roller coaster.

Variability of a set of numerical data indicates how widely spread or closely clustered the data values are.

For each situation below, do you expect the data to be more similar to or different from each other? Why?

Each student records the number of each color of M&M™ candies found in his or her own bag of candies.

Each student measures the same student's head size in centimeters.

Each student collects his or her reaction times on five trials using a computer reaction-time game.

Each student records his or her grade level—sixth grade, seventh grade, or eighth grade—as part of the data collected on a school survey.

Investigation 1 Making Sense of Variability   **5**

Notes _____

_____

_____

_____

1.1 Variability in Categorical Data

Data that are specific labels or names for categories are called **categorical data.** Suppose you ask people in which months they were born or what their favorite rock groups are. Their answers are categorical data. When displaying categorical data using tables or graphs, you usually report the *frequency*, or "how many," of each category in the data set as a count or a percent.

Did You Know?

M&M™ candies have been around for a long time. They are named after Mars and Murrie, the people who started the candy company in the early 1940s. M&M candies began as a high-energy field snack for American soldiers, because "they melt in your mouth, not in your hand." They were later introduced to the public.

For many years, M&M candies came in six colors: brown, yellow, orange, green, tan, and red. Blue replaced tan in 1995, but in early 2004, M&M candies were available only in black and white! The same six, but brighter, 1995 colors returned in March 2004.

Did the Mars Company plan a specific distribution of colors of M&M candies before March 2004?

- What kinds of data would help answer the question?
- How might you collect such data?
- How would you analyze the data?
- How would you use your analysis to help answer the question?

Notes _____

_____

_____

_____

One student uses a database that gives data for 200 bags of pre-2004 M&M's. The database shows how many of each color candy were in each of the 200 bags. She uses the counts from the first bag to make a bar graph that shows the *percent* of each color of candies in the bag.

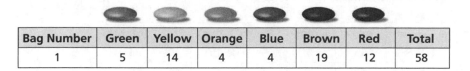

Bag Number	Green	Yellow	Orange	Blue	Brown	Red	Total
1	5	14	4	4	19	12	58

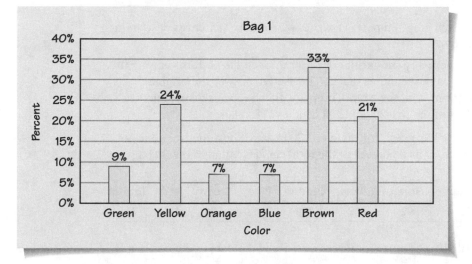

How did the student use the counts of the data to graph the percents?

The student noticed that the percent varied considerably from color to color.

There were more yellow, brown, and red candies than green, orange, and blue candies.

Brown candies took up the greatest percentage of the bag; $\frac{1}{3}$, or about 33%, of the bag of candies was brown.

The yellow and the red candies were close in quantity, with yellow a little less than $\frac{1}{4}$, or 25%, of the bag and red a little more than $\frac{1}{5}$, or 20%, of the bag.

The green, orange, and blue candies were each less than $\frac{1}{10}$, or 10%, of the bag.

Investigation 1 Making Sense of Variability   **7**

Notes _____

_____

_____

_____

A. 1. The table shows data from two other bags of candies. Make a bar graph for each set of data. Show the frequency of each color as a percent of the total candies in that bag.

Bag Number	Green	Yellow	Orange	Blue	Brown	Red	Total
2	5	15	2	7	15	10	54
3	3	13	5	5	19	10	55

2. For each graph in part (1), write two or more sentences describing the data.

3. Are there any similarities or differences in the patterns among the three bags of candies that can be used to answer the original question, "Did the Mars Company plan a specific distribution of colors of the pre-2004 M&M candies?" Explain.

B. 1. Make a bar graph for these pre-2004 data. Show the frequency of each color as a percent of the total candies found in the 30 bags.

Bag Number	Green	Yellow	Orange	Blue	Brown	Red	Total
1–30	92	449	109	90	576	415	1,731

2. Write two or more sentences describing the data in the bar graph.

3. How would you now answer the question, "Did the Mars Company plan a specific distribution of colors of the pre-2004 M&M candies?"

C. Look at the eight graphs on the next page. Did the company make a change in the distribution of colors in March 2004? If so, describe the change. Explain your reasoning.

ACE Homework starts on page 17.

1.2 Variability in Numerical Counts

Data that are counts or measures are called **numerical data.** We often count to gather numerical data. For example, we count people to find the population of each state in the United States in order to answer the question, "How much do state populations vary in size?"

Notes _____

_____

_____

_____

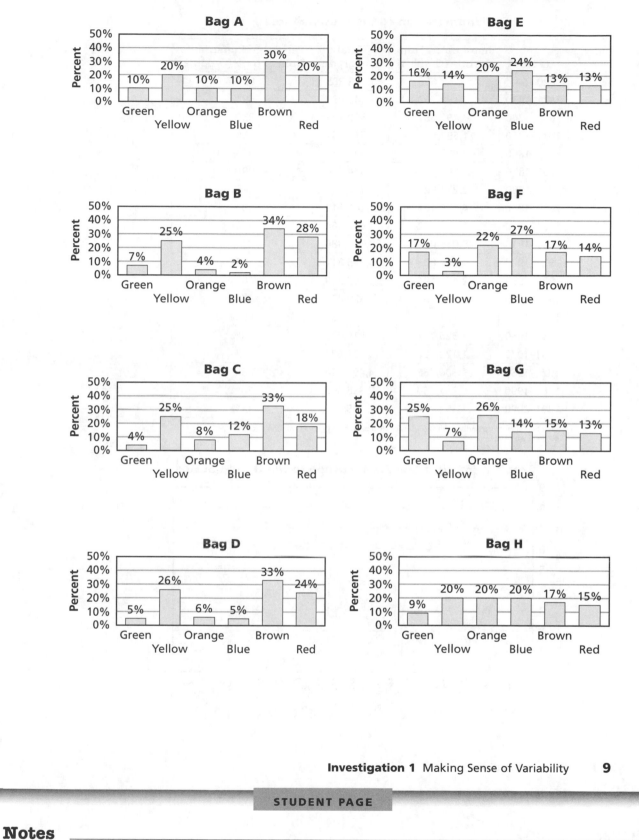

Before March 2004

Bag A

Bag B

Bag C

Bag D

After March 2004

Bag E

Bag F

Bag G

Bag H

Notes _____

_____

_____

_____

Use the table and related graphs to answer the questions in Problem 1.2.

Immigration to the United States

Decade	Immigrants From Europe (Graph 1)	Total Immigrants	Percent of Immigrants From Europe (Graph 2)
1820	7,650	8,385	82%
1821–1830	98,797	143,439	69%
1831–1840	495,681	599,125	83%
1831–1850	1,597,442	1,713,251	93%
1851–1860	2,452,577	2,598,214	94%
1861–1870	2,064,141	2,314,824	89%
1871–1880	2,271,925	2,812,191	81%
1881–1890	4,735,484	5,246,613	90%
1891–1900	3,555,352	3,687,564	96%
1901–1910	8,056,040	8,795,386	92%
1911–1920	4,321,887	5,735,811	75%
1921–1930	2,463,194	4,107,209	60%
1931–1940	347,566	528,431	66%
1941–1950	621,147	1,035,039	60%
1951–1960	1,325,727	2,515,479	53%
1961–1970	1,123,492	3,321,677	34%
1971–1980	800,368	4,493,314	18%
1981–1990	761,550	7,338,062	10%
1991–2000	1,359,737	9,095,417	15%

SOURCE: U.S. Citizenship and Immigration Services. Go to www.PHSchool.com for a data update.
Web Code: ang-9041

Graph 1: Immigration From Europe to the United States

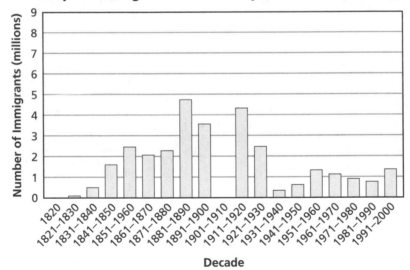

Notes

Graph 2: Immigration From Europe to the United States

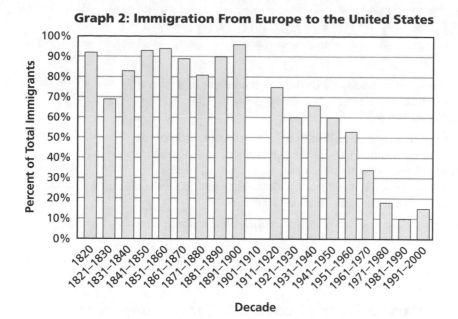

How did immigration from Europe to the United States change from 1820 to 2000?

Problem 1.2 **Variability in Numerical Counts**

A. 1. a. In the decade from 1901 to 1910, how many immigrants came from Europe?

b. Copy Graph 1 and add the bar for 1901–1910.

c. Write two comparison statements about how the 1901–1910 data value is similar to or different from the values for other decades.

2. a. In the decade from 1901 to 1910, how many immigrants came from all countries?

b. What percent of this number were immigrants from Europe?

c. Copy Graph 2 and add the bar for 1901–1910.

d. Write two comparison statements about how the percent in part (b) is similar to or different from the percents for other decades.

B. Describe any trends or patterns you notice in immigration to the United States from Europe from 1820 to 2000.

ACE **Homework starts on page 17.**

Investigation 1 Making Sense of Variability **11**

Notes _____

_____

_____

_____

1.3 Variability in Numerical Measurements

Measurements, such as the time to run a mile or the height of a student, are another kind of numerical data. You already know that any measurement is approximate.

The measurement tools we use to gather data affect the precision of the measures we obtain. For example, one scale measures mass to the nearest tenth of a gram while another scale measures mass to the nearest thousandth of a gram. Also, when different people measure the same object, the results may differ even when they use the same tool.

What tool(s) might you use to measure heads in order to determine sizes needed for fitted baseball caps?

Problem 1.3 Variability in Numerical Measurements

Suppose your class wants to order fitted baseball caps with the *Mugwump* as a logo.

A. 1. Your teacher will choose one boy and one girl from the class to represent two different head sizes. Measure these two students' head sizes to the nearest tenth of a centimeter and record the data.

2. Measure your own head size to the nearest tenth of a centimeter and record the data.

B. Use the data gathered by your class for Question A. Make a line plot for each of the following:

1. the head-size measurements for the girl chosen

2. the head-size measurements for the boy chosen

3. the head-size measurements of all the students in the class

C. For each line plot in Question B:

1. What are the minimum and maximum values of the distribution?

2. What is the range of the distribution?

3. Do you think the range of the measurements is great enough that recommending a single cap size would be difficult? Explain.

4. Are there any unusually high or low data values, or *outliers*? If so, what are they?

5. Do some or most of the data cluster in one or more locations? If so, where does this occur?

6. Are there gaps in the data? If so, where do they occur?

12   Data Distributions

Notes _____

_____

_____

_____

7. What would you describe as a typical head size for these data? Explain.

8. Use these ideas to describe the variability in the data.

ACE Homework starts on page 17.

1.4 Two Kinds of Variability

Each of 13 students measured the circumference of Jasmine's head. The results are shown using a table and a graph called a **value bar graph.**

Head Measurements

Name	Measure (cm)
Santo	56.0
Sara	55.8
Pam	56.0
Melosa	55.9
Malik	55.5
Martin	56.0
Ming	55.2
Manny	56.5
Juanita	55.0
Jun	55.5
Tai	56.0
Kareem	55.5
Chip	55.8

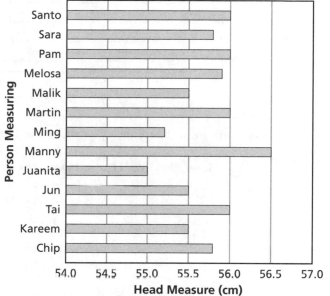

How are the table and the value bar graph related?

What is a value bar graph?

The variability results from measurement errors as different students measured the circumference of Jasmine's head.

How do you think measurement errors occur?

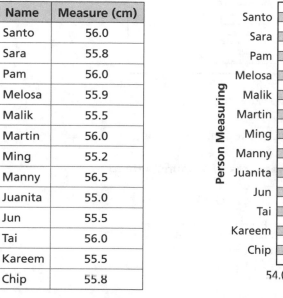

Investigation 1 Making Sense of Variability **13**

Notes _____

_____

_____

_____

The **ordered value bar graph** shows the data in order from minimum to maximum values.

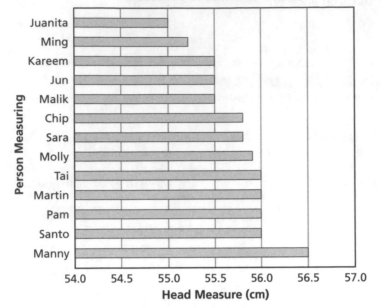

The **line plots** show the frequency of each measurement.

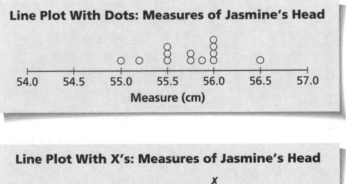

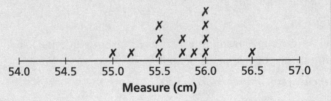

How are the ordered value bar graph and the line plots related?

What does each graph tell you about the distribution of these data?

Notes _____

_____

_____

_____

Problem 1.4 Two Kinds of Variability

Use the ordered value bar graph and the line plots on the facing page.

A. 1. Examine the distribution of the measurements. What are the minimum and maximum values?

   2. What is the range?

   3. Is the range of the measurements great enough that choosing a cap size for Jasmine would be difficult? Explain.

   4. Are there any outliers? If so, what are they?

   5. Do some or most of the data cluster in one or more locations? Explain.

   6. Are there gaps in the data? If so, where do they occur?

   7. What measurement would you recommend using to choose a cap size for Jasmine? Explain.

   8. Use these ideas to describe the variability in the data set.

B. 1. Jasmine's classmates measured their own head sizes and recorded them in the table below. Make an ordered value bar graph and a line plot for these data.

Class Head Sizes

Initials	CK	KN	TB	JG	JW	MD	MG
Measure (cm)	55.8	58.0	56.5	58.0	55.5	58.0	55.2

Initials	MJ	MR	MS	PM	SF	SK
Measure (cm)	58.5	55.2	55.5	54.0	57.0	56.4

   2. What are the minimum and maximum values?

   3. What is the range?

   4. Is the range of the measurements great enough that recommending one cap size for all the students would be difficult? Explain.

   5. Are there any outliers? If so, what are they?

   6. Do some or most of the data cluster in one or more locations? Explain.

   7. Are there gaps in the data? If so, where do they occur?

   8. What would you describe as the typical cap size for these students? Explain.

   9. Use these ideas to describe the variability in the data set.

ACE Homework starts on page 17.

Investigation 1 Making Sense of Variability **15**

Notes _____

_____

_____

_____

Applications

1. a. Use the M&M™ data for Bag 1, Bag 2, and Bag 3. For each bag, make a bar graph that shows the percent of each color found.

M&M™ Candy Colors

Bag Number	Green	Yellow	Orange	Blue	Brown	Red	Total
1	3	10	9	5	10	18	55
2	5	12	4	6	19	11	57
3	7	10	9	4	16	12	58
4	4	14	2	1	14	19	54
5	12	7	8	7	14	13	61
6	10	9	6	5	15	8	53
7	11	11	6	6	12	12	58
8	8	15	5	3	16	10	57
9	2	11	4	4	24	12	57
10	5	7	4	1	26	13	56
11	6	13	4	4	15	18	60
12	5	8	4	2	23	16	58
13	9	13	4	4	14	11	55
14	9	10	5	5	14	14	57
15	5	19	5	2	13	14	58
Total	101	169	79	59	245	201	854

b. Write two or more comparison statements that describe the distribution of colors for the three bags.

c. Is there some plan to the distribution of colors in the bags? Explain.

2. a. Use the totals in the last row of the table for each color of candies. Make a bar graph for these data that shows the percent of each color found in the 15 bags.

b. Describe the data by writing two or more comparison statements.

c. Look back at the bar graph you made for Problem 1.1, Question B. Compare this graph with the graph you made in part (a). How would you now answer the question, "Did the Mars Company plan a specific distribution of colors of M&M candies?" Explain.

16 Data Distributions

Notes _____

_____

_____

_____

3. a. The line plot below shows the head measurements of several seventh-grade students. What are the minimum and maximum values?

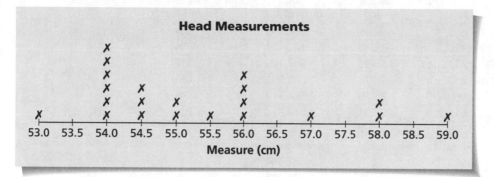

b. What is the range?

c. Is the range of the measurements great enough that recommending one cap size for all the students would be difficult? Explain.

d. Are there any outliers? If so, what are they?

e. Do some or most of the data cluster in one or more locations? If so, where?

f. Are there gaps in the data? If so, where do they occur?

g. What would you describe as the typical cap size for these students?

h. How might you use these ideas to describe the variability in the data?

For each situation in Exercises 4–7, tell whether the data collected are categorical or numerical. Then, tell whether the data are widely spread out or closely clustered.

4. Each student records the number of people living in his or her household.

5. Each student measures the length of the same table in centimeters.

6. Each student randomly chooses a number from 1 to 10.

7. Each student records the time spent viewing television, videos, and DVD movies in the past week.

Homework Help Online
——PHSchool.com
For: Help with Exercises 4–7
Web Code: ane-8104

Investigation 1 Making Sense of Variability **17**

Notes _____

_____

_____

_____

For Exercises 8–11, use the table below.

Immigration to the United States

Decade	Immigrants From Mexico	Total Immigrants	Percent of Immigrants From Mexico
1820	1	8,385	0%
1821–1830	4,817	143,439	3%
1831–1840	6,599	599,125	1%
1831–1850	3,271	1,713,251	0%
1851–1860	3,078	2,598,214	0%
1861–1870	2,191	2,314,824	0%
1871–1880	5,162	2,812,191	0%
1881–1890	1,913	5,246,613	0%
1891–1900	971	3,687,564	0%
1901–1910	49,642	8,795,386	1%
1911–1920	219,004	5,735,811	4%
1921–1930	459,287	4,107,209	11%
1931–1940	22,319	528,431	4%
1941–1950	60,589	1,035,039	6%
1951–1960	299,811	2,515,479	12%
1961–1970	453,937	3,321,677	14%
1971–1980	640,294	4,493,314	14%
1981–1990	1,655,843	7,338,062	23%
1991–2000	2,249,421	9,095,417	25%

SOURCE: U.S. Citizenship and Immigration Services. Go to www.PHSchool.com for a data update.
Web Code: ang-9041

8. **a.** In each of the decades 1961–1970 and 1971–1980, how many people were immigrants from Mexico?

   b. Copy the graph below. Add the bars for 1961–1970 and 1971–1980.

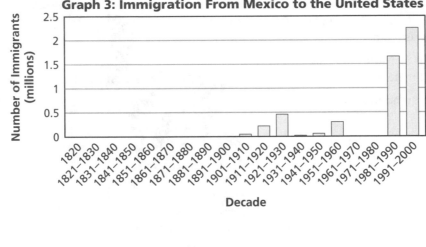

Graph 3: Immigration From Mexico to the United States

18 Data Distributions

Notes _____

_____

_____

_____

9. **Multiple Choice** Which statement is true?

   A. More immigrants came to the United States in the decade
   1941–1950 than in the decade 1961–1970.

   B. About the same number of immigrants came to the United States in
   the decade 1921–1930 as in the decade 1961–1970.

   C. The number of immigrants in the decade 1991–2000 is about 50,000
   more than the combined number of immigrants for the two decades
   1971–1990.

   D. None of the above.

10. **a.** In each of the decades 1961–1970 and 1971–1980, how many people
   total were immigrants to the United States?

   b. What percent of each of the numbers in part (a) were immigrants
   from Mexico?

   c. Copy the graph below. Add the bars for 1961–1970 and 1971–1980.

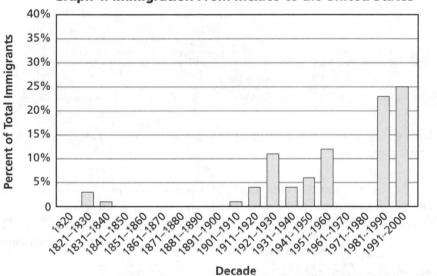

Graph 4: Immigration From Mexico to the United States

   d. Write two comparison statements
   about how the data values in part (c)
   are similar to or different from the
   data values for other decades.

11. How has the pattern of immigration
   from Mexico to the United States
   changed from 1820 to 2000? Explain.

Investigation 1 Making Sense of Variability   **19**

Notes _____

_____

_____

_____

12. a. One of the line plots below shows several measures of Yukio's head. The other shows one measure of Yukio's head and one of each of his classmates' heads. Identify the line plot that shows Yukio's head measurements. Explain your reasoning.

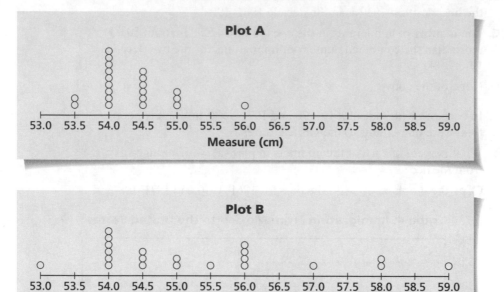

b. Identify the line plot that shows the head measurements of Yukio and his classmates.

13. a. The table below shows the data for the brown candies from Bags 4–9 of Exercise 1. Make an ordered value bar graph and a line plot for these data.

Brown M&M's

Bag Number	4	5	6	7	8	9
Number of Brown Candies	14	14	15	12	16	24

b. What are the minimum and maximum values?

c. What is the range?

d. Are there gaps or clusters of data? Explain.

e. Would an ordered value bar graph or a line plot better represent the data? Explain.

20 Data Distributions

Notes _____

_____

_____

_____

Connections

14. There are 100 candies in Bag A. Given the following statements, how many candies of each color are there?

- $\frac{3}{10}$ are brown
- 0.25 are yellow

- 0.1 are green

- $\frac{2}{10}$ are red
- the ratio of red candies to blue candies is 2 : 1
- 0.05 are orange

15. There are 80 candies in Bag B. Given the following statements, how many candies of each color are there?

- 30% are brown
- 0.25 are yellow
- the ratio of brown candies to blue candies is 3 : 1

- 20% are red
- 0.05 are green
- the ratio of orange candies to green candies is 2 : 1

16. Multiple Choice The stem-and-leaf plot shows the heights of a group of students. What percent of the students are more than 5 feet tall?

Student Heights

4	3 3 4 5 6 7 7 8 9
5	0 0 1 1 2 2 2 6 8 8 9
6	0 0 3 5 5

Key: 5 | 2 means 52 inches

F. 44%   **G.** 20%   **H.** 12%   **J.** 80%

Notes

17. a. Describe any trends or patterns in immigration to the United States from Asia from 1820 to 2000 using the graph below.

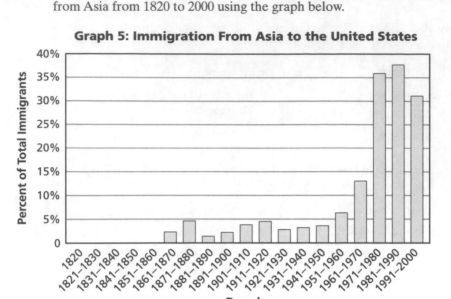

Graph 5: Immigration From Asia to the United States

Source: U.S. Citizenship and Immigration Services. Go to www.PHSchool.com for a data update. Web Code: ang-9041

b. Write two comparison statements about the trends in immigration from Mexico to the United States (Exercises 8–11) and from Asia to the United States from 1820 to 2000.

c. Look back at Graph 2 in Problem 1.2. As the trend for immigration from Europe was decreasing from 1961 to 2000, what happened to the trends for immigration from Mexico and Asia?

18. Multiple Choice Ms. Turini's math class took a test on Monday. The scores for the exam were: 98, 79, 65, 84, 87, 92, 90, 61, 93, 76, 72, and 93. Which stem-and-leaf plot correctly displays these data?

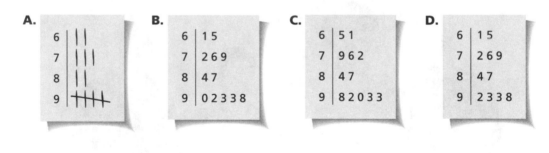

A.

6	ǀ ǀ
7	ǀ ǀ ǀ
8	ǀ ǀ
9	ǀ ǀ ǀ ǀ ǀ

B.

6	1 5
7	2 6 9
8	4 7
9	0 2 3 3 8

C.

6	5 1
7	9 6 2
8	4 7
9	8 2 0 3 3

D.

6	1 5
7	2 6 9
8	4 7
9	2 3 3 8

Notes _____

_____

_____

_____

19. a. The tables below show prices for skateboards at four different sporting goods stores. For each store, make a stem-and-leaf plot that will show the distribution of prices for skateboards from that store.

Store A			Store B			Store C			Store D	
$60	$50		$13	$70		$40	$50		$179	$145
$40	$50		$40	$50		$20	$60		$160	$149
$13	$60		$45	$70		$60	$70		$149	$149
$45	$50		$60	$50		$35	$70		$149	$149
$20	$25		$50	$10		$50	$50		$149	$149
$30	$15		$30	$120		$30	$90		$145	$145
$35	$70		$15	$90		$13	$120		$149	$150
$60	$120		$35	$120		$45	$120		$100	$149
$50	$90		$15			$40	$200		$179	$149
$70										

b. How do the prices for skateboards compare across the four stores? Write statements that make your reasoning clear.

c. Look at the four stem-and-leaf plots. What is the typical price for skateboards? Explain your reasoning.

d. Describe the variability in the prices of skateboards.

20. Make a line plot to show the distribution of head-size measures that matches the criteria below.

- There are 10 data points.
- The measures vary from 54 cm to 57.5 cm.
- The mode is 55 cm; there are three data values at the mode.
- The median is 55.5 cm.

Investigation 1 Making Sense of Variability   **23**

Notes _____

_____

_____

_____

Extensions

For Exercise 21, use the data in the table below.

Presidential Fitness Test Standards

Tests	Time (seconds)			
	Age 11	Age 12	Age 13	Age 14
Boys—Shuttle Run	10.0	9.8	9.5	9.1
Girls—Shuttle Run	10.5	10.4	10.2	10.1
Boys—Mile Run	452	431	410	386
Girls—Mile Run	542	500	493	479

SOURCE: The President's Council on Physical Fitness and Sports

21. Each graph is marked with a reference line that shows the Presidential Fitness Standard Time for the age group.

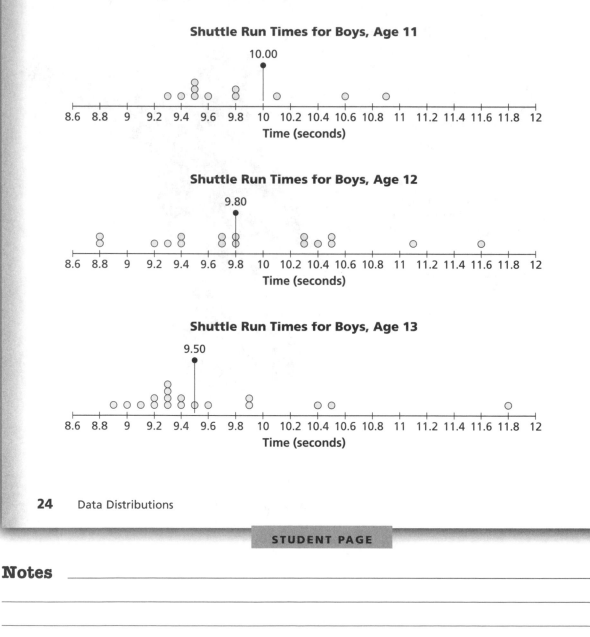

Notes _____

_____

_____

_____

a. Estimate the minimum and maximum times in each distribution.

b. Estimate the range of each distribution.

c. Does the range seem "large" or "small" for each set of data? Explain your reasoning.

d. Are there any outliers? If so, what are they?

e. Do some or most of the data in each distribution cluster in one or more locations? If so, where?

f. Are there gaps in any set of data? If so, where do they occur?

g. How would you describe the typical shuttle run time for each age group of boys?

h. Describe the variability in each of the three distributions.

i. How do the fitness test results in each graph compare to the Presidential Standards for that age level? Explain.

STUDENT PAGE

22. a. Estimate the minimum and maximum shuttle run times shown in the scatter plot.

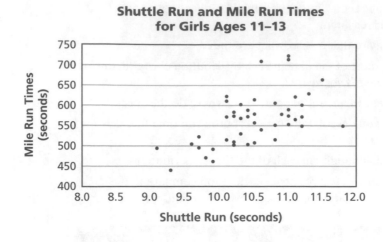

Shuttle Run and Mile Run Times for Girls Ages 11–13

b. Estimate the minimum and maximum mile run times.

c. Copy the scatter plot. Sketch the line $y = 50x$ where y is the time for the mile run and x is the time for the shuttle run.

d. What can you say about the times that are on this line? Times that are above this line? Times that are below this line?

e. Is there a relationship between Times for Mile Run and Times for Shuttle Run? Explain.

23. Multiple Choice Janelle makes a scatter plot that shows the relationship between the number of music downloads she has made and the amount of unused disk space she has left. Which statement is true?

F. As the number of music downloads increases, the amount of unused disk space increases.

G. As the number of music downloads increases, the amount of unused disk space stays the same.

H. As the number of music downloads decreases, the amount of unused disk space increases.

J. As the number of music downloads decreases, the amount of disk space used decreases.

26   Data Distributions

Notes _____

_____

_____

_____

Mathematical Reflections 1

In this investigation, you explored how data in a distribution vary. These questions will help you summarize what you have learned.

Think over your answers to these questions. Discuss your ideas with other students and your teacher. Then write a summary of your findings in your notebook.

1. Use the situation below to help you answer parts (a)–(e).

   Students collected data from their classmates to answer each of these three questions:

   - *What is the typical bedtime for students?*
   - *What are students' favorite kinds of pets?*
   - *What is the typical number of pets students have?*

   a. What measures are used to describe variability?

   b. Define the range of a distribution of data so a sixth-grader would understand.

   c. How would you help a sixth-grade student understand the difference between categorical data and numerical data?

   d. What does it mean when we say categorical data vary?

   e. What does it mean when we say numerical data vary?

2. In which situations might you report frequencies of data using actual counts? In which might you use percents? How do you decide?

3. Describe how displaying data in tables or graphs can help you identify patterns or determine what is typical about a distribution.

Investigation 1 Making Sense of Variability   **27**

Notes

Investigation ①

ACE
Assignment Choices

Differentiated Instruction
Solutions for All Learners

Problem 1.1
Core ACE 1, 2
Other ACE *Connections* 14, 15

Problem 1.2
Core ACE 8–11
Other ACE *Connections* 16, 17; unassigned choices from previous problems

Problem 1.3
Core ACE 3–7
Other ACE *Connections* 18; unassigned choices from previous problems

Problem 1.4
Core ACE 12, 13
Other ACE *Connections* 19, 20; *Extensions* 21–23; unassigned choices from previous problems

Adapted For suggestions about adapting Exercise 2 and other ACE exercises, see the CMP *Special Needs Handbook.*
Connecting to Prior Units 14, 15, 17: *Comparing and Scaling*; 17: *Bits and Pieces II*; 16, 18, 19: *Data About Us*

Applications

1. a.

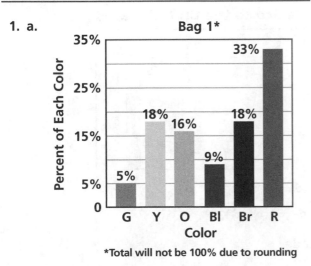

Bag 1*

*Total will not be 100% due to rounding

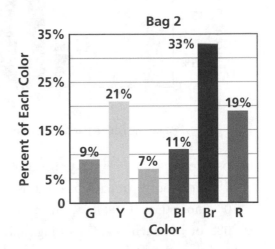

Bag 2

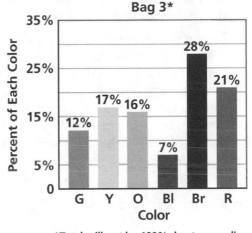

Bag 3*

*Total will not be 100% due to rounding

b. Possible answer: In Bag 1, red took up the greatest percent of the bag at 33%, or $\frac{1}{3}$ of the bag, and brown took up 18%, or a little less than $\frac{1}{5}$ of the bag. The reverse was true for Bag 2, in which brown took up 33%, or $\frac{1}{3}$ of the bag, and red took up 19%, or a little less than $\frac{1}{5}$ of the bag.

c. It seems as though red, brown, and yellow tend to have the highest percentage, and green and blue seem to have the lowest. Orange seems to be in the middle range between the highest and the lowest percentage.

2. a.

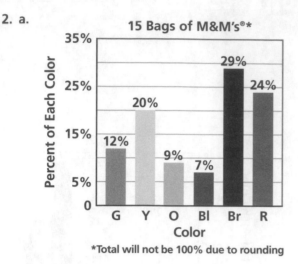

15 Bags of M&M's®*

*Total will not be 100% due to rounding

b. Possible answers. Brown candies took up 29%, or about $\frac{3}{10}$ of each bag. This is about 10% more than the yellow, which took up 20%, or $\frac{1}{5}$ of each bag. The orange and blue candies each consisted of a little less than 10% of each bag. Green was in between the percent of yellow and orange with 12%.

c. Brown still seems to be the highest, with red and yellow having the next highest percent of candies in each bag. Orange, blue, and green have the lowest percents of candies in each bag. The above statements apply to both graphs leading one to believe there is a plan to the distribution of colors in M&M's candies.

3. a. 53 cm and 59 cm

b. The range is 6 cm.

c. Possible answer: Yes. The range is quite large, so if one cap size was used, it may be too large or too small for the students at either end of the distribution.

d. There is a possible outlier at 59 cm. The median is 55. Interquartile range is 2. There are no outliners.

e. Most of the data cluster from 54 to 56 cm.

f. Gaps occur at 53.5 cm, 56.5 cm, 57.5 cm, and 58.5 cm.

g. The typical head size is between 54 and 56 cm, where most of the data clusters. The median is at 55 cm, so that may be referred to as a typical head/cap size.

h. The data have a fairly large range without any significant gaps, however there seems to be a cluster of data at 54–56 cm.

4. Numerical; the data can vary widely.

5. Numerical; measures of the length of the same table should be roughly the same.

6. Students might choose "categorical" here, thinking of these numbers as labels rather than values. Or they might say "numerical," thinking of the numbers as quantities. The distribution should be uniform and spread from 1 to 10.

7. Numerical; the data can vary widely.

8. a. From 1961–1970 there were 453,937 immigrants from Mexico. From 1971–1980 there were 640,294 immigrants from Mexico.

b. (Figure 3)

9. D

Figure 3

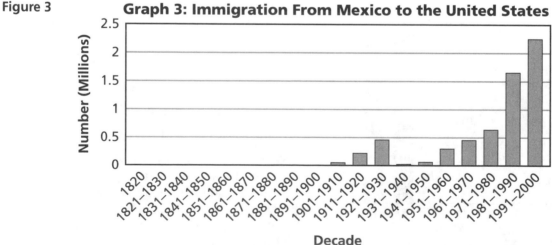

Graph 3: Immigration From Mexico to the United States

10. a. During the decade 1961–1970 there were 3,321,677 immigrants to the U.S. from all countries, and during 1971–1980 there were 4,493,314 immigrants to the U.S. from all countries.

b. During the decade 1961–1970 about 14% of the immmigrants were from Mexico. From 1971–1980 also about 14% of the immigrants were from Mexico.

c. (Figure 4)

d. Possible answer: These data values are slightly above the immigration rate of Mexicans from 1921–1930 and about double the immigration rate from 1941–1950.

11. Possible answer: From 1821–1830, the immigration from Mexico was close to 5% but from 1831–1910 it was close to 0%. In 1911, there began an increase to about 5%. In 1921, there was a surge to 10% and, in 1931, immigration reverted back to 5%, and from 1931 there was a steady increase to 25% in 1991–2000. Another possible answer: Throughout the 19th century, Mexican immigration was very low but throughout the 20th century, it increased greatly.

12. a. Figure A shows less variability, which leads you to believe that it is the measure of Yukio's head. The variability is not great because it is probably due to measurement error.

b. The variability in Figure B shows the head measures of Yukio and each of his classmates. The variability is greater than in Figure A, probably due to the natural difference in the size of each person's head.

13. a.

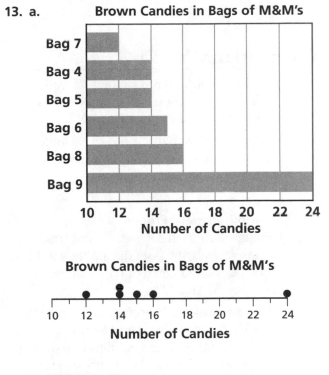

b. 12–24 candies

c. 12

d. There is a cluster from 12–16 candies, then a gap from 16–24 candies.

Figure 4

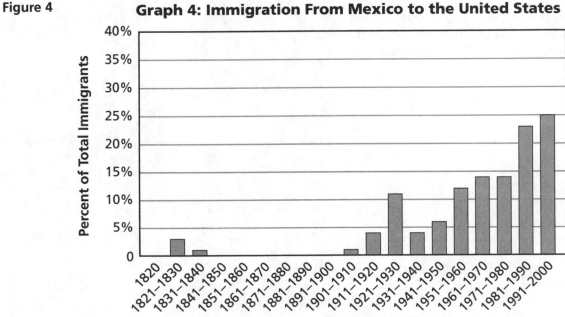

e. Answers may vary. It is easy to see the values in the line plot. The lengths of the bars in the ordered value bar graph allow you to immediately make a comparison of which are longer or shorter. The line plot makes more visible the repeated values in a set of data.

Connections

14. 30 brown candies, 20 red candies, 25 yellow candies, 10 blue candies, 10 green candies, and 5 orange candies

15. 24 brown candies, 16 red candies, 20 yellow candies, 8 blue candies, 4 green candies, and 8 orange

16. H

17. a. Possible answers: From 1820–1850, immigration from Asia was about 0%. Immigration from Asia during the 1971 to 2000 period remained fairly constant between 31 and 37%.

b. Possible answers: Immigration from Asia and Mexico have increased over the period 1820 to 2000. Mexican immigration during the period 1971 to 2000 was not as great as the immigration from Asia. The immigration from Mexico (1981–2000) was about 25% of the total immigration to the United States, and the immigration from Asia was between 30% and 35%.

c. They were increasing.

18. B (Note to teacher: Although C does have the correct data, it is not ordered correctly, which is the proper way to display a stem-and-leaf plot.)

19. a.

Store A

1	3 5
2	0 5
3	0 5
4	0 5
5	0 0 0 0
6	0 0 0
7	0 0
8	
9	0
10	
11	
12	0

Key: 9 | 0 means $90

Store B

1	0 3 5 5
2	
3	0 5
4	0 5
5	0 0 0
6	0
7	0 0
8	
9	0
10	
11	
12	0 0

Key: 9 | 0 means $90

Store C

1	3
2	0
3	0 5
4	0 0 5
5	0 0 0
6	0 0
7	0 0
8	
9	0
10	
11	
12	0 0
13	
14	
15	
16	
17	
18	
19	
20	0

Key: 9 | 0 means $90

Store D

1	
2	
3	
4	
5	
6	
7	
8	
9	
10	0
11	
12	
13	
14	5 5 5 9 9 9 9 9 9 9 9 9 9 9
15	0
16	0
17	9 9

Key: 9 | 0 means $90

b. Possible answers: The most expensive skateboards are in Store D because 94% of their prices fall between $145 and $180, whereas 0% of Stores A's and B's prices, and 5% of Store C's prices fall in or above this interval.

c. Possible answers for the typical price for skateboards: Store A: $50 since that is where the data cluster. (The actual mean is about $50, and the median is $50.) Store B: Somewhere between $50 and $60 because that takes into account where the data cluster and the effect of possible outliers. (The actual mean is about $52, and the median is $50.) Store C: Somewhere between $60 and $70, which takes into account where the data cluster and where the effect of possible outliers are. (The actual mean is about $65, and median is $50.) Store D: About $149 because that takes into account where the data cluster and the effect of possible outliers. (The actual mean is about $150, and the median is $149.)

d. Possible answers: Store A and B have some variability. The prices for Store A vary from $13 to $120 (range $107) with a couple of gaps, and the prices for Store B vary from $10 to $120 (range of $110) with a few gaps. There is greater variability in the prices for Store C where the prices vary from $13 to $200 (range of $187) with a few gaps and a possible outlier. Store D does not have as great a variability in its data because its prices vary from $100 to $179 (range of $79) and almost all of these are between $145 and $150.

20. Possible answer: (Figure 5)

Extensions

21. a. The boys' times for age 11 vary from 9.3 seconds to 10.9 seconds. The boys' times for age 12 vary from 8.8 seconds to 11.6 seconds. The boys' times at age 13 appear to have the most variation, varying from 8.9 seconds to 11.8 seconds.

b. The boys' times for age 11 have a range of 1.6 seconds. The boys' times for age 12 have a range of 2.8 seconds. The boy's times for age 13 have a range of 2.9 seconds.

c. The range seems fairly small for these data, with a difference of at most 3 seconds separating the fastest from the slowest runner.

d. There appears to be a possible outlier at 11.8 seconds for the age 13 group.

e. The boys' times for age 11 cluster around 9.5 seconds. The boys' times for age 12 appear to have no major clusters of times. The boy's times at age 13 cluster around 9.3 seconds.

f. The boys' times for age 11 have a gap between 10.1 and 10.6 seconds, and a smaller gap between 9.8 and 10.1 seconds, as well as between 10.6 and 10.9 seconds. The boys' times for age 12 have a number of gaps: with the largest between 10.5 and 11.1 seconds, and others between 11.1 and 11.6 seconds, and 9.8 and 10.3 seconds. The boys' times at age 13 have a large gap between 10.5 and 11.8 seconds, with two smaller ones from 9.9 to 10.4 seconds, and between 9.6 and 9.9 seconds.

Figure 5

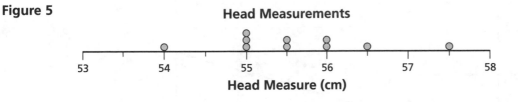

Head Measurements

Head Measure (cm)

g. Possible answers: The typical time for 13-year-old boys is about 9.3 because that is where the data cluster. The typical time for 12-year-old boys is about 9.8 because that marks a time that seems to balance the data. The typical time for 11-year-old boys is about 9.7 because time seems to take into account where the data cluster and the effect of the possible outlier. (In case the students use measures of center to describe what is typical: age 13: mean is about 9.6, median 9.4; age 12: mean is about 10, median 9.8; and age 11: mean is about 9.8, median 9.6.)

h. The boys' times for age 11 clump around 9.5 seconds with a few gaps. The boys' times for age 12 appear to have the most variation with a range of 8.8 to 11.6 seconds with a number of gaps and no major clusters of times. The boys' times at age 13 have a spread from 8.9 to 11.8 seconds, clump around 9.3 seconds, and have a few gaps including a possible outlier.

i. For the 11-year-old boys, about 73% of their times fell slightly above the standards of 10 seconds for Presidential Fitness Tests. For the boys at age 12, more than 50% performed at or above the standard. For the boys at age 13, about 61% exceeded the standards for Presidential Fitness Tests.

22. a. about 9.1 to 11.75 seconds

b. about 440 to 720 seconds

c. (Figure 6)

d. Times for the mile run are 50 times the number of seconds for the Shuttle Run. Times below the line are less than 50 times the number of seconds for the Shuttle Run. Times above the line are more than 50 times the number of seconds for the Shuttle Run.

e. There appears to be the general relationship that as the time for the Shuttle Run increases, so does the time for the mile run. Using the $y = 50x$ line as a marker, about 75% of the girls' times for the mile run were more than the 50 times their Shuttle Run times.

23. H

Possible Answers to Mathematical Reflections

1. a. Frequencies (counts or percents) describe variability. There may be more of certain categories or numerical values while fewer of others. The range also is used with numerical data to describe variability.

b. The range describes the difference between the maximum and minimum values in a distribution of numerical data. It is a measure of variability and provides some information about the variability in a data set.

c. Categorical data are grouped by category like months of the year, kinds of pets, etc. You cannot do calculations with categorical data like find the mean or median. Numerical data are usually represented by numbers. When you use counted data, you

Figure 6

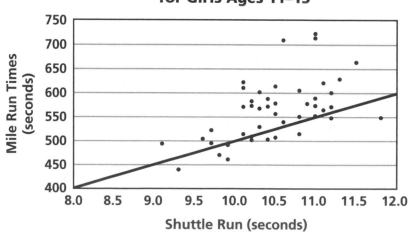

Shuttle Run and Mile Run Times for Girls Ages 11–13

are often using whole numbers, so there are no values between two consecutive whole numbers. For example, counting the number of students in a class, there would not be a value between 25 and 26 students. You cannot have half of a student. When you use measurement data, you typically have values that are between two whole numbers, such as in measuring head sizes. You could have a head size of 54.5 cm or 54.8 cm.

d. There are a variety of different categories.

e. The values of the data are not the same; they may be spread out.

2. You might use actual counts or percents to report frequencies for both categorical and numerical data. The percent frequency will show how much your data count represents out of the total. When comparing two data sets, whether categorical or numerical data, you can use counts if the numbers of data values in the sets are the same. Often it is better to use percents if the numbers of data values in the data sets are different.

3. You can see a change in the count or percent over time. You can find out what is typical by finding the mean or the median.

Investigation 2

Making Sense of Measures of Center

Mathematical and Problem-Solving Goals

- Read and understand line plots, and bar graphs used to display data distributions

- Recognize that variability occurs whenever data are collected

- Use properties of distributions to describe the variability in a given data set

- Understand and use different models to make sense of the mean

- Decide if a difference among data values and/or summary measures matters

- Decide when to use the mean, median, or mode to describe a distribution

- Develop and use strategies for comparing equal-size and unequal-size data sets

- Understand when and how changes in data values affect the median or the mean

- Relate the shape of a distribution to the location of its mean and median

Summary of Problems

 **The Mean as an Equal Share**

Students examine situations in which they learn to interpret the mean visually and mentally through sharing equally among the data values in a data set.

 **The Mean as a Balance Point in a Distribution**

Students examine situations in which they learn to interpret the mean visually and mentally using the balance model. The number line is viewed as a strip with weights representing data values in a distribution. The mean is the fulcrum that balances the distribution. Determining distances from the fulcrum is the key element in balancing the distribution.

Problem 2.3 Repeated Values in a Distribution

Students explore graphical displays for different situations, take into account the presence of repeated values, and make decisions about using measures of center or clusters to answer questions. The presence of repeated values in a distribution influences the kinds of representations that are chosen, determines the location of the mode, and impacts ways we think about the mean and median as markers in a distribution.

Problem 2.4 Measures of Center and Shapes of Distributions

Students explore the ways changing data values in a distribution affects the locations of the mean and the median. They do a sorting activity that focuses on shapes of distributions and the locations of the mean and the median.

Mathematics Background

For background on the concept of variability and strategies for data reduction, see pages 4–10.

	Suggested Pacing	Materials for Students	Materials for Teachers	ACE Assignments
All	$6\frac{1}{2}$ days	Calculators, student notebooks	Blank transparencies and transparency markers (optional)	
2.1	1 day	Counters (optional, for the Getting Ready); Labsheet 2.1	Transparency of Labsheet 2.1 (optional); Transparencies 2.1A, 2.1B (optional)	1, 2, 13, 17
2.2	1 day	Ruler; half cardboard tube (paper towel tube works); several coins of the same value (optional); small stick-on notes (optional)	Transparencies 2.2A–2.2C (optional)	3, 14, 15
2.3	2 days		Transparencies 2.3A–2.3E	4–6, 16
2.4	2 days	Computers with *TinkerPlots*™ software (optional); Labsheet A.1 (optional)	Stick-on notes; Transparency 2.4 (optional); transparency of Labsheet A.1 (optional)	7–12, 18, 19
MR	$\frac{1}{2}$ day			

2.1 The Mean as an Equal Share

Goals

- Read and understand bar graphs used to display data distributions

- Recognize that variability occurs whenever data are collected

- Use properties of distributions to describe the variability in a given data set

- Understand and use an equal share model to make sense of the mean

- Decide if a difference among data values and/or summary measures matters

In this problem, students examine a variety of situations in which they are encouraged to interpret the mean visually and mentally as the results of a process of evening out or sharing equally among the data values in a data set.

Launch 2.1

Use the introduction to the Investigation to set up the context and also present the mathematical issues.

Suggested Questions These questions can help start discussion:

- *RBI, Free throw percentage, ERA, and Yards per game: What sports are these letters or phrases from? What do they mean? How do you know?* [Runs batted in (baseball), Free throw percentage (basketball), Earned run average (baseball), Yards per game (football)]

- *Each of these is a statistic. What do you think a statistic is?* (A number that is computed from data.)

Explore the Getting Ready. If you want, have four students act out the situation. Let each student be one of the students named. Give each student his/her "beads" (e.g., cubes, counters, etc.). Have them start sharing with each other. When a pair of students meets, the one with more beads gives beads to the other until they both to have the same number (or as close as possible). This continues until it is not possible to share any more (i.e., everyone has the same number of beads).

Suggested Questions

- *What quantity does each person have now?* (15 beads)

- *Are there other ways that you could have solved this problem?*

Different solutions result from different starting points. For example:

- Jude could give Marie 5 beads. Then Marie and Sarah would have 10 beads each and Jude and Sri would have 20 beads each. Each person with 20 beads gives a person with 10 beads five of their beads; now each person has 15 beads.

- Doing it another way, Sri and Sarah could share beads evenly; they each would have 15 beads. Jude and Marie could do the same thing; they each would have 15 beads.

Discuss the idea of equal shares and its relation to the mean as a number that describes a distribution.

Have students work in pairs.

Explore 2.1

Students will need Labsheet 2.1 for this problem.

As you move around the room, you will find students for whom the questions in the problem are challenging; these students may not have a well-developed concept of the mean, and this problem provides opportunities for them to make sense of it.

You may also encounter students who just want to perform the algorithm for computing the mean. You will need to press the students to think about solutions that are more visual and that don't rely on the algorithm. One way to make sure this happens is to ask these students to find a second solution that does not use the algorithm. This is important because, while they may be able to use the algorithm and recognize that it can be used in these situations, they may not have a firm conceptual understanding of what the mean tells about a distribution.

Summarize 2.1

Share strategies for answering the questions. This can be a very rich discussion. It gives you an informal way to assess students' understanding of the evening-out interpretation of the mean.

It is likely that some student will suggest the standard algorithm as a way to find the equal share for each person. Press students to explain why this makes sense. Using the standard algorithm with understanding is an important goal. If students raise this issue, take advantage of the suggestion to ask:

- *Why does this make sense?*

- *What does the standard algorithm look like in terms of the 4 girls sharing the beads?* (Make a pile of all the beads and divide it into 4 equal piles, instead of trading.)

- *How is the mean a typical value for the entire data set?* (The mean is, *more or less*, what each person has, or each test scores, etc.)

Check for Understanding

- *The coach of the high school girls swim team thinks that a mean time of 52.5 seconds for his team in the 4×100 freestyle relay race will win an upcoming event. (This means each of the four swimmers on a team swims 100 meters.) His first three swimmers have these times: 52.0, 53.3, and 52.1. What time does the last swimmer need for the team to win if the coach is correct?* (52.6 seconds)

The Mean as an Equal Share

Mathematical Goals

- Read and understand bar graphs used to display data distributions
- Recognize that variability occurs whenever data are collected
- Use properties of distributions to describe the variability in a given data set
- Understand and use an equal share model to make sense of the mean
- Decide if a difference among data values and/or summary measures matters

Launch

Explore the Getting Ready for Problem 2.1. If you want, have four students act out the situation. Let each student be one of the students named. Give each student his/her "beads" (e.g., cubes, counters, etc.). Have them start sharing with each other. If a pair of students meets, the one with more beads gives the other beads until they each have the same amounts (or as close as possible). This continues until it is not possible to share any more (i.e., everyone has the same number of beads).

- *What quantity does each person have now? Are there other ways that you could have solved this problem?*

Different solutions result from different starting points. See the extended Launch for examples. Discuss the idea of equal or fair shares and its relation to the mean as a number that describes a distribution.
Have students work in pairs.

Materials
- Calculators
- Counters of some sort to act out the Getting Ready (optional)
- Transparency 2.1A (optional)

Explore

Students will need Labsheet 2.1 for this problem.

As you move around the room, you will find students for whom the questions in the problem are challenging; these students may not have a well-developed concept of the mean and this problem provides opportunities for them to make sense of the mean.

You may also encounter students who just want to perform the algorithm for computing the mean. You will need to press the students to think about solutions that are more visual and that don't rely on the algorithm. One way to make sure this happens is to ask these students to find a second solution that does not use the algorithm. This is important because, while they may be able to use the algorithm and recognize that it can be used in these situations, they may not have a firm conceptual understanding of the mean.

Materials
- Labsheet 2.1
- Transparency 2.1B (optional)

Share strategies for answering the questions. This can be a very rich discussion.

- *How does the standard algorithm relate to the sharing idea?*
- *In what way is the mean a typical value for a data set?*

Materials
- Student notebooks
- Transparency of Labsheet 2.1 (optional)

ACE Assignment Guide for Problem 2.1

Differentiated Instruction Solutions for All Learners

Core 1
Other *Applications* 2; *Connections* 13; *Extensions* 17; unassigned choices from previous problems

Adapted For suggestions about adapting ACE exercises, see the CMP *Special Needs Handbook*.
Connecting to Prior Units 13: *Bits and Pieces II*

Answers to Problem 2.1

A. 1. a. The mean is 17. The mean bar is the height that all bars would be if Malaika received the mean score on all her projects. Project 4 would need a score of 19 points.

   b. The minimum and maximum values are 15 points and 19 points, for a range of 4 points. Some students might argue that there is not much variability in her scores. Others may convert scores to percentages (i.e., 15 points is 75% and 19 points is 95%) that they interpret as grades and decide that there is, indeed, more variability as the impact on final grades definitely matters.

2. a. His mean score would be 15 points.

   b. Answers will vary; the four scores should sum to 60 points.

   c. Answer depends on part (b).

d. Answer depends on part (b) and then is compared to Question A, part (1).

B. 1. a. Range is $1.75. Students may consider that this is not a lot of variability in the amount of tips received by the four friends. Some students will consider that $1.75 is a large amount of variability.

   b. Each friend receives $5.65.

2. They will receive more. Imala gets $5.65; then the remainder of her tips ($0.45) is shared among the five people, so each gets $5.74.

3. a. It is entirely possible that this is not the case. Here are two sets with a mean of $6.45, yet no one received this amount in tips: ($6.30, $6.30, $6.40, $6.50. $6.75) and ($6.50, $6.50, $6.50, $6.50, $6.25).

   b. Answers will vary. See part (a) for examples.

4. a. Yes, it could happen. Isabel could have made a low amount of tips but others made high tips, so the result would be $5.25. Here is one example: ($7.10, $5.25, $5.25, $5.25, $3.40).

   b. Information is incomplete but we know that Isabel has a smaller amount of tips than the mean, so this suggests that there have to have been larger tips to offset this amount to make the mean $5.25. So, the range of the data must be greater than $1.85.

2.2 The Mean as a Balance Point in a Distribution

Goals

- Read and understand line plots used to display data distributions

- Recognize that variability occurs whenever data are collected

- Use properties of distributions to describe the variability in a given data set

- Understand and use a balance model to make sense of the mean

In this problem, students examine a variety of situations in which they are encouraged to interpret the mean visually and mentally using the balance model. In this model, the number line is viewed as a board with weights distributed to show data values in a distribution; the mean is the fulcrum that balances the distribution.

Launch 2.2

A situation involving data about grams of sugar in servings of cereal is set up. Students are asked to visualize this as a representation that uses a balance beam and a fulcrum. You may want to actually create and carry out the suggested experiment using a ruler and a one-half paper towel cardboard tube.

Work through the introductory material with the class to review line plots made to represent data.

Have students work in pairs.

Note: Your ruler and cardboard tube models may not balance exactly as you would wish. This is because the ruler adds unintended weight to the balance model. These models (or neutral images of them) are more useful for visualizing the approximate location for the mean than for finding the mean exactly.

Explore 2.2

You may want to have students work on Questions A and B for a while and then stop and have a class discussion about strategies that students have used. Students should be able to call on the sharing model, the balance model, and the standard algorithm to help create their distributions.

Midway Summary

Question A You can look at the many different ways students can make distributions with a mean of 6. One way to do this is to post chart paper and set up several number lines; have students use small stick-on notes to display their distributions. You can discuss the variety of ways that students made distributions. As you discuss each distribution, ask students to figure out the sum of distances from the mean of 6 that the values greater than the mean are and that the values less than the mean are (they should be the same). Encourage students to notice the pattern and also speculate on why this would be true (i.e., in a balance, the weights are balanced in relation to the fulcrum so the sum of distances from the fulcrum have to be equal on either side).

Question B You can do similar kinds of sharing with the problems in Question B as you have done for Question A.

Then, students should complete Questions C and D.

Summarize 2.2

Use Questions C and D to firm up the idea that the distances from the mean are the same on each side of the fulcrum or mean.

2.2 The Mean as a Balance Point in a Distribution

Mathematical Goals

- Read and understand line plots used to display data distributions
- Recognize that variability occurs whenever data are collected
- Use properties of distributions to describe the variability in a given data set
- Understand and use a balance model to make sense of the mean

Launch

A situation involving data about grams of sugar is set up. Students are asked to visualize this as a representation, which uses a balance beam and a fulcrum. You may want to actually create and carry out the suggested experiment using a ruler and a one-half paper towel cardboard tube.

Have students work in pairs.

Materials
- Transparency 2.2A (optional)

Explore

You may want to have students work on Questions A and B for a while and then stop and have a class discussion about strategies that students have used.

Midway Summary

Question A: You can look at the many different ways students can make distributions with a mean of 6. One way to do this is to post chart paper and set up several number lines; have students use small stick-on notes to display their distributions. You can discuss the variety of ways that students made distributions. As you discuss each distribution, ask students to figure out the sum of distances from the mean of 6 that the values greater than the mean are and that the values less than the mean are (they should be the same). Encourage students to notice the pattern and also speculate on why this would be true (i.e., in a balance, the weights are balanced in relation to the fulcrum so the sum of distances from the fulcrum have to be equal on either side).

Question B: You can do similar kinds of sharing with the problems in Question B as you have done for Question A.

Then students should complete Questions C and D.

Materials
- Calculators
- Ruler (optional)
- Half cardboard tube (paper towel tube works, optional)
- Several coins of the same value (optional)
- Small stick-on notes
- Transparency 2.2B, 2.2C (optional)

Summarize

Use Questions C and D to tie up the idea of the distances from the mean being the same on each side of the mean (balancing).

Materials
- Student notebooks

ACE Assignment Guide for Problem 2.2

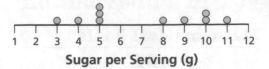

Core 3
Other *Connections* 14, 15; unassigned choices from previous problems

Adapted For suggestions about adapting Exercise 3 and other ACE exercises, see the CMP *Special Needs Handbook*.
Connecting to Prior Units 15: *Bits and Pieces I*

Answers to Problem 2.2

A. 1. Possible answer:

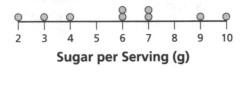

Sugar per Serving (g)

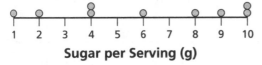

Sugar per Serving (g)

2. Possible answers:

a. 8 g and 9 g

b. Range is greater for the second line plot.

B. 1. a. Line plot:

Sugar per Serving (g)

b. 6 g

2. a. Possible answer (range = 9 g):

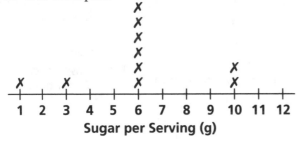

Sugar per Serving (g)

b. Possible answer (range = 11 g):

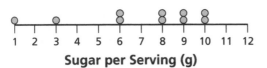

Sugar per Serving (g)

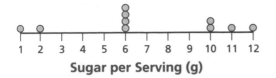

Sugar per Serving (g)

c. Possible answer (range = 8 g):

Sugar per Serving (g)

C. 1. The arrows indicate the distance each data value is from the mean.

2. The distances of values greater than the mean: 1, 4, 6; sum = 11
The distances of the values less than the mean: 1, 3, 3, 4; sum = 11

3. The two sums are equal. This reflects the fact that the mean is a balance point.

4. It will always be true.

5. If you think of the distribution as a seesaw, then balancing involves positioning the fulcrum so that the weights balance. If a weight is positioned far from the fulcrum on one side and weight of the same mass is positioned closer to the fulcrum on the other side, then the weight positioned farther out will tilt the board that way. Only when they are equal distances from the mean will the board balance. Similarly, the location of a data value in relation to the mean determines its effect on the mean's computation. If one data value is 8 and the other is 2, the mean is 5. This means the balance point, or fulcrum, is positioned halfway between the two points. When there are multiple data values at different locations, the sums of the distances will be the same for balance to occur at the mean.

D. 1. Graph A: 9 for values above the mean
Graph B: 14 for values greater than the mean

2. Graph A: 9 for values less than the mean
Graph B: 14 for values below the mean

3. No, the mean would not change. The mean is 6 grams of sugar; adding additional values at 6 grams does not change the overall balance of the differences from the mean that we found originally.

Repeated Values in A Distribution

Goals

- Read and understand line plots and bar graphs used to display data distributions

- Recognize that variability occurs whenever data are collected

- Use properties of distributions to describe the variability in a given data set

- Decide if a difference among data values and/or summary measures matters

- Understand and decide when to use the mean, median, or mode to describe a distribution

- Develop and use strategies for comparing equal-sized and unequal-sized data sets to solve problems

In this problem, students explore graphical displays for different situations, take into account the presence of repeated values, and make decisions about using measures of center or clusters to answer questions.

Launch 2.3

The first two problems focused students' attention on the mean and two different ways to interpret this statistic. This problem addresses all three measures of center (mean, median, and mode) with a particular emphasis on appropriateness of the mode in categorical data and the inappropriateness with numerical data.

Use the Getting Ready and Transparencies 2.3A and 2.3B to help you introduce this problem.

Answers to the Getting Ready

- Range: 21

- Mean: 6; It is close to the large cluster of values. Students should try to visualize the balance point rather than to actually calculate the mean.

- The median of 3.5 sits to the left of the mean because many students have just a few animals, but the few students who have many animals increase the mean. Half the students have more than 3.5 pets and half have fewer.

- Clusters: The data cluster from 0 to 6.

- Relation of clusters to locations of median and mean: the many students who have just a few animals keep both the mean and the median low.

The idea of repeated values is emphasized as a way to help students think about distributions of data values. The presence or lack of repeated values in a distribution provides information about the nature of the variability in the data. Counts vs. measurements impact whether there will be repeated values; often measurements are more variable in that there are few repeated measures (see Investigation 3 in this unit). It may also be that there is greater spread in the data; for example, counting how many jumps a person can do in jumping rope results in data that are quite spread out (see the sixth-grade unit *Data About Us*).

Work through the questions posed about each of the graphs in the introduction to the problem, making sure the students recall how to identify the mode and compute the median. The mode is an actual data value that occurs in a distribution; it may be numerical or categorical data. The median and mean are *computed* numerical values determined only when using numerical data. Each is a *marker* that marks a location in the distribution (i.e., marks a location along the *x*-axis number line); it may or may not be the same as one or more data values in a distribution.

There is a lot of reading in this problem. You may want to explore the first two problems together as a class to help students understand the issues that are being raised and to be able to think about choices that need to be made (Question B). If you do this, use Questions A and B from the Summarize so that you can complete the discussions of these two Questions.

Have students work in pairs.

If you find that students are having trouble reading information from the graph in Question B, you might ask a few questions that focus on different aspects of reading the graph:

Suggested Questions Read the data:

- *How many cereals have 3 grams of sugar in a serving size?* (11 cereals)

Read between the data:

- *How many cereals have 10 or more grams of sugar in a serving size?* (24 cereals or about one-third of the cereals)

Read beyond the data:

- *How many grams of sugar are typically found in a serving of cereal?* (Students make choices from those provided or offer a different answer.)

Help students address the fact that the mode is not a good descriptor of typical value in this case.

Summarize **2.3**

All the graphs on Transparencies 2.3A–2.3E can be used as you discuss each question.

Question A The purpose of this problem is to help students so that they can identify the mode *but* they need to think about whether the mode provides *useful* information in answering a question. Looking at this graph, it would make sense to buy half thin crust and half thick crust.

Question B In the discussion of this question, use the language of 1) read the data, 2) read between the data, and 3) read beyond the data. As students discuss their work on B, ask which of these is at play in answering the question.

Question C For this situation, ask the students questions like those posed for Question B.

Again, help students address the fact that the mode is not a good descriptor of typical value in this case.

Question D Students apply the work they have been doing with variability and measures of center. Together, consider these questions:

- *Look at the distribution of data for each shelf. Describe the variability in grams of sugar for cereals located on that shelf.*

- *Do the data cluster in any locations?*

- *Locate the mean and median for the data on this shelf. Are they similar or different? Why do you think this might be so?*

- *Use the results of the discussion and compare the three distributions.*

As part of the discussion, introduce students to using one or more *reference lines*—vertical lines drawn across the three line plots. For example, draw a reference line at 3 grams of sugar; talk about data that are below, at, or above this reference line. Draw another reference line at 10 grams of sugar; again, talk about data that are below, at, or above this reference line. Also, talk about the data that are between the two reference lines (between 3 and 10 grams of sugar per serving).

- *How does the use of reference lines help you compare distributions?*

Classroom Dialogue Model

Repeated Values in a Distribution

Teacher I want people to volunteer and speak about which crust we decided to go with in Question A (thin) and why.

Janelle Thick crust is only 2% behind thin crust, and that is very small, so it is unfair for the other kids.

Sean You should go half and half because thick crust was only 2% behind thin crust and 6% of the people do not care.

Teacher Jason wondered how many grams of sugar are typically found in a serving of cereal. Which statement seems to be a sensible answer given the distribution of data from 70 cereals in Question B?

Janelle No one went with the mode because it doesn't explain much and there are a lot closer ones. 6–12 are closer.

Sean You wanted to find the typical—the mode is the most if you want typical, so you figure out the mean.

Teacher So you would go with the mean. Did you figure out what the mean was? Can you take a guess?

Sean Probably somewhere between 3 and 12.

Teacher Can you find that real quick? Sean wants to use the mean, so let's figure out what it is. Austin just added them all up and got 513. Did anyone else do this? Do we agree on this total? So then you have to figure out how many sugar grams per serving for an average cereal. I just saw Austin divide by 70. Austin, why did you do that?

Austin I was looking at all the numbers and I saw that there are 70 cereals.

Raj About 7.3. Looks like a good mean but I do not want use it. Some have just 1. I would probably use clusters 8–12; that's where most of the cereal are set. The data varies too much.

Pedro What do you mean they vary?

Maria It goes from 1 through 15 sugars—some even have zero sugars.

Teacher It is kind of evenly distributed through 8–12 grams?

Raj Yeah.

Teacher Yeah. Gwen said something earlier about 8–12 being a better number. . . do you see that, Shannon?

Teacher In Question C is a graph of data about the length of time people spent listening to a telephone message advertising a product. The advertiser is changing the message length in hopes that people will spend more time listening to it. What choice would you suggest as a good length of message to use?

Janelle Three, because you are trying to see how many people hung up after a certain amount of time. . . it tells you a third of the people hung up before a minute, and half the people hung up before 1.5 minutes. It tells you when they hung up. . . after how much time people are still listening.

Sean I would not choose number 3 because no one would want to listen to 3 minutes because even though it's mode, because it doesn't make sense because no one would want to listen to it.

Teacher Really! Sean, 6 people wanted to listen to it.

Sean Well, 3 people wanted to listen to 1 minute and that would be better.

Teacher Well, why would that be better?

Sean Because it is shorter.

Teacher How do you use the data to prove that point, because there were 6 people that wanted to listen for 3 minutes? Everyone needs to help out.

Sean Because there is a cluster between 0.2 minutes and 1.5 minutes.

Teacher There is a cluster, a bunch of people in that range. What else?

Austin 0.2 minutes to about 1.5, then, if you add it all up there is more there than in 3 minutes.

Teacher About how many people were surveyed?

Raj I say about 30.

Teacher It was around 30 people. We have 6 as the mode there. 6 out of 30.

Pedro 20%.

Teacher So 20%. If we take away 20% and ignore them, even though they were important,. where would we see the cluster of data?

Maria 0.2 and 1.5—that's where most of it is. 2.1 to 3.0 are 40% in all. And so the total is 60%.

2.3 Repeated Values in a Distribution

Mathematical Goals

- Read and understand line plots and bar graphs used to display data distributions
- Recognize that variability occurs whenever data are collected
- Use properties of distributions to describe the variability in a given data set
- Decide if a difference among data values and/or summary measures matters
- Understand and decide when to use the mean, median, or mode to describe a distribution
- Develop and use strategies for comparing equal-size and unequal-size data sets to solve problems

Launch

This problem addresses all three measures of center: mean, median, and mode. Use Transparencies 2.3A and 2.3B to help you introduce this problem. The transparencies display the questions and the two graphs that are used to review the mode and the median. Work through the questions posed about each of the graphs in the introduction to the problem, making sure the students recall how to identify the mode and compute the median.

Have students work in pairs.

Materials
- Transparencies 2.3A, 2.3B

Explore

There is a lot of reading in this problem. You may want to explore the first two problems as a class to help students understand the issues that are being raised and to be able to think about choices that need to be made (Question B). If you do this, then use Questions A and B from the Summarize so that you can complete the discussions of these two questions. Students can work in pairs on Questions C and D. See the extended Summarize section for questions to ask as you visit groups.

Materials
- Calculators

Summarize

All the graphs on Transparencies 2.3A–2.3E can be used to discuss each question.

Question A This problem helps students identify the mode, but they need to think about whether the mode provides useful information in answering a question.

Question B Ask a few questions on different aspects of reading the graph. Read the data:

Materials
- Student notebooks
- Transparencies 2.3A–2.3E

continued on next page

    • *How many cereals have 3 grams of sugar in a serving size?*

Read between the data:

    • *How many cereals have more than 10 grams of sugar in a serving size?*

Read beyond the data:

    • *How many grams of sugar are typically found in a serving of cereal?*

Question C: Ask the students questions like those posed for Question B.

Question D: Students apply their work with variability and measures of center. Together consider these questions:

    • *Look at the distribution of data for each shelf. Describe the variability in grams of sugar for cereals located on that shelf.*

    • *Do the data cluster in any locations?*

    • *Locate the mean and median for the data on this shelf. Are they similar or different? Why do you think this might be so?*

    • *Use the results of the discussion and compare the three distributions.*

    As part of the discussion, introduce students to using one or more "reference lines"—vertical lines drawn across the three line plots. Also, talk about the data that are between the two reference lines.

    • *How does the use of reference lines help you compare distributions?*

ACE Assignment Guide for Problem 2.3

Differentiated Instruction
Solutions for All Learners

Core 6

Other *Applications* 4, 5; *Connections* 16; unassigned choices from previous problems

Adapted For suggestions about adapting Exercises 4–6 and other ACE exercises, see the CMP *Special Needs Handbook*.

Answers to Problem 2.3

A. Disagree; there are clearly two choices for pizza.

B. Answers will vary. The mode is at the lower end of the data set, so most students will choose a median or a mean. The median indicates the middle of the distribution. Students may opt for the mean to describe the typical number of grams of sugar, which is about 7.3 grams. If they choose the mean they should practice visualizing the balance point rather than only calculating it. Option 3, using clusters, is a reasonable way to describe this distribution.

C. Answers will vary. Possible answer: Option 3, since it gives the advertiser specific information about one-third of the callers hanging up before 1 minute, and over one-half of the callers hanging up before $1\frac{1}{2}$ minutes.

D. 1. Top shelf: mean 4.55 (students can estimate 4–5 by the balancing method), median 3, mode 3
Middle shelf: mean 10.22 (students can estimate 10), median 11, mode 12
Bottom shelf: mean 6.93 (students can estimate 7 by the balancing method), median 7, mode 8
The middle shelf had considerably more sugar than the other shelves using all three statistics, followed by the bottom shelf. The top shelf had the fewest grams of sugar per serving.

    2. The middle shelf has cereals with the greatest numbers of grams of sugar per serving. The top shelf has cereals with fewer grams of sugar per serving.

Goals

- Read and understand line plots used to display data distributions

- Recognize that variability occurs whenever data are collected

- Use properties of distributions to describe the variability in a given data set

- Understand when and how changes in data values in a distribution affect the median or the mean

- Relate the shape of a distribution to the location of its mean and median

Technology Option For an optional approach using *TinkerPlots*™ software, see the Teacher's Guide Appendix for Problem 2.4, beginning on page 168. Blackline masters of student pages for use with this investigation begin on page A5.

Launch 2.4

Introduce the problem by discussing when means and medians are similar or different in the two cereal and shelves distributions.

Suggested Question

- *What is it about the data distribution that impacts where the mean or median will be located?*

As a class first (and then students working in pairs or triples replicate), use stick-on notes to set up the distribution shown in the Student Edition (Figure 1).

Have the students compute the sum of these data values and discuss how they determine the mean.

Have them locate the mean and median and place markers.

Look at Question A, part (1). Have students make predictions about what will happen to the mean and the median if they replace one cereal having 6 grams of sugar per serving with one that has 9 grams of sugar per serving. Remind them to think about the mean as a "balance point" in the distribution.

Suggested Questions Ask:

- *When a data value is changed to one that is larger, how does the mean change to keep everything in "balance?" What about when a data value is changed to one that is smaller?* (Mean moves to the right—gets larger, too; same for smaller—mean moves to the left.)

Then have them re-compute both the mean and the median. To re-compute mean, have the students look at the previous sum (91 grams of sugar). Ask:

- *How will this sum change if a cereal with 6 grams of sugar was replaced with a cereal with 9 grams of sugar?* (The new sum will be 94 grams of sugar.)

Figure 1

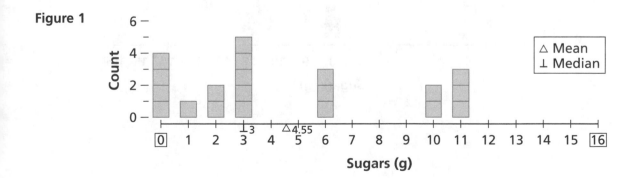

- *How does this one change affect the mean?* (The mean is increased from 4.55 to 4.7.)

- *How does this one change affect the median?* (The median does not change.) (Figure 2)

Explore 2.4

Have students work in pairs to continue with Question A, parts (1) and (2). They will need to set up their own distribution using stick-on notes (one distribution per pair of students). Make sure that they make a prediction before they make a set of changes.

Suggested Questions For Question A, part (1), only the mean will change in value. Once students make this observation, as you visit with groups, ask:

- *Why do you think the median did not change in this situation?* (Answers will vary; students may not yet have enough information to sort

this out. The median separates the data into two equal-sized parts; to make a change, you will need to change a data value so that it moves across the median.)

Have students continue with the rest of the problem, being deliberate in making predictions, changing one data value at a time, and then making sure they see what the change created. In Question A, part (2), the median will shift when students move to part (b). If students have been careful in maintaining their graph, they will be able to anticipate this change. Before part (c), their graphs should look like Figure 3 (two of the 3 data values have been changed to 8 grams).

Suggested Questions As you visit groups, ask:

- *Why has the median changed to 5.5?* (Because there are 10 data values below and 10 data values above this value, which is the midpoint between 3 and 8 grams.)

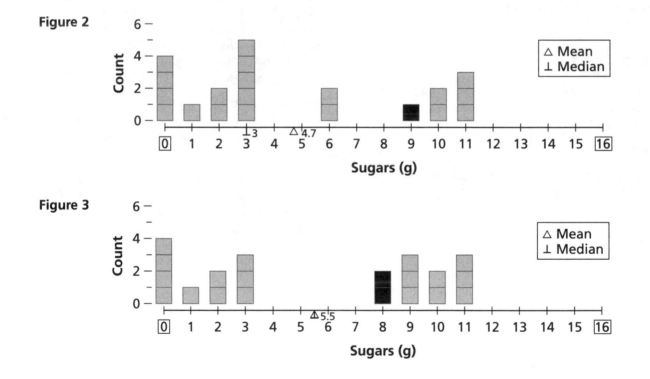

Figure 2

Figure 3

After Question A, part (2c), their graphs should look like Figure 4 (three data values have been changed to 8 grams).

Suggested Question As you visit groups, ask:

• *Why has the median changed to 8?* (Because there are 10 data values below and 10 data values above the median of 8.)

Have students continue to explore Questions A and B. For Question B, they can experiment with distributions using 20–25 stick-on notes.

Stop and do a summary of findings from these two questions.

Launch Question C by looking at the distributions in the Student Edition. Have students complete this part of the problem.

Summarize 2.4

The goals are to summarize how the mean and median behave in response to data changes, and to be able to estimate where the mean and median are located in a distribution.

When you stop and do a summary of Question A in order to answer Question B, make sure you continue to "act out" all changes to the two graphs that occur in your discussions. Students need to see visually what is happening.

Figure 4

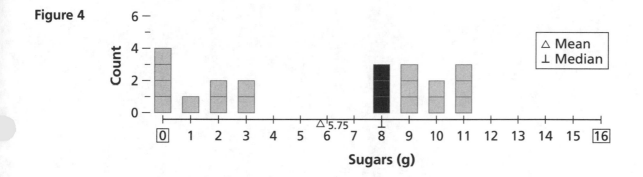

2.4 Measures of Center and Shapes of Distributions

Mathematical Goals

- Read and understand line plots used to display data distributions
- Recognize that variability occurs whenever data are collected
- Use properties of distributions to describe the variability in a given data set
- Understand when and how changes in data values in a distribution affect the median or the mean
- Relate the shape of a distribution to the location of the mean and median

Launch

Introduce the problem by discussing when means or medians are similar or are different in the cereal and shelves distributions (Problem 2.3D).

- *What is it about the data distribution that impacts where the mean and median might be located?*

Have students work in pairs completing the problem using the stick-on representations.

For an optional approach using data analysis software, see the Teacher's Guide Appendix for Problem 2.4, beginning on page 168, and the blackline masters of student pages beginning on page A5.

Materials
- Stick-on notes
- Transparency 2.4 (optional)
- Computers with *TinkerPlots*™ software (optional)
- Labsheet A.1 (optional)
- Transparency of Labsheet A.1 (optional)

Explore

Have students work in pairs to explore Questions A and B.

Stop and do a summary of findings from these two questions. Use information learned to work as a class to answer Question B.

Launch Question C by looking at the distributions in the Student Edition. Then have students complete this part of the problem.

Summarize

The goal is to summarize how each of the measures of center behaves and how easily changed a measure is or is not.

Materials
- Student notebooks

ACE Assignment Guide
for Problem 2.4

Differentiated Instruction
Solutions for All Learners

Core 7

Other *Applications 8–12; Extensions* 18, 19; unassigned choices from previous problems

Adapted For suggestions about adapting ACE exercises, see the CMP *Special Needs Handbook*.

Answers to Problem 2.4

A. Original top shelf: mean 4.55, median 3

1. Mean changes to 5; median remains the same.

2. **a.** Mean changes to 5.25; median remains the same.

   b. Mean changes to 5.50; median changes to 5.5.

   c. Mean changes to 5.75; median changes to 8.

   The distribution has shifted to the right; more than half the data values are greater than or equal to 8 grams of sugar.

B. 1. Distributions will vary; changing smaller data values to larger data values shifts the mean toward the larger values. If data values that were smaller than the median are changed to data values larger than the median, then the median will increase.

2. Distributions will vary; changing larger data values to smaller data values shifts the mean toward the smaller values. If data values that were larger than the median are changed to data values smaller than the median, then the median will decrease.

3. Changing values in this way MAY shift the mean and the median toward the clustering.

C. 1. Means and medians close: 1, 4, 5, 6

   Means and medians not close: 2, 3, 7, 8

2. When means and medians are close, there appears to be some kind of symmetry or balance in the data located on either side of these measures. When the means and medians are not close, the distribution appears not to be symmetrical on both sides of these measures and seems to be lacking in balance. Statisticians talk about distributions being symmetrical (like what we mean with symmetry but not with the exactness we are used to dealing with when we look at symmetrical figures) or asymmetrical (lacking symmetry).

The student edition pages for this
investigation begin on the next page.

Notes _____

_____

_____

_____

Making Sense of Measures of Center

Statistics are numbers that are part of your everyday world. They are used in reporting on baseball, basketball, football, soccer, the Olympics, and other sports. Statistics are used to highlight the top hitters in baseball or top free-throw shooters in basketball. Identifying gold-medal skating champions depends on the statistics used to interpret scores from their performances during different events.

- What sports are these stats from? What do they mean?

  RBI   free-throw percentage
  ERA   yards per game

When you analyze data, the variability in a distribution is important. However, you also want to describe what is typical about a distribution. Three statistics that are often used to help describe what is typical about distributions are the *mean*, the *median*, and the *mode*.

Means, medians, and modes are called **measures of center.**

How is a measure of center influenced by the variability in a distribution of data?

There are other statistics you can use to describe variability. You can describe the distribution of data by its *range*. The **range** is the difference between the maximum and minimum values in a distribution. You can also give the minimum and maximum values to show how the data vary. You may notice unusual values and wonder if any of these data are **outliers.** Or you may notice that data with similar values form *clusters* in a distribution or that there are *gaps* with no data values.

28   Data Distributions

Notes _____

_____

_____

_____

2.1 The Mean as an Equal Share

The mean is one way to describe what is typical for a distribution. The **mean** is often called the "average" of the data. You can also think of the mean as the amount each person gets if everyone gets an equal share.

Getting Ready for Problem 2.1

Students are using beads for a class project. Marie has 5 beads, Sarah has 10 beads, Sri has 20 beads, and Jude has 25 beads. The students distribute their beads until everyone has the same number of beads. Each now has an equal share of the beads.

1. How many beads will each student have in the end?

2. How did you solve this problem?

When the redistributing is finished, each student has an equal share of the beads. This equal share of beads is the mean number of beads per person.

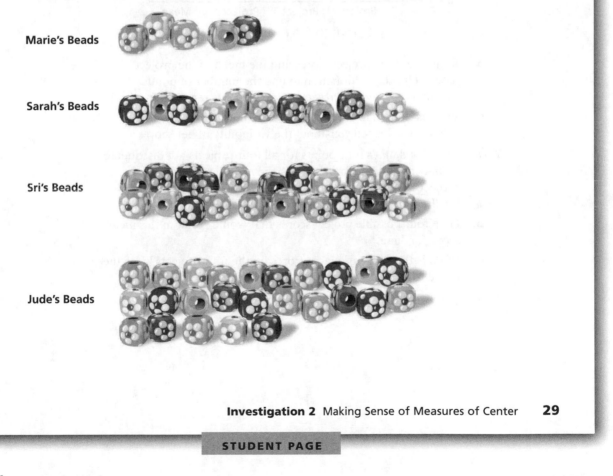

Marie's Beads

Sarah's Beads

Sri's Beads

Jude's Beads

Investigation 2 Making Sense of Measures of Center   **29**

Notes _____

_____

_____

_____

Problem 2.1 The Mean as an Equal Share

Use the idea of mean as an equal share as you answer these questions.

A. Malaika has four 20-point projects in her science class.

1. The bar graph shows Malaika's scores on three of these projects. There is also a bar that shows Malaika's mean score for all four projects.

Malaika's Project Scores

Projects 1–4 and Mean

a. Read the three project scores and the mean of the project scores. Use this information to find the number of points Malaika received on Project 4. Explain your reasoning.

b. What is the range of Malaika's scores on the four projects? What does this tell you about the variability of her scores?

2. a. When Malaika's total points for all four projects are distributed equally among the four projects, the result is 17 points per project, which is her mean score. Juan has a total of 60 points for the four projects. What is his mean score?

b. Give four possible project scores that would result in this mean score for Juan.

c. What is the range of Juan's scores on the four projects? Use the range to write a sentence about the variability of his scores.

d. Do Juan's scores vary more than Malaika's scores? Explain.

30 Data Distributions

Notes _____

_____

_____

_____

B. 1. a. On Monday, four servers receive the following amounts as tips while working at the Mugwump Diner. What is the range of the tips earned on Monday? What does this tell you about the variability of the tips?

Monday's Diner Tips

Server	Tip Amount
Maisha	$5.25
Brian	$4.75
Isabel	$6.50
Joe	$6.10

b. The four servers decide to share the tips equally. How much money per server is this?

2. Imala was forgotten when tips were shared. She received $6.10, the same amount that Joe originally received. Suppose Imala's tips are included with the others' tips and shared equally among the five servers. Would the first four servers receive less than, the same as, or more than they did before Imala's tips were included? Explain your reasoning.

3. a. On Tuesday, the five servers share their tips equally. The result is a mean of $6.45 per server. Does this tell you that one of the servers originally received $6.45 in tips? Why or why not?

b. What is a possible set of tips that would result in this mean?

4. a. On Wednesday, Isabel receives $3.40 in tips. When all of the tips are shared equally among the five servers, the result is $5.25 per server. Do you think this could happen? Explain.

b. Based on the information in part (a), what can you say about the range of tips earned on Wednesday? Explain.

ACE Homework starts on page 44.

Notes _____

_____

_____

_____

You can look at the mean as the balance point in a distribution. It acts like the fulcrum (FUL krum) for a seesaw. You can simulate this situation with a ruler, a cardboard tube (cut in half lengthwise), and some coins (all of the same type). The coins are placed along the board so that the board remains in balance on the cardboard tube. Look at the picture below for an example.

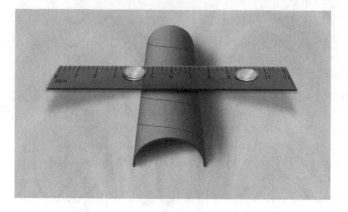

Notice that a coin placed far from the balance point can be balanced by a coin the same distance away on the other side of the balance point, by two coins half the distance away on the other side, or by three coins $\frac{1}{3}$ of the distance away on the other side.

The mean is a kind of fulcrum in a distribution of data. The data balance around the mean, much as the coins on the ruler balance around the fulcrum created by the tube.

Notes _____

_____

_____

_____

The table below shows the number of calories and the amount of sugar per serving for nine cereals in the store.

Content Sugar of Cereals

Cereal	Calories	Sugar (g)
Cereal 1	90	5
Cereal 2	110	12
Cereal 3	220	8
Cereal 4	102	2
Cereal 5	120	6
Cereal 6	112	9
Cereal 7	107	12
Cereal 8	170	12
Cereal 9	121	6

SOURCE: Bowes & Church's Food Values of Portions Commonly Used

You can make a line plot to show the distribution. The mean is 8 grams of sugar, the data vary from 2 to 12 grams of sugar, and the range is 10 grams of sugar. The distribution balances at 8 grams of sugar.

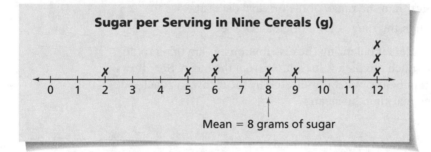

You can show this using a ruler and a cardboard tube. The ruler is marked with 13 main tick marks, one at 0 and one at each inch mark up to 12. Use nine coins of the same type. Place the ruler on the tube at the 8-inch mark, and place the coins along the ruler so they match the distribution shown above.

Notes

Problem 2.2 The Mean as a Balance Point in a Distribution

Use the idea of mean as a balance point as you answer these questions.

A. 1. There are nine cereals in a data set. The mean amount of sugar in the cereals is 6 grams per serving. One of the cereals has 10 grams of sugar in one serving. Make a line plot that shows a distribution of the amount of sugar. Then make a different line plot that meets the criteria. Explain how you designed each distribution.

   2. a. What is the range of each distribution you made?

   b. How do the ranges compare? Are they the same, or is one range greater than the other?

B. 1. Here is a set of data showing the amount of sugar in a serving for each of ten cereals, in grams:

   1   3   6   6   6   6   6   6   10   10

   a. Make a line plot to show this new distribution.

   b. What is the mean for these data?

   2. Make one or more changes to the data set in part (1) so that the mean is 7 and the range is:

   a. the same as the range of the original data set

   b. greater than the range of the original data set

   c. less than the range of the original data set

C. 1. Anica wonders if balancing the distribution has anything to do with how much the data values differ from the mean. She draws the diagram below. What is indicated by the arrows on each side of the line marking the mean?

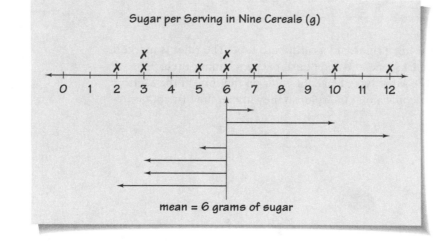

Sugar per Serving in Nine Cereals (g)

mean = 6 grams of sugar

34   Data Distributions

Notes _____

_____

_____

_____

2. Determine the length of each arrow. Find the sum of the lengths of the arrows on each side of the mean.

3. How do the two sums compare? Why do you think this is so?

4. Do you think this will always be true? Explain.

5. How might balancing the distribution relate to the distances of the data values from the mean? Explain.

D. Graph A and Graph B show two different distributions. Latoya guesses that each distribution has a mean of 5 grams of sugar per serving. For each distribution, answer parts (1)–(3).

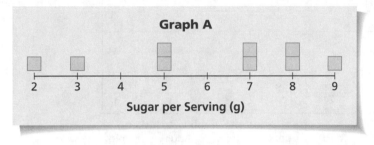

Graph A

Sugar per Serving (g)

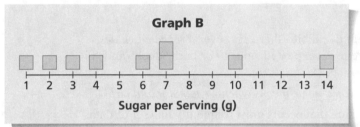

Graph B

Sugar per Serving (g)

1. Find the difference from Latoya's guess of 5 for each data value that is greater than 5. What is their sum?

2. Find the difference from Latoya's guess of 5 for each data value that is less than the mean. What is their sum?

3. Is Latoya correct that the mean is 5? Does the distribution "balance?" If so, explain. If not, change one or more of the values to make it balance.

 **Homework starts on page 44.**

Notes _____

_____

_____

_____

The graph below shows categorical data collected about the kinds of pets that 26 students have.

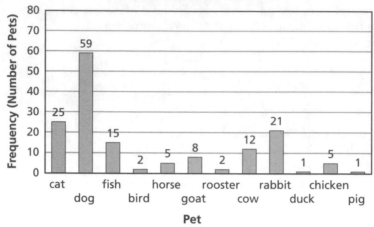

Pets Students Have

For "cat," "dog," "fish," and "rabbit," there are several *repeated values*. For other data, there are fewer repeated values. For both "duck" and "pig," there are no repeated values.

What do you think a repeated value means when we talk about data?

The **mode** is the data value that occurs most frequently in a set of data. For pets in this graph, the mode is "dog." When the data are categorical data, the mode is the only measure of center that can be used. It tells you the data value that is repeated the most often. For example, you can say that the mode kind of pet in the graph is a dog.

36 Data Distributions

Notes
_____
_____
_____
_____

The **median** is the midpoint in an ordered distribution. In the graph of a distribution, data values are located below, above, or at this midpoint. The graph below shows numerical data about the numbers of pets each of the 26 students has.

Number of Pets Students Have

Are there repeated values in this distribution?

Where would you mark the location of the median for these data?

Getting Ready for Problem 2.3

In Problem 2.2, you saw that the mean is like a fulcrum in a distribution. The data balance around the mean. Look at the graph above and consider these questions.

- What is the range of the data?
- What is the mean and where is it located?
- How does the location of the median compare to the location of the mean?
- Why do you think this is so?
- Do the data seem to cluster in some parts of the distribution?
- Does clustering of the data appear to be related to the locations of the median and the mean?

Notes _____

_____

_____

_____

A. Jorge is ordering pizza for a party. Tamika shows Jorge the graph at the right. She tells him to order only thin-crust pizzas because thin crust is the mode. Do you agree or disagree? Explain.

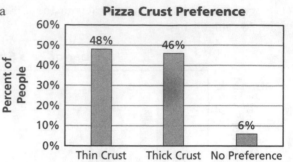

Pizza Crust Preference

B. The data from 70 cereals are shown below. Which option do you suggest using to find the typical amount of sugar in a serving of cereal? Explain.

Option 1 Use the mode, 3 grams. The typical amount of sugar in a serving of cereal is 3 grams.

Option 2 Use the median, 7.5 grams. The typical amount of sugar in a serving of cereal is 7.5 grams.

Option 3 Use clusters. There are several cereals that have either 3 or 6 grams of sugar per serving. 40% of the data seem to be evenly spread between 8 and 12 grams of sugar.

Option 4 Use something else. Write your own statement about what you consider to be the typical amount of sugar in a serving of cereal.

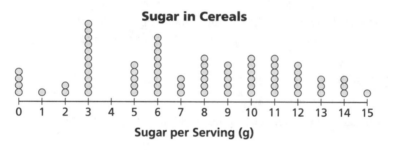

Sugar in Cereals

Sugar per Serving (g)

C. An advertiser wants more people to listen to a phone message. He uses the graph below.

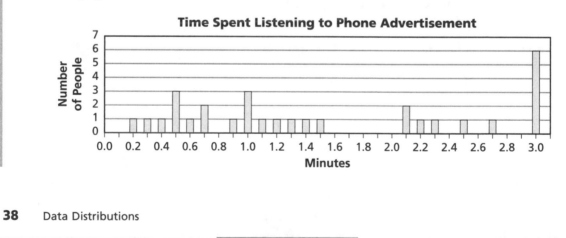

Time Spent Listening to Phone Advertisement

Minutes

38 Data Distributions

Notes _____

_____

_____

_____

Which of the options below should the advertiser use to decide how long the message should be? Explain.

Option 1 Use the mode. The most frequent amount of time spent listening to the phone advertisement was 3 minutes.

Option 2 Use the mean. Listening times lasted, on average, 1.51 minutes per person.

Option 3 Use clusters. One third of the people listened less than 1 minute and more than half listened less than 1.5 minutes. Only 20% of the people listened for 3 minutes.

Option 4 Use something else. Write your own response.

D. 1. In the plots below, the data for the 70 cereals in Question B are organized by the cereals' locations on the shelves in a supermarket. Use means, medians, clusters, or other strategies to compare the three distributions. Explain your reasoning.

2. Use the information from part (1) to make a prediction about the sugar content per serving of a cereal based on its shelf location.

Sugar in Top Shelf Cereals

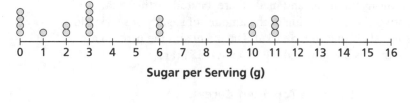

Sugar per Serving (g)

Sugar in Middle Shelf Cereals

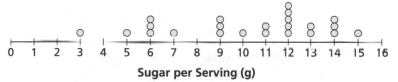

Sugar per Serving (g)

Sugar in Bottom Shelf Cereals

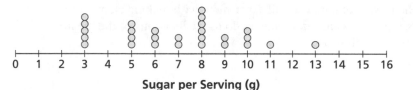

Sugar per Serving (g)

ACE Homework starts on page 44.

STUDENT PAGE

Notes _____

_____

_____

_____

Unlike with categorical data, the mode is not always useful with numerical data. Sometimes there is no mode and sometimes there is more than one mode.

Sometimes the mean and median of a distribution are located close together. The graph below shows the distribution of the amount of sugar in cereals located on the bottom shelf in a supermarket. The mean and the median are marked. The median is 7 grams and the mean is 6.9 grams.

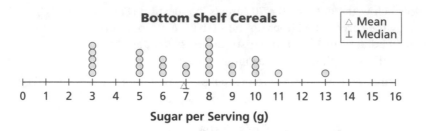

In some distributions the mean and median are located further apart. The graph below shows the distribution of the amount of sugar per serving in cereals on the top shelf in a supermarket. The mean and the median are marked. The median is 3 grams and the mean is 4.55 grams.

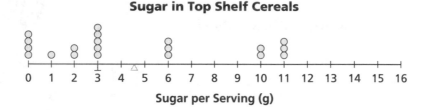

The overall shape of a distribution is determined by where the data cluster, where there are repeated values, and how spread out the data are. The shape of a distribution influences where the median and mean are located. In the next problem, you will experiment with making changes to distributions. Observe what these changes do to the locations of the mean and median in a distribution.

40   Data Distributions

Notes _____

_____

_____

_____

Problem 2.4 Measures of Center and Shapes of Distributions

For Questions A–C, predict what will happen. Then do the computation to see whether you are correct.

A. The graph below shows the distribution of the amount of sugar in 20 cereals found on the top shelf. The sum of the values in this distribution is 91 grams. Use stick-on notes to make a copy of the distribution. Note the location of the mean at 4.55 grams of sugar and the median at 3 grams of sugar.

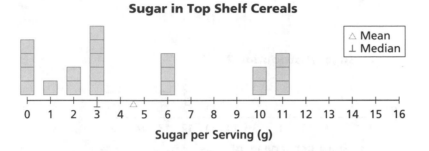

Sugar in Top Shelf Cereals

Sugar per Serving (g)

△ Mean
⊥ Median

1. Suppose you remove the three cereals with 6 grams of sugar per serving and add three new cereals, each with 9 grams of sugar per serving. What happens to the mean and the median? Why do you think this happens?

2. **a.** Use the new distribution from part (1). Suppose you remove a cereal with 3 grams of sugar and add a cereal with 8 grams of sugar. How do the mean and the median change?

   b. Suppose you remove another cereal with 3 grams of sugar and add another cereal with 8 grams of sugar. How do the mean and the median change?

   c. Suppose you remove a third cereal with 3 grams of sugar and add a third cereal with 8 grams of sugar. How do the mean and the median change?

B. Use the new distribution from Question A, part (2). Experiment with removing data values and replacing them with new data values.

1. How does replacing smaller data values with larger data values affect the mean and the median?

2. How does replacing larger data values with smaller data values affect the mean and the median?

3. How does replacing larger and smaller data values with values that are closer to the middle of the distribution affect the mean and the median?

Notes _____

_____

_____

_____

C. 1. Sort these eight distributions into two groups: one where the means and medians are the same or almost the same and one where they are not.

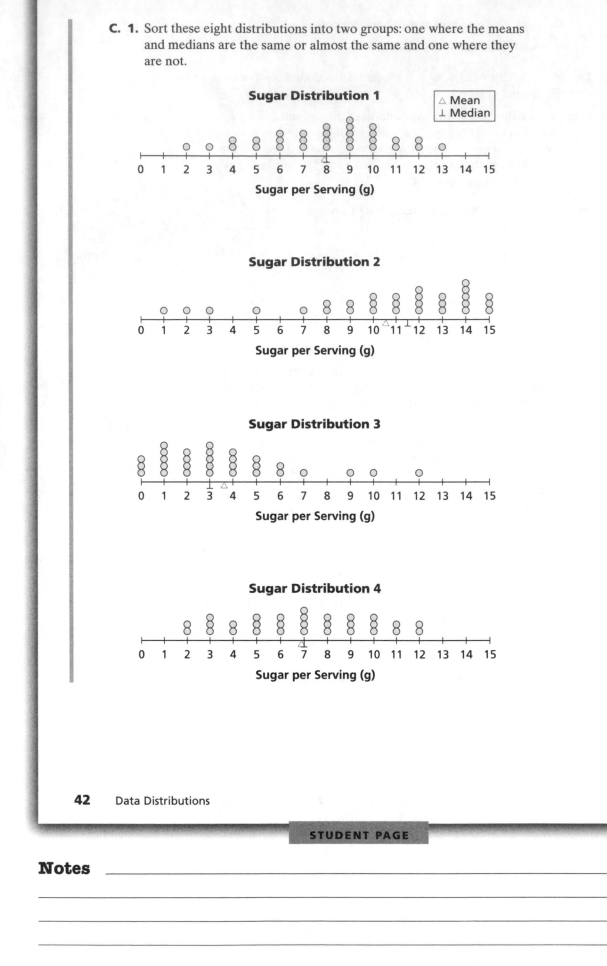

42　Data Distributions

Notes _____

_____

_____

_____

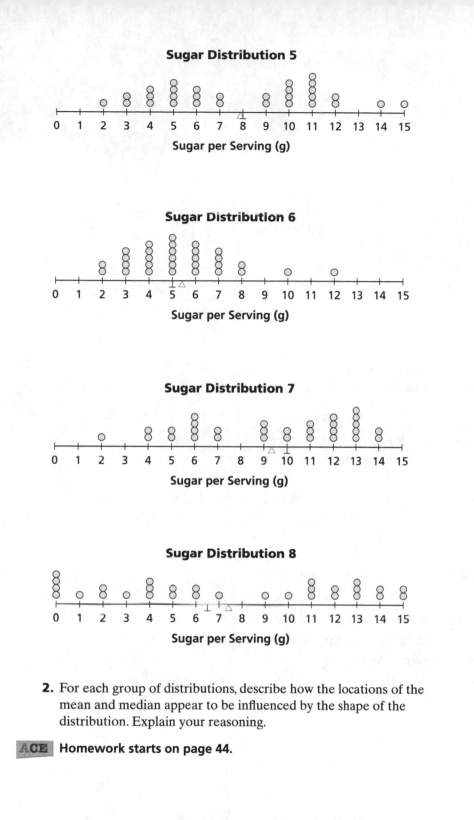

Sugar Distribution 5

Sugar per Serving (g)

Sugar Distribution 6

Sugar per Serving (g)

Sugar Distribution 7

Sugar per Serving (g)

Sugar Distribution 8

Sugar per Serving (g)

2. For each group of distributions, describe how the locations of the mean and median appear to be influenced by the shape of the distribution. Explain your reasoning.

ACE Homework starts on page 44.

Investigation 2 Making Sense of Measures of Center **43**

Notes _____

_____

_____

_____

Applications

1. a. Use the table at the right. What is the mean tip for each of the days?

b. Suppose Server 2 keeps her own tips. Does she get more for the week? Explain.

Tips

Day	Server 1	2	3	4	5
Monday	$3.55	$6.20	$4.70	$3.85	$4.95
Tuesday	$5.10	$5.20	$5.70	$3.15	$3.55
Wednesday	$7.25	$8.30	$4.00	$6.20	$5.85
Thursday	$4.05	$2.10	$7.60	$2.75	$8.40
Friday	$9.75	$8.50	$9.25	$6.20	$7.35

2. On Saturday, Server 4 forgets to count her tips. Server 3 gathers all of the tip money and distributes an equal share to each server.

Tips

Server 1	Server 2	Server 3	Server 4	Server 5	Mean
$5.65	$6.80	$4.45	■	$7.55	$6.50

a. How much tip money did Server 4 receive originally? Explain.

b. Suppose the mean is $7.75. How much tip money did Server 4 receive originally?

Use the table on the next page for Exercises 3–6.

3. a. What is the mean amount of caffeine in the soda drinks?

b. Make a line plot for the soda drinks.

c. What is the mean amount of caffeine in the other drinks?

d. Make a line plot for the other drinks.

e. Write three statements comparing the amount of caffeine in soda and in other drinks.

44 Data Distributions

Notes _____

_____

_____

_____

4. Indicate whether each statement is true or false.

   a. Soda B has more caffeine than Soda F or Soda D.

   b. Energy Drink C has about three times as much caffeine as the same amount of Energy Drink A.

   c. Of the drinks in the table, 75% have 25 mg or less of caffeine in an 8-ounce serving.

Caffeine Content of Selected Beverages

Soda Drinks

Name	Caffeine in 8 Ounces (mg)
Soda A	38
Soda B	37
Soda C	27
Soda D	27
Soda E	26
Soda F	24
Soda G	21
Soda H	15
Soda J	23

Other Drinks

Name	Caffeine in 8 Ounces (mg)
Energy Drink A	77
Energy Drink B	70
Energy Drink C	25
Energy Drink D	21
Iced Tea A	19
Iced Tea B	10
Coffee Drink	83
Hot Cocoa	2
Juice Drink	33

5. Moderate caffeine intake for adults is 300 mg per day, but it is recommended that 10- to 12-year-olds have no more than 85 mg per day. Has a middle-school student who drinks three 12-ounce cans of Soda F consumed more of his or her recommended intake of caffeine than an adult who drinks two servings of Coffee Drink?

6. Predict whether or not the mean and the median for caffeine content in the graph below have almost the same values. Explain.

Caffeine in Drinks

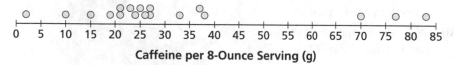

Caffeine per 8-Ounce Serving (g)

Notes _____

_____

_____

_____

7. a. Compare the three sets of data. Which group of students has longer names? Explain your reasoning.

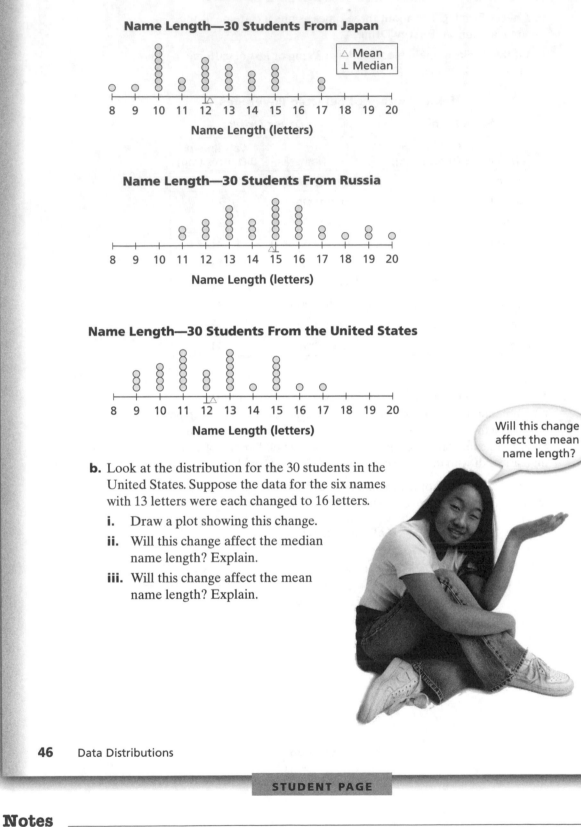

Name Length—30 Students From Japan

△ Mean
⊥ Median

Name Length (letters)

Name Length—30 Students From Russia

Name Length (letters)

Name Length—30 Students From the United States

Name Length (letters)

Will this change affect the mean name length?

b. Look at the distribution for the 30 students in the United States. Suppose the data for the six names with 13 letters were each changed to 16 letters.

i. Draw a plot showing this change.

ii. Will this change affect the median name length? Explain.

iii. Will this change affect the mean name length? Explain.

46 Data Distributions

Notes _____

_____

_____

_____

8. a. The next plots group the same 90 name lengths by gender. Compare the two plots. Which group of students has longer names? Explain.

Homework Help Online
PHSchool.com
For: Help with Exercise 8
Web Code: ane-8208

Name Lengths—Males

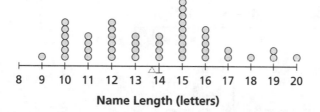

Name Length (letters)

Name Lengths—Females

Name Length (letters)

b. Look at the distribution for the females. Suppose that the data for four names with 18 or more letters were changed. These students now each have name lengths with 10 or fewer letters.

   i. Draw a plot showing this change.

   ii. Will this change affect the median name length for females?

   iii. Will this change affect the mean name length for females?

9. Multiple Choice Send It Quick Mail House mailed five packages with a mean weight of 6.7 pounds. Suppose the mean weight of four of these packages is 7.2 pounds. What is the weight, in pounds, of the fifth package?

A. 3.35   **B.** 4.7   **C.** 6.95   **D.** 8.7

Notes _____

_____

_____

_____

10. **Multiple Choice** In test trials for two new sneaker designs, performance was judged by measuring jump heights. The results are shown below.

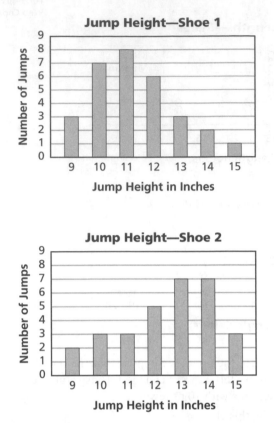

Jump Height—Shoe 1

Jump Height—Shoe 2

Which response below helps the shoe designer decide which sneaker, Shoe 1 or Shoe 2, performs better?

F. Use the mode. The most frequent height jumped for Shoe 1 was 11 inches. The most frequent height jumped for Shoe 2 was 13 or 14 inches.

G. Use the mean. The average jump height for Shoe 1 was 11.3 feet. For Shoe 2, the average was 12.5 feet.

H. Use clusters. Overall, 70% of the students jumped 10 to 12 feet with Shoe 1 while the data varied from 9 to 15 feet. About 63% of the students jumped 12 to 14 feet with Shoe 2 while the data varied from 9 to 15 feet.

J. All of the above.

48   Data Distributions

Notes _____
_____
_____
_____

11. a. What aspect of the shape of a distribution tells you that the mean is greater than the median? Explain.

b. What aspect of the shape of a distribution tells you that the mean is less than the median? Explain.

c. What aspect of the shape of a distribution tells you that the mean and the median are about the same value? Explain.

12. Multiple Choice Del Kenya's test scores are 100, 83, 88, 96, and 100. His teacher tells the class that they can choose the measure of center she will use to determine final grades. Which measure should Del Kenya choose?

A. Mean **B.** Median **C.** Mode **D.** Range

Go Online
PHSchool.com
For: Multiple-Choice Skills Practice
Web Code: ana-8254

Connections

13. a. A gymnast receives these scores from five judges:

   7.6   8.2   8.5   8.2   8.9

What happens to the mean of the scores when you multiply each data value by 2? By $\frac{2}{3}$? By 0.2?

b. Why do you think the mean changes as it does in each situation?

Investigation 2 Making Sense of Measures of Center   **49**

Notes _____

_____

_____

_____

14. **Multiple Choice** Suppose a number is selected at random from a set of data. The data set has an even number of data values, no two of which are alike. What is the probability that this number will be greater than the median?

   F. $\frac{1}{4}$ **G.** $\frac{5}{8}$ **H.** $\frac{1}{2}$ **J.** 1

15. Brilliant Candle Company claims their candles have longer mean burning times than those of other companies. Jaime chooses the same size candles from Brilliant Candle, Firelight Candle, and Shimmering Candle. He burns 15 candles from each company and records the number of minutes that each candle burns.

Burning Time (min)

Candle Number	Brilliant Candle	Firelight Candle	Shimmering Candle
1	60	66	68
2	49	68	65
3	58	56	44
4	57	59	59
5	61	61	51
6	53	64	60
7	57	53	61
8	60	51	63
9	61	60	49
10	62	50	56
11	60	64	59
12	56	60	62
13	61	60	64
14	59	51	57
15	58	49	54

For each company:

a. Make a line plot or bar graph to display the distribution of the data.

b. Describe the variability within the set of data.

c. Estimate the mean and the median for each distribution.

d. Determine the mean and the median for each distribution. How do these values compare with your estimates in part (c)?

e. Do Brilliant Candle's products burn longer than the other two companies' products? Explain.

Notes _____

_____

_____

_____

16. a. Make a circle graph that shows these results.

A survey about favorite colors reports that *exactly*:

12% of those surveyed prefer red
14% of those surveyed prefer orange
28% of those surveyed prefer purple
30% of those surveyed prefer blue
16% of those surveyed prefer green

b. What is the smallest number of people that could have taken the survey? Explain.

Extensions

17. A student gets 40 points out of 100 points on a test. Her teacher announces that this test and next week's test will be averaged together for her grade. The student wonders if she could still get a C if she gets a 100 on the next test. She reasons, "I think my average (mean) would be 70 because half of 40 is 20 and half of 100 is 50. That is a C because 20 plus 50 is 70." Does her method always work? Explain your thinking.

Notes _____

_____

_____

_____

18. If you know the number of chirps made by a cricket in a specific amount of time, you can estimate the temperature in degrees Fahrenheit or degrees Celsius. There are different ways you might do this. For example, one formula involves counting the chirps (the number of wing vibrations per second) over a 13-second period and adding 40 to get the temperature in degrees Fahrenheit. This formula works for the snowy tree cricket.

a. It is possible to turn cricket-chirp recordings into sound intensity versus time graphs. Then you can see each individual chirp and the chirp rate. Look at the four graphs below. Describe how you can tell that the chirp rates vary with the changes in temperature.

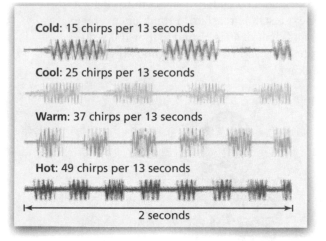

b. Another formula for estimating the temperature is more complicated. Count the chirps per minute, subtract 40, divide by 4, and add 50 to get the temperature in degrees Fahrenheit. Write this formula using x for the number of chirps per minute.

$$y = \text{Temperature in } °F = \underline{\ \ ?\ \ }$$

c. Use your formula from part (b). Draw a line on a coordinate graph that will allow you to relate the number of chirps per minute to temperatures from 0°F to 212°F. Use this line to predict the number of chirps expected for each temperature.

| 0°F | 50°F | 100°F | 212°F |

Notes _____

_____

_____

_____

19. a. The chirp frequency for a different kind of cricket lets you estimate temperatures in Celsius rather than in Fahrenheit. Make a coordinate graph of the data below.

Cricket Chirps per Minute

Frequency	Temperature (°C)
195	31.4
123	22
212	34.1
176	29.1
162	27
140	24
119	20.9
161	27.8
118	20.8
175	28.5
161	26.4
171	28.1
164	27
174	28.6
144	24.6

b. Determine a formula that lets you estimate the temperature in degrees Celsius for a given number of chirps.

c. Use the formula from part (b) to draw a line on the graph from part (a). Describe how well the line "matches" the data. Explain your thinking.

Investigation 2 Making Sense of Measures of Center **53**

Notes _____

_____

_____

_____

Mathematical Reflections 2

In this investigation, you explored three measures of center. These questions will help you summarize what you have learned.

Think about your answers to these questions. Discuss your ideas with other students and your teacher. Then write a summary of your findings in your notebook.

1. **a.** Explain how the mean can be interpreted as an equal share in a situation. Use examples.

   b. Explain how the mean can be interpreted as a balance point in a distribution. Use examples.

   c. In what kinds of situations can you use the mode, but not the mean or the median, to identify what is typical? Use examples.

2. Give an example of each method of summarizing data. Explain why you might choose to use this method with your example.

   a. clusters   **b.** mode

   c. median   **d.** mean

3. **a.** When the mean and the median are the same or very similar, what does this indicate about the shape of the distribution?

   b. When the mean and median are more different than similar, what does this indicate about the shape of the distribution?

   c. Medians and means are called measures of center. Why do you think this is so?

Notes

Investigation 2

ACE Assignment Choices

Differentiated Instruction
Solutions for All Learners

Problem 2.1

Core 1
Other 2, 13, 17; unassigned choices from previous problems

Problem 2.2

Core 3
Other 14, 15; unassigned choices from previous problems

Problem 2.3

Core 6
Other 4, 5, 16; unassigned choices from previous problems

Problem 2.4

Core 7
Other 8–12, 18, 19; unassigned choices from previous problems

Adapted For suggestions about adapting Exercises 3–6 and other ACE exercises, see the CMP *Special Needs Handbook.*
Connecting to Prior Units 13: *Bits and Pieces II*; 15: *Bits and Pieces III*; 16: *How Likely Is It?*

Applications

1. a.   **Tips**

Day	Mean
Monday	$4.65
Tuesday	$4.54
Wednesday	$6.32
Thursday	$4.98
Friday	$8.21

   b. Yes, she would have gotten $30.30 if she kept her own tips. By sharing she gets $28.70.

2. a. $8.05. The total for all of the tips is $5 \times \$6.50 = \$32.50$. If you subtract the total of the four tips given, you have $\$32.50 - \$24.45 = \$8.05$.

   b. $14.30

3. a. $26.4\overline{4}$

   b. (Figure 5)

   c. $37.7\overline{7}$

   d. (Figure 6)

Figure 5

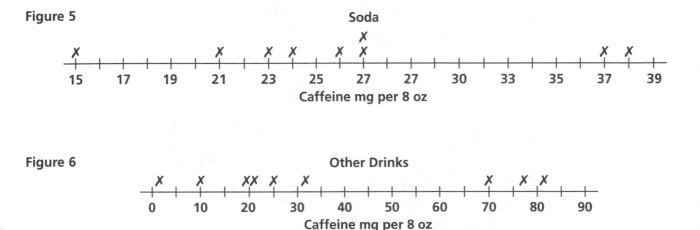

Soda

Caffeine mg per 8 oz

Figure 6

Other Drinks

Caffeine mg per 8 oz

e. Some possibilities: The soda drinks have a smaller mean than the other drinks. If you remove the three high-caffeine drinks, the rest of the other category has a mean of $18.3\overline{3}$, less than the soda-drink mean. The soda drinks have a smaller range of caffeine than the other drinks even if you remove the Hot Cocoa Mix.

4. a. True; Soda B has 37 milligrams of caffeine compared to 24 milligrams for Soda F and 27 milligrams for Soda D.

   b. False; Energy Drink C has 25 mg and Energy Drink A has 77 milligrams, so Energy Drink A has about 3 times as much caffeine as Energy Drink C.

   c. false; It is $\frac{9}{18}$, or 50%.

5. Yes; the 72 mg out of the recommended maximum of 85 mg for a middle-school student is greater than the 166 mg out of the moderate caffeine intake of 300 mg for an adult $(\frac{72}{85} > \frac{166}{300})$.

6. No; the data has 3 possible outliers that will probably affect the mean and not the median.

7. a. The Russians have longer names because their name lengths vary from 11 to 20 letters and they cluster around 15 letters. Name lengths in Japan vary from 8 to 17 letters with all but 2 names being 15 letters or shorter. The name lengths in the United States vary from 9 to 17 letters with all but 2 names being 15 letters or shorter. The means and medians for Japanese and United States name lengths are very similar; the Russian mean and median name lengths are longer.

   b. i. (Figure 7)

      ii. No, the median name length will remain at 12 letters because there will still be the same number of data values on either side of it when you move those data values.

      iii. Yes, the mean name length will change. It will increase to about 13 letters because when you increase data values the mean as the "balance" of the distribution will increase.

8. a. The females seem to have longer names. Their mean name length is almost 14 letters, with a median of 14 letters. The males have a mean name length of about 12.5, with a median of 13 letters. The females have a spread from 9 to 20 letters as opposed to the males that have a spread of 8 to 17.

   b. i. One example is shown in Figure 8.

Figure 7

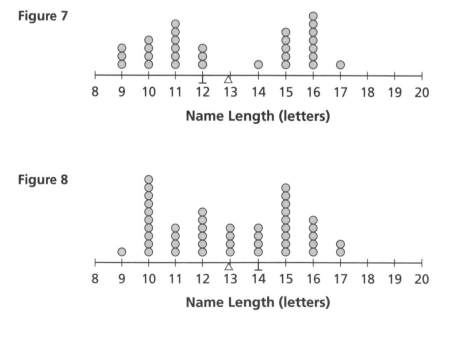

Name Length (letters)

Figure 8

Name Length (letters)

ii. The median would mark a lower value from 14 to 13.

iii. This change will lower the mean.

9. B

10. H; this choice highlights where each clusters and describes variability.

11. a. When the distribution is skewed to the right the mean is greater than the median.

b. When the distribution is skewed to the left the mean is less than the median.

c. The mean and median will be the same value when the distribution is symmetrical or uniform.

12. C. The mode is 100.

Connections

13. a. i. It doubles the mean of the scores.

ii. It is $\frac{2}{3}$ of the mean of the scores.

iii. It is 0.2 of the mean of the scores.

b. If you multiply the individual scores by a factor, then by the distributive property we can pull the factor out and multiply the sum of the individual scores by this factor. Since we multiplied the sum of the scores by a factor this means we multiply the mean by this very same factor.

14. H

15. a. (Figures 9–11)

b. Brilliant Candle: The data vary from 49 to 62 (range of 13) with a cluster from 56 to 62 and 2 gaps in the data: between 49 and 53, and between 53 and 56.

Firelight Candle: The data are fairly uniformly distributed and vary from 49 to 68 (range of 19) with 4 gaps in the data: between 51 and 53, between 53 and 56, between 56 and 59, and between 61 and 64. These gaps are all small in comparison to the overall spread of the data. No large clusters appear.

Shimmering Candle: The data are fairly uniformly distributed and vary from 44 to 68 (range of 24). There are about 5 gaps, most of which are small.

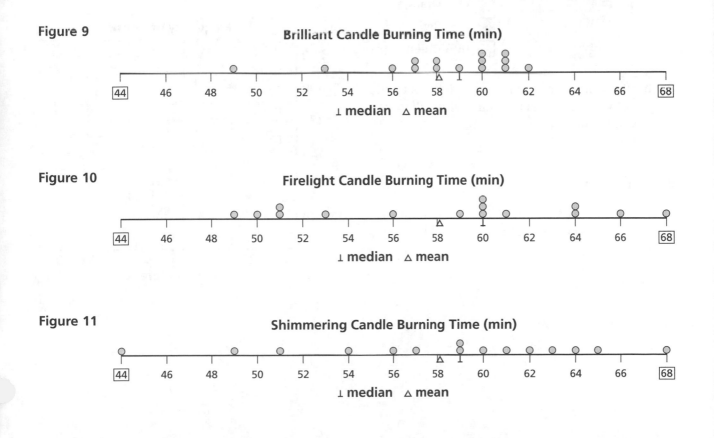

Figure 9

Brilliant Candle Burning Time (min)

⊥ median △ mean

Figure 10

Firelight Candle Burning Time (min)

⊥ median △ mean

Figure 11

Shimmering Candle Burning Time (min)

⊥ median △ mean

c. Possible estimates:

Brilliant Candle: estimated mean 59, estimated median 59

Firelight Candle: estimated mean 57, estimated median 59

Shimmering Candle: estimated mean 59, estimated median 59

d. Brilliant Candle: mean is a little over 58, median is 59

Firelight Candle: mean is a little more than 58, median is 60

Shimmering Candle: mean is 58, median is 59

e. By looking at the means you could not say that Brilliant Candle's products typically burn longer. However, you could say that the burn time is more consistent than the other two companies because their products' burning time has a smaller range, has fewer gaps, and has a cluster between 56 and 62 where the other companies' products' burning time is more spread out with many gaps and no significant clusters.

16. a.

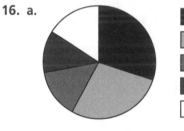

■ 30% Blue
■ 28% Purple
■ 14% Orange
■ 12% Red
□ 16% Green

b. 50 people; since the percents are exact and not rounded, 50 is the smallest number with whole number results.

Extensions

17. Yes; dividing each score by two and adding is the same as adding both scores and dividing by two.

18. a. When it is colder the chirps are longer and less frequent which is evidenced by the chirps changing from 15 to 49 chirps in number when the temperature went from cold to hot.

b. $y = \dfrac{x - 40}{4} + 50$

c. 0°: None (this part of graph would not be used in this context)

50°F: about 40

100°F: about 240

212°F: about 688

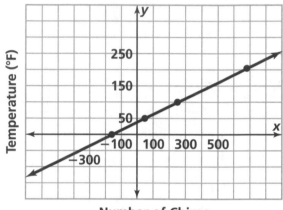

Number of Chirps

19. a.

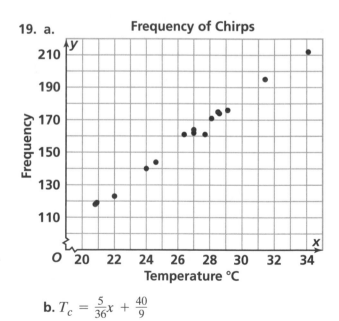

Frequency of Chirps

b. $T_c = \dfrac{5}{36}x + \dfrac{40}{9}$

c. Possible answer:

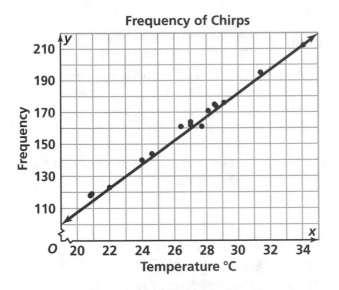

Frequency of Chirps

Although all of the data are not exactly on line, they match it fairly well because they are clustered very close to it.

Possible Answers to Mathematical Reflections

1. a. The mean can be interpreted as an equal share situation because it is the value that all values would be if the data were "evened out." For example, when a number of people have different amounts of beads and they redistribute them evenly to each person, the new amount each person has is the mean.

b. The mean is a balance point because the data values on one side of the mean need to balance the data values on the other side of the mean. The mean is a kind of fulcrum in a distribution; the total distances from the mean for all data values greater than the mean or less than the mean are equal.

c. You can use the mode with categorical data. For example, when your data represented favorite pets, you could find out what pet was chosen most frequently, but you could not find the mean or median.

2. a. Clusters are used with numerical data to help show where data values are clumped together. For example, the data set (2, 3, 15, 15, 16, 16, 16, 17, 17, 17, 25) has a cluster of data between 15 and 17.

b. The mode is useful primarily with categorical data but can be used with numerical data. For example, this data set (red, green, green, blue, blue, blue, red) representing favorite colors, has a mode of blue, and this data set (2, 2, 3, 3, 3, 4, 4, 4, 4, 5) representing number of people in students' households has a mode of 4.

c. The median is a useful way to summarize numerical data because it is a measure of center that is unaffected by outliers. The median marks the midpoint in the distribution that has the same number of values on either side of it. For example, the median of the data set 2, 3, 7, 8, 100 is 7.

d. The mean is a useful way to summarize numerical data because, as a measure of center, it marks where the distribution balances or the value when the data are "evened out." For example, the mean for the data set 2, 3, 7, 8, 100 is 24.

3. a. When the mean and median are similar, the distribution may have a bell or mound shape or a fairly symmetric shape.

b. When the mean and median are different, the distribution may be asymmetrical with some outliers and thus have a skewed shape, possibly with clusters.

c. The mean and median are measures of center in the following way: The median is the midpoint in the ordered distribution. The mean is a kind of fulcrum in a distribution; the total distances from the mean for all data values greater than the mean or less than the mean are equal.

Investigation  Comparing Distributions: Equal Numbers of Data Values

Mathematical and Problem-Solving Goals

- Use tables, line plots, and bar graphs to display data distributions

- Recognize that variability occurs whenever data are collected

- Use properties of distributions to describe the variability in a given data set

- Decide when to use the mean or median to describe a distribution

- Decide if a difference among data values and/or summary measures matters

- Recognize the importance of having the same scales on graphs that are used to compare data distributions

- Develop and use strategies for comparing equal-size data sets to solve problems

Summary of Problems

Problem 3.1 Measuring and Describing Reaction Times

Students write comparison statements about two sets of reaction times collected from two seventh-grade students who used a computer reaction time game.

Problem 3.2 Comparing Reaction Times

Students use the two sets of reaction times collected from the two seventh-grade students in Problem 3.1 and consider data for two other students. They analyze each and make comparisons, addressing both consistency and quickness. They make a recommendation about which student to choose for a class competition.

Problem 3.3 Comparing More Than a Few Students

Students examine forty cases of reaction time data of five trials each. They compare distributions of both the fastest and the slowest reaction times for girls and boys.

Problem 3.4 Comparing Fastest and Slowest Trials

Students make comparisons between fastest reaction times and slowest reaction times for a class of 40 students' data. They consider the use of *benchmark* locations (in addition to mean or median) to mark graphs of two different data sets and use the results to make comparisons. They make recommendations for timing of a video game based on these analyses.

Technology Option for Investigation 3: *TinkerPlots*™ Software

This Investigation has been written so that students can explore the central mathematics ideas without computer software support. However, if you have access to *TinkerPlots* software and to computers, the exploration can be greatly enhanced. The following paragraph is to help you think about your options.

If you have access to *TinkerPlots* and sufficient computers, 2 or 3 students working together on a computer is ideal. This allows all students to work on the problems at the same time. Other options are also workable but require planning. If computers are limited, it may be that students have staggered time on computers prior to discussing a problem. Another option—least desirable—is that all the computer explorations are done as demonstrations.

Ideally, you would have ways to project the software when summarizing. As students describe strategies and/or discuss findings, the actual screen they created can be re-created. Another option is for students to print out their displays and then make transparencies of the displays that you want to have the class consider prior to summarizing the problem.

Using TinkerPlots™ *With CMP Problems: Students' Guide* is provided as an appendix in the Teacher's Guide for students to use as they learn how to use *TinkerPlots*. There are four sections, the first is an introduction and then each section that follows is designed to accompany one of the investigations in *Data Distributions*.

	Suggested Pacing	Materials for Students	Materials for Teachers	ACE Assignments
All	$6\frac{1}{2}$ days	Calculators, student notebooks	Blank transparencies and transparency markers (optional)	
3.1	1 day	Computers with access to applet that measures reaction time (optional)	Transparencies 3.1A–3.1C (optional); chart paper and magic markers	1, 2, 9–13
3.2	1 day	Labsheets 3.2 (one copy for each team, optional); 3ACE Exercise 17	Transparencies 3.2A, 3.2B; transparency of Labsheet 3.2 (optional)	3, 4, 14–17
3.3	2 days	All: Labsheets 3.3A–3.3K (1 set for each group of 2–3 students), 3.3L (one per student) If not using software: Labsheets 3.3M–3.3R (optional) If using software: Computers with *TinkerPlots*™ software; *Using TinkerPlots*™ *With CMP Problems: Students' Guide*	All: Transparency 3.3A, 3.3B (optional) If using software: *Using TinkerPlots*™ *With CMP Problems: Teacher's Guide*	5, 6, 18–22
3.4	2 days	If not using software: Labsheets 3.4A, 3.4B (optional) If using software: Computers with *TinkerPlots*™ software; *Using TinkerPlots*™ *With CMP Problems: Students' Guide*	All: Transparency of Problem 3.4 (optional) If using software: *Using TinkerPlots*™ *With CMP Problems: Students' Guide*	7–8, 23–29
MR	$\frac{1}{2}$ day			

Goals

- Use tables and value bar graphs to display data distributions

- Recognize that variability occurs whenever data are collected

- Use properties of distributions to describe the variability in a given data set

- Decide when to use the mean or median to describe a distribution

- Recognize the importance of having the same scales on graphs that are used to compare data

- Develop and use strategies for comparing equal-size data sets to solve problems

Launch 3.1

Suggested Questions Talk with the students about the context of the problem. Explain that "dominant hand" means the hand that works faster for the game. Usually, this is a student's writing hand.

- *Do you know what a reaction time is?* (See introduction to Problem 3.1 in Student Edition.)

- *In what circumstances might reaction times be important?* (See introduction to Problem 3.1 in Student Edition.)

- *One way to consider reaction time is to measure how long it takes you to press a button when an object appears anywhere on a computer screen. This is a measure of your reaction time. Another way is to measure the distance a yardstick falls between the time you see it falling and the time you catch it.*

Use Transparencies 3.1A and 3.1B. Transparency 3.1A gives an idea of the game. Transparency 3.1B is one example of data from a middle-grades student who used a reaction-time computer game. The data are recorded in a table and displayed in a value bar graph. You can use this context to help students understand these representations and to think about how to write statements about a student's performance.

- *From the table of data, what do we know about Jalin's reaction times?* (the actual time in seconds it took for each of the trials)

- *How are the data in the table related to the value bar graph displaying Jalin's times?* (Each data value is represented by a value bar on the graph; the data are in order by trial with trial 5 nearest the horizontal axis.)

We want to write statements about Jalin's times and about any differences or similarities that we notice. There are three kinds of statements we can think of about writing. (Show Transparency 3.1B; see page 9 to revisit each type of statement—read the data, read between the data, read beyond the data.)

Read the Data

Use the information on Transparency 3.1B about one student's times to guide the initial discussion. For each of the kinds of statements, first look at the name and the description. Then look at each of the examples provided. With the students, discuss how each example fits the category of the statement. Ask whether students can add any other statements. The primary goal is to make meaningful statements. Two statements, one about fastest time and one about slowest time, are meaningful because they (1) individually are special scores among the list of five scores and (2) together provide information about the range of the data. Students might suggest these possible statements: "Jalin's second fastest score was 0.88 seconds. Or Jalin's second slowest score was 1.06 seconds."

Read Between the Data, Read Beyond the Data

Do the same as above. It is important to work with the students on writing these kinds of statements so that they will have some idea of how to tackle Problem 3.1.

Then look at what students need to do to complete Problem 3.1. Some teachers have given students an opportunity to actually use a reaction time game and collect their own data. Here are some options:

- There are several ways that students can test their own reaction times. Links to Web sites that offer computer-game methods may be found on www.PHSchool.com/cmp2. Links providing instructions on measuring reaction times using yardsticks may also be found on that site.

- If you do a computer reaction time activity, organize students so they can go one-at-a-time to one or more computers and play one round of the game and record their respective times. Some teachers have done this using only one computer; students can be working on Problem 3.1 when they are not collecting their data.

    Organize students in teams of two.

Explore 3.1

For Questions A and B1, the situations are similar to the one the students did with the data about Jalin. Teachers have found that there is a need to support students as they work to articulate quantitative observations that involve statements with some substance.

You can talk with students as they work, helping them clarify what would be a "read the data" or a "read between the data" statement and press them to move to "read beyond the data" statements. For example, below are sample statements that can be made when describing Jasmine's scores. You may need to encourage students to think about these ways of writing observations:

Read the data:

- Jasmine's fastest time was 0.84 second.

- Jasmine's slowest time was 1.05 seconds.

Read between the data:

- Jasmine's times have a range of 0.21 second.

- Jasmine's median time is 0.93 second, just a bit less than one second.

Read beyond the data:

- Jasmine's times seem somewhat inconsistent; her second and fourth trials were her better times.

- 4 out of 5 trial times occurred in the interval of 0.80–1.00 second so this is probably a good estimate of times to expect when she plays the game.

    (**Note:** If students ask, "decisecond" and "centisecond" can be used to describe times that are less than one second.)

For Question B, part (1), you may find that you need to encourage students to think about these ways of writing observations:

Read the data:

- Nathaniel's fastest time was 0.70 second.

- Nathaniel's slowest time was 0.93 second; he had this time twice.

Read between the data:

- Nathaniel's times have a range of 0.23 second.

- Nathaniel's median time is 0.88 second which is closer to his slowest time of 0.93 second than to his fastest time of 0.70 second.

Read beyond the data:

- Nathaniel's times seem somewhat consistent; his first few trials were his better times and were less than 0.8 second; his last three trials were all in the interval of 0.88 – 0.93.

- Nathaniel seemed to do less well with the game in the later rounds than during the early rounds.

    For Question B, part (2), students can use the two sets they just completed writing, and then write comparisons between Jasmine and Nathaniel using the ways of comparing that they considered in *Comparing and Scaling*. For example:

Using differences: Both Jasmine's and Nathaniel's ranges are similar (about 0.20 second) but their scores are different. Nathaniel's fastest time is 0.14 second faster than Jasmine's fastest time.

Using ratios: 4 out of 5 of Jasmine's times are in an interval of 0.80 second to 1.00 second; 3 out of 5 of Nathaniel's times are in the same interval. The rest of Nathaniel's times are less than Jasmine's times (i.e., less than 0.8 second).

Using fractions: Jasmine's median time is $\frac{93}{100}$ second. Nathaniel's median time is $\frac{88}{100}$ second. The difference is $\frac{5}{100}$ second.

Using percents: 80% of Jasmine's times are less than 1 second and 100% of Nathaniel's times are less than 1 second.

Going Further

- *What score would Jasmine need on a sixth trial to have a mean less than 0.85?* (Any score less than 0.40 will work.)

Summarize 3.1

This discussion is pivotal to "pressing" students to make more than simple vague statements like "more" or "less" or simple quantitative statements about the data (i.e., "read the data" statements).

You may want to post two sheets of chart paper, one for statements about Jasmine's times and one for statements about Nathaniel's times. You can post these pages next to each other; ask students to share their observations for "read the data statements" and record. Do the same for the other two categories of observations, i.e., "read between the data" and "read beyond the data" statements. Then, have students share comparison statements that are recorded on a third sheet of chart paper.

Make sure to press them to think about using differences, fractions, ratios, and percents.

If students have computed both the median and the mean, have a discussion about which measure they think is helpful. With only the five scores, the median will always mark the middle value which will or will not be reflective of all the values. If the mean is used, it will reflect some of the inconsistencies or consistencies in times because it responds to unusual values.

Finally, ask students to state and justify which of the two students they think is more *consistent* overall and which of the two students they think is *quicker*. Leave the final charts displayed so that students can refer to them as they complete the rest of the problems in this investigation.

3.1 Measuring and Describing Reaction Times

Mathematical Goals

- Use tables and value bar graphs to display data distributions
- Recognize that variability occurs whenever data are collected
- Use properties of distributions to describe the variability in a given data set
- Decide when to use the mean or median to describe a distribution
- Decide if a difference among data values and/or summary measures matters
- Recognize the importance of having the same scales on graphs that are used to compare data
- Develop and use strategies for comparing equal-size data sets to solve problems

Launch

Talk with students about the problem's context.

- *What is a reaction time? In what circumstances is it important?*

One way to consider reaction time is to measure your response time in clicking on an object appearing on a computer screen. Another way is to measure the distance a yardstick falls between the time you see it falling and the time you catch it. Use Transparency 3.1A to show how a computer game might look. Use Transparency 3.1B as an example of data from a middle-grades student's reaction time game.

- *From the table of data, what do we know about Jalin's reaction times?*
- *How are the data in the table related to the value bar graph displaying Jalin's times?*
- *Write statements about Jalin's times and about differences or similarities we notice.*

Read the data, Read between the data, Read beyond the data

There are three kinds of statements. For each kind of statement, look at the name and description, then at the examples provided and, with the students, discuss how each example fits the statement's category.

- *Can students add more statements?*

Organize students in teams of two.

Materials

- Transparencies 3.1A–3.1C

For Question A, the situation is similar to the one with Jalin's data. Talk with students as they work, help them clarify what is a "read the data" or a "read between the data" statement, and move them to "read beyond the data" statements. For Question B, part (1), students can probably write similar statements to those written about Jasmine's times. If necessary encourage students to think about these ways of writing observations: "read the data," "read between the data," and "read beyond the data." Students can then write comparisons between Jasmine and Nathaniel using ways of comparing considered in *Comparing and Scaling*.

Materials
- Calculators
- Access to computer applet that measures reaction time (optional)

Summarize

This discussion is pivotal to "pressing" students to move beyond simple statements like "more" or "less" or to stick only with simple quantitative statements about the data (i.e., "read the data" statements). Post two sheets of chart paper next to each other, one for statements about Jasmine's times and one for statements about Nathaniel's times. Ask students to share their statements and record. Then, have students share comparison statements on a third sheet of chart paper. Finally, have students justify which of the two students is more *consistent* overall. Who is *quicker*? Keep the final charts displayed for students to refer to in completing Investigation 3.

Materials
- Student notebooks
- Chart paper
- Markers

ACE Assignment Guide for Problem 3.1

Differentiated Instruction
Solutions for All Learners

Core 1, 2, 9–13
Adapted For suggestions about adapting ACE exercises, see the CMP *Special Needs Handbook*.
Connecting to Prior Units 9–13: *Data About Us*

Answers to Problem 3.1

A. Possible answers: Jasmine's fastest time was 0.84 seconds and her slowest time was 1.05 seconds; Jasmine's median time is 0.93 seconds, just a bit less than one second; Jasmine's time seems somewhat inconsistent, her second and fourth trials were her better times. See the Explore section for further discussion on the types of answers to elicit from students.

B. 1. Possible answers: Nathaniel's fastest time was 0.70 second and his slowest time was 0.93 second—he had this time twice; the range was 0.23 second; Nathaniel seemed to do worse with the game in the later rounds than during the earlier rounds. See the Explore section for further discussion on the types of answers to elicit from students.

2. Possible answer: Both Jasmine's and Nathaniel's ranges are similar (about 0.20 second) but Nathaniel's fastest time is 0.14 second faster than Jasmine's fastest time. See the Explore section for further discussion on the types of answers to elicit from students.

3.2 Comparing Reaction Times

Goals

- Use tables and value bar graphs to display data distributions

- Recognize that variability occurs whenever data are collected

- Use properties of distributions to describe the variability in a given data set

- Decide when to use the mean or median to describe a distribution

- Decide if a difference among data values and/or summary measures matters

- Recognize the importance of having the same scales on graphs that are used to compare data

- Develop and use strategies for comparing equal-size data sets to solve problems

Launch 3.2

Begin with Transparency 3.2A. This shows the two students' data from the reaction time game on a single page. It is very important to see both graphs on the same page in order to create the "effect" we want.

Suggested Questions Ask:

- *Who performed better, Diana or Henry?*

You can have some fun with this. Students immediately claim, "Henry." Then, eventually, some student will say, "Wait a minute. The two scales on the graphs aren't the same." Once students realize that the scales are different, they have to rethink their claims about "better." Once students raise the question of scale, you can ask:

- *Suppose we want to show both sets of data on the same graph. Do we put Diana's data on Henry's graph or put Henry's data on Diana's graph in order to have the same scale? Which should we do?* (Because Henry's times are greater than Diana's, it makes sense to put Diana's results as bars on Henry's bar graph.)

You can use an overhead pen and draw in Diana's bars over Henry's bars, making sure you match Trial 1 with Trial 1 and so on. It might look like Transparency 3.2B. (Figure 1)

Figure 1

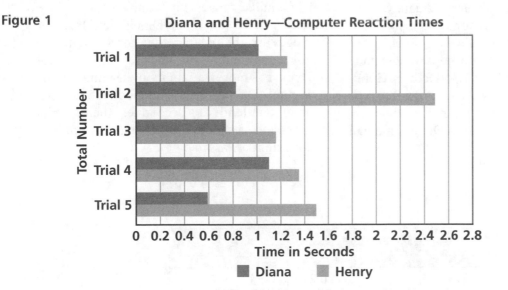

Suggested Questions Now, have students talk about:

- *When we talk about one student being "better" than another student in this context, what do we mean?* (one student is quicker, more consistent, has shorter trials as the game progresses than the other student)

- *Suppose we decide to look at quickness. Who is quicker, Diana or Henry? Explain your reasoning using statements about each person's performance.*

- *Suppose we decide to look at consistency. Who is more consistent, Diana or Henry? Explain your reasoning using statements about each person's performance.*

Remember to make statements that use comparisons among individual data values (read the data), among clusters of data values (read between the data), or among statistics, predictions, or interpretations of the data (read beyond the data). You can use differences, fractions, ratios, and percents in making any comparisons.

While students will not write something like this immediately, you may decide to share this with them if you think it will help: Diana is more *consistent* and *quicker* than Henry, two desirable traits when playing this kind of game. Each of her times is less than the comparable time for Henry. Her data vary from 0.59 second to 1.08 seconds, so her range is 0.43 second; Henry's data vary from 1.15 seconds to 2.48 seconds, so his range is 1.33 seconds or about triple Diana's range. Diana's mean time of 0.85 second is almost half Henry's mean time of about 1.54 seconds. Henry's mean time is influenced by the one possible outlier of 2.48 seconds. Henry's median time (1.34 seconds) is about 1.6 times Diana's median time (0.83 second).

Take time with the students to articulate points like those above. Also, discuss what "quicker" and "consistent" mean and why they might be important to define and consider when looking at reaction times. Suggest that these are ways to think about describing comparisons.

Organize students in teams of 2 or 4 and have them complete Problem 3.2. They will need a copy of Labsheet 3.2 (all graphs have same scales), one for each team. Have them cut the graphs so that they have individual sheets they can move around for each of Diana, Henry, Nathaniel, and Jasmine. (You might have these already cut to save time.)

Explore 3.2

For Questions A–E, students need to use quantitative arguments to justify their reasoning like the work that has been done so far.

Summarize 3.2

The summary statistics for each student are shown in Figure 2.

Have the students discuss the ways they went about making comparisons. Together, build a table like that below. Examine the data for "consistency" and for "quickness." Both Jasmine and Nathaniel have similar ranges but Jasmine's times visually appear more consistent. Diana's and Henry's ranges are greater than the others'. Henry is really not in the running for quickness or consistency. Diana has more variability in her times than Jasmine. Diana's mean and median times are about one-tenth of a second less than Jasmine's times. Diana can be quicker but may not be as consistent as Jasmine.

Labsheet 3ACE Exercise 17 is provided if Exercise 17 is assigned.

Figure 2

Name	Minimum Value	Maximum Value	Range	Mean	Median
Jasmine	0.84	1.05	0.21	0.94	0.93
Nathaniel	0.70	0.93	0.23	0.84	0.88
Diana	0.59	1.08	0.43	0.85	0.83
Henry	1.15	2.48	1.33	1.54	1.34

3.2 Comparing Reaction Times

Mathematical Goals

- Use tables and value bar graphs to display data distributions
- Recognize that variability occurs whenever data are collected
- Use properties of distributions to describe the variability in a given data set
- Decide when to use the mean or the median to describe a distribution
- Decide if a difference among data values and/or summary measures matters
- Recognize the importance of having the same scales on graphs that are used to compare data
- Develop and use strategies for comparing equal-size data sets to solve problems

Launch

Begin with Transparency 3.2A, which shows the two students' results from the reaction time game on a single page. Ask:

- *Who is quicker, Diana or Henry?*

Students immediately claim, "Henry." Some students will notice that the two scales on the graphs aren't the same. Once students question the scale, ask: Suppose we want to show both sets of data on the same graph.

- *Do we put Diana's data on Henry's graph or put Henry's data on Diana's graph in order to have the same scale?*

At this point, you can use an overhead pen and draw in Diana's bars over Henry's bars, making sure you match Trial 1 with Trial 1 and so on. Have students talk about:

- *Who is quicker, Diana or Henry? Explain your reasoning using statements about each person's performance.*

- *Who is more consistent? Explain your reasoning using statements about each person's performance.*

- *Write statements that use comparisons among individual data values (read the data), among clusters of data values (read between the data), or among statistics, predictions, or interpretations of the data (read beyond the data). You can use differences, fractions, ratios, and percents in making any comparisons.*

Organize students in teams of 2 or 4 and have them complete Problem 3.2. Each team will need a copy of Labsheet 3.2. Have them cut the graphs to have individual sheets to move around for Diana, Henry, Nathaniel, and Jasmine.

Materials

- Transparencies 3.2A, 3.2B
- Labsheet 3.2 (one copy per team with multiple copies of blank paper if needed, optional)
- Transparency of Labsheet 3.2 (optional)
- Labsheet 3ACE 17

Explore

For Questions A–E, students need to use quantitative arguments to justify their reasoning like the work that has been done so far.

Materials

- Calculators

See Summarize 3.2 for the summary statistics for each student. Have the students discuss the ways they went about making comparisons. Together, build a table like that in Summarize 3.2. Examine the data for "consistency" and for "quickness."

Materials
- Student notebooks

ACE Assignment Guide for Problem 3.2

Differentiated Instruction
Solutions for All Learners

Core 3, 4, 17

Other *Connections* 14–16; unassigned choices from previous problems

Adapted For suggestions about adapting ACE exercises, see the CMP *Special Needs Handbook*.
Connecting to Prior Units 14, 15: *Bits and Pieces I*; 16: *Shapes and Designs*

Labsheet 3ACE Exercise 11 is provided if Exercises 8–10 are assigned.

Answers to Problem 3.2

A. When the graphs have the same scale, the reaction times are easier to compare.

B. 1. Jasmine's times vary from 0.84 to 1.02 seconds; Nathaniel's times vary from 0.70 to 0.93 second; Diana's times vary from 0.59 to 1.08 seconds; Henry's times vary from 1.15 to 2.48 seconds.

2. Jasmine's range is 0.18 second; Nathaniel's range is 0.23 second; Diana's range is 0.43 second; Henry's range is 1.33 seconds.

3. Ranges sometimes give information about variability (consistency) so, for example, Jasmine's and Nathaniel's ranges are smaller than the other two students', which could suggest greater consistency in reaction times.

4. Ranges help describe consistency. However, we also would want to know minimum and maximum times. Someone could have a small range but longer overall times, so we wouldn't necessarily call this person quicker.

C. 1. Jasmine's median reaction time is 0.93 second; Nathaniel's is 0.88 second; Diana's is 0.83 second, and Henry's median reaction time is 1.34 seconds.

2. Jasmine's mean reaction time is 0.93 second; Nathaniel's is 0.84 second; Diana's is 0.85 second; Henry's mean reaction time is 1.54 seconds.

3. Possible answer: Henry's mean is higher than his median reaction time due to a possible outlier, which indicates some variability in his data. Whereas Jasmine's mean and median reaction times are close, which indicates that there are probably no outliers and her data is more consistent than Henry's. However, other information such as range may be helpful in comparing whether a student's reaction time is more consistent than another's.

4. Mean or median are measures of center and are useful to compare reaction times. The mean marks the balance point of the reaction times, and the median marks the midpoint of the data. The student with the smallest mean or median reaction times is quicker than the others.

D. Possible answer: Determining the amount of trials or percentage of trials that were below 1 second might help determine which student is quicker than another.

E. Possible answer: Recommend Nathaniel because, although Diana is quicker than Nathaniel, he is more consistent.

Goals

- Recognize that variability occurs whenever data are collected

- Use properties of distributions to describe the variability in a given data set

- Decide when to use the mean and the median to describe a distribution

- Decide if a difference among data values and/or summary measures matters

- Develop and use strategies for comparing equal-sized data sets to solve problems

Technology Option For an optional approach using *TinkerPlots*™ software, see the Teacher's Guide Appendix for Problem 3.3, beginning on page 172. Blackline masters of student pages for use with this investigation begin on page A13.

Launch 3.3

Begin Problem 3.3 using Labsheets 3.3A–3.3K to make a set of Reaction Time Cards. Be sure each group of 2–3 students has a card set. If not already done, students should cut the pages so that each graph is a single card that can be moved around. There are 40 cards in the card set; each card is a *case* that shows all data about one student's trials. All the graphs have the same scales.

Suggested Questions Ask:

- *Look at the cards you have. What can you tell about the different students who are represented in the card set?* (You can tell first name, gender, age, time it took for each trial, and can compare the trials visually.)

- *We can describe each card as a case or one individual in the data set. Let's list the attributes that we know from looking at the cases.* [Name, Gender, Age, Trial 1(sec), Trial 2(sec), Trial 3(sec), Trial 4(sec), Trial 5(sec)]

- *Can we determine any other information? Fastest trial? Slowest trial? Mean or median trials? How would you determine these values*

for a single case? (All this information can be determined; each card looks like the cards used in the previous problem.)

- *With your partners, sort the cards in any way you want. Be prepared to describe how you sorted the cards.* (Students use a variety of methods; some like to sort by gender, others by age; let students offer their methods and things they noticed. The goal is for them to get familiar with this data set.)

- *Are there any attributes where the values for several cases are the same [constant]?* (Gender is M or F; age is eleven, twelve, or thirteen.)

- *Which attributes have values that are categorical data?* (Gender and age are written as categorical data; age could be written as numerical data in some other situation.)

- *Which attributes have values that are numerical data?* (the trial times)

Have students look at the attribute of fastest trial.

- *What is the range of the values for the fastest trials?* (Have students use their card sets to look for the fastest trials with the lowest and highest values; the fastest trials vary from 0.58 second to 1.18 seconds, with a range of 0.60 second.)

- *Based on the range, how might we make a number line so we can make a line plot to show the distribution of these data?*

Discuss the use of decimal data and setting up a scale that permits marking decimal data (e.g., the data for the entire data set of fastest trials vary from 0.58 second to 1.18 seconds so we might use 0.5 second to 1.2 seconds with ticks at every tenth of a second). Have the students look at their cards and share ten of the fastest trials so you can mark these times on the number line to make a line plot.

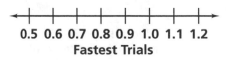

0.5 0.6 0.7 0.8 0.9 1.0 1.1 1.2
Fastest Trials

INVESTIGATION 3

Here are two possible ways to proceed at this point:

1. Have students use the data card set and the empty table (Labsheet 3.3L) that has name, gender, and age listed for each student and some empty columns. They can add a column title (e.g., Fastest Time) and then enter the data from the card set. They can use these data when they make their graphs. Each group makes a line plot, marking locations for fastest trials for each of the 40 students. You may want to prepare a large line plot on chart paper. This will make it easier to mark the locations. Have them also locate the mean and the median times.

2. Use Labsheets 3.3M–3.3R that show sorted tables of data and graphs of these data with the mean and median already marked.

Suggested Questions Here is a discussion using Transparency 3.3B (Figure 3):

- *Can you tell me how the data in the table are related to the top graph?* (Have students locate individual students' fastest times and then point to the dot that marks each time on the graph.)

- *How can we use the bottom graph to do the same activity?* (The bottom graph is identical to the top graph; it is scaled by 0.05 increments and the top graph is scaled by 0.1 increments.)

- *What are some "read the data" statements we can make about the class's fastest reaction times?* (E.g., the fastest time is 0.58 second and the slowest time is 1.18 seconds.)

- *What are some "read between the data" statements we can make about the class' fastest reaction times?* (E.g., there are 12 reaction times less than 0.7 second; there are very few repeated values in reaction times.)

- *What are some "read beyond the data" statements we can make about the class' fastest reaction times?* (E.g., the mean and median differ by about 0.25 second, not a very big difference even in a timed situation; the range of reaction times is 0.6 second; 32 out of 40 [or 80%] of the fastest reaction times are less than 1.0 second.)

Have students work in teams of two to complete Questions A and B.

Here are two possible ways to proceed at this point:

1. Have students make all their own graphs by hand. You will need a copy of the database for each pair of students working together.

2. Provide Labsheets 3.3Q and 3.3R that have the needed graphs for exploring the problem.

Figure 3

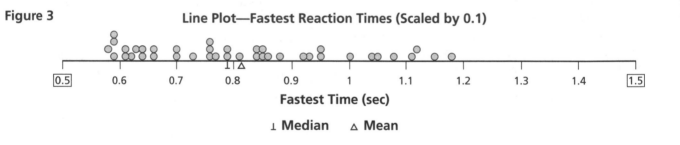

Line Plot—Fastest Reaction Times (Scaled by 0.1)

Fastest Time (sec)

⊥ Median   △ Mean

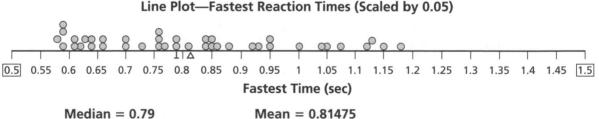

Line Plot—Fastest Reaction Times (Scaled by 0.05)

Fastest Time (sec)

Median = 0.79   Mean = 0.81475
Minimum Value = 0.58   Maximum Value = 1.18   Range = 0.60

Explore 3.3

Comparing the boys and girls on the fastest and slowest times gives students opportunities to compare equal-size data sets. Students can compare statistics both within a distribution and between distributions: mean, median, range. They can also look for clusters and use benchmarks at specific times to make comparisons.

They are focusing on two ways of characterizing reaction times: using the characteristic of *quickness* and using the characteristic of *consistency*. They will need to think about what this means when comparing between two groups.

Summarize 3.3

You can use the framework of read the data, read between the data, and read beyond the data to organize data analysis.

Question A

Read the Data

- The fastest fast time for girls is 0.58 second and the slowest fast time is 1.08.

- The fastest fast time for boys is 0.59 second and the slowest fast time is 1.18.

- The distributions have few repeated values since measurement data are being used.

Read Between the Data

- The minimum and maximum values for the girls are 0.58 second and 1.08 seconds. The range is 0.50 second.

- The minimum and maximum values for the boys are 0.59 second and 1.18 seconds. The range is 0.59 second.

- There is a difference between the two ranges of about one-tenth of a second.

- The data seem to cluster in two locations for each distribution (see graphs marked below); the girls' data seem to be more clumped than the boys'. (Figure 4)

Read Beyond the Data

- The median is 0.8 seconds (girls) and 0.775 seconds (boys) and the mean is 0.796 seconds (girls) and 0.8335 seconds (boys). The girls' mean and median are between the boys' mean and median.

- The girls' mean and median are almost identical values; there is a difference of 0.004 second.

- The difference between the boys' mean and median is 0.037 second or about 4 hundredths of a second, which is a small difference that may not matter much in this context since there is a range from about 0.5 to 1.2 seconds.

Figure 4

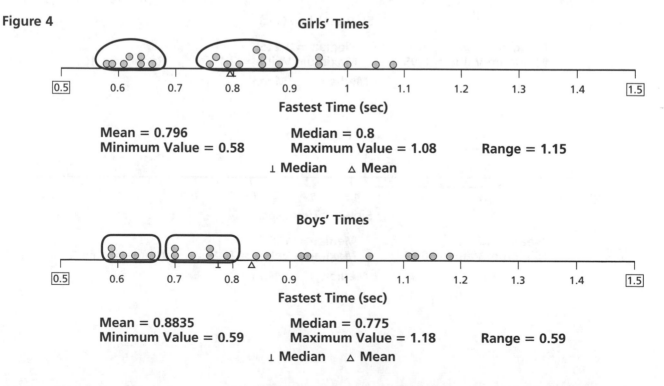

Girls' Times

Fastest Time (sec)

Mean = 0.796   Median = 0.8
Minimum Value = 0.58   Maximum Value = 1.08   Range = 1.15
⊥ Median   △ Mean

Boys' Times

Fastest Time (sec)

Mean = 0.8835   Median = 0.775
Minimum Value = 0.59   Maximum Value = 1.18   Range = 0.59
⊥ Median   △ Mean

Investigation 3   Comparing Distributions: Equal Numbers of Data Values   **85**

INVESTIGATION 3

- About 35% of the reaction times for boys and girls together are less than or equal to 0.7 second.

- About 25% of the girls' and 38% of the boys' times are greater than 0.9 second.

- The boys have some higher times than the girls: 10% of their times are greater than 1.10 seconds; none of the girls had times greater than 1.10 seconds.

Question B Slowest Trials

Read the Data

- The fastest slow time for girls is 0.95 second and the slowest slow time is 2.1.

- The fastest slow time for boys is 0.84 second and the slowest slow time is 2.48.

- The distributions have few repeated values since measurement data are being used.

Read Between the Data

- The data for the girls vary from 0.95 second to 2.1 seconds, with a range of 1.15 seconds.

- The data for the boys vary from 0.84 second to 2.48 seconds, with a range of 1.64 seconds.

- There is a difference between the two ranges of about half a second.

- The data seem to cluster in one (similar) location for each distribution. (Figure 5)

- There is a possible outlier in each distribution; without the possible outliers, the two ranges are quite similar. (Figure 5)

Read Beyond the Data

- The median is 1.215 seconds (girls) and 1.235 seconds (boys) and the mean is 1.288 seconds (girls) and 1.282 seconds (boys). The girls' mean and median are similar and the boys' mean and median are very similar.

- The girls' mean and median are almost identical values; there is a difference of 0.073 seconds.

- The boys' mean and median are almost identical values; there is a difference of 0.047 second or about 5 hundredths of a second.

- About 20% of the girls' slowest reaction times and about 10% of the boys' slowest reaction times are greater than or equal to 1.6 seconds.

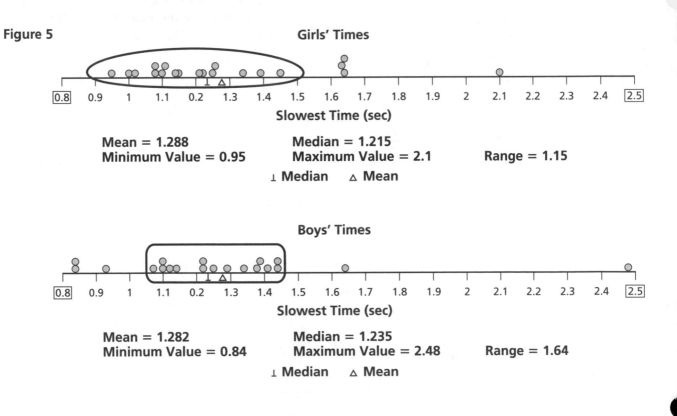

Figure 5

Girls' Times

Slowest Time (sec)

Mean = 1.288
Minimum Value = 0.95

Median = 1.215
Maximum Value = 2.1

Range = 1.15

⊥ Median   △ Mean

Boys' Times

Slowest Time (sec)

Mean = 1.282
Minimum Value = 0.84

Median = 1.235
Maximum Value = 2.48

Range = 1.64

⊥ Median   △ Mean

3.3 Comparing More than a Few Students

At a Glance

PACING 2 days

Mathematical Goals

- Recognize that variability occurs whenever data are collected
- Use properties of distributions to describe the variability in a given data set
- Decide when to use the mean or median to describe a distribution
- Decide if a difference among data values and/or summary measures matters
- Develop and use strategies for comparing equal-size data sets to solve problems

Launch

Begin Problem 3.3 using Labsheets 3.3A–3.3K to make a set of Reaction Time Cards. Make sure each group of 2–3 students has a card set. If not already done, students should cut the pages so that each graph is a single sheet or card that can be moved around.

- *Look at the cards you have. What do you know about the different students who are represented in the card set?*
- *We can describe the information you have as a case or one individual in the data set. Let's list the attributes that we know from looking at the cases. Name, Gender, Age, Trial 1(sec), Trial 2(sec), Trial 3(sec), Trial 4(sec), Trial 5(sec)*
- *Can we determine any other information? Fastest trial? Slowest trial? Mean or median trials?*
- *How would you determine these values for a single case?*
- *With your table partners, sort the cards in any way you want. Be prepared to describe how you sorted the cards. Are there any attributes where the values for several cases are the same (constant)?*
- *Which attributes have values that are categorical data?*
- *Which attributes have values that are numerical data?*
- *Have students look at the attribute of fastest trial.*
- *What is the range of the values for the fastest trials?*
- *Based on the range, how might we make a number line so we can make a line plot to show the distribution of these data?*

Have the students look at their cards and share ten of the fastest trials so you can make these times on the number line to make a line plot.

For an optional approach using data analysis software, see the Teacher's Guide Appendix for Problem 3.3, beginning on page 172, and the blackline masters of student pages beginning on page A13.

Materials

All:
- Labsheets 3.3A–3.3K (1 set for each group of 2–3 students), 3.3L (one per student)
- Transparency 3.3

If not using software:
- Labsheets 3.3M–3.3R

If using software:
- Computers with *TinkerPlots™* software
- *Using TinkerPlots™ with CMP Problems: Students' Guide*
- *Using TinkerPlots™ with CMP Problems: Teacher's Guide*

Investigation 3 Comparing Distributions: Equal Numbers of Data Values **87**

When students are directed to make graphs, it is anticipated that they will make line plots. Students can continue to use Labsheets 3.3A–3.3K if needed.

Summarize

You can use the framework of *read the data*, *between the data*, and *beyond the data* to organize data analysis. See the extended Summary section for a discussion.

Materials
- Student notebooks

ACE Assignment Guide for Problem 3.3

Differentiated Instruction
Solutions for All Learners

Core 5, 6, 18–22
Other unassigned choices from previous problems

Adapted For suggestions about adapting ACE exercises, see the CMP *Special Needs Handbook*.
Connecting to Prior Units 18–22: *Data About Us*

Answers to Problem 3.3

See the extended Explore section for discussion of ways to compare the data.

A. 1. Consistent: Girls' mean and median are similar; boys' mean is noticeably higher than boys' median, indicating the presence of unusually high data values. Girls' range is smaller than boys' range. Girls appear somewhat more consistent.

   2. Quicker: Girls' data values have both max and min values that are less than boys; girls' range is less than boys'; girls have 3 out of

20 times greater than or equal to 1 second while boys have 5 out of 20 such times. The means and medians are very similar, making a useful comparison difficult. Based on max, min, range, and benchmarks, girls appear to be somewhat quicker than boys, but these measures of center do not definitively support this. It is too close to call.

B. 1. Yes; girls' and boys' means and medians are similar. Most of the data for both are less than 1.5 seconds. However, there are 4 out of 20 girls with reaction times greater than 1.5 seconds but only 2 out of 20 boys with such reaction times. The range for boys is greater than the range for girls.

   2. Yes; the girls' range is less than the boys' range but boys only have one possible outlier whose value is influencing the range. There is a cluster of boys that have quicker times than any of the girls; the boy's data seems a bit more tightly clustered than the girls. It is too close to call.

Comparing Fastest and Slowest Trials

Goals

- Recognize that variability occurs whenever data are collected

- Use properties of distributions to describe the variability in a given data set

- Decide when to use the mean or median to describe a distribution

- Decide if a difference among data values and/or summary measures matters

- Develop and use strategies for comparing equal-size data sets to solve problems

Technology Option For an optional approach using *TinkerPlots*™ software, see the Teacher's Guide Appendix for Problem 3.4, beginning on page 178. Blackline masters of student pages for use with this investigation begin on page A13.

Launch 3.4

Suggested Questions With the students, read the initial introduction to the problem.

- *How many of you play video games?* (Many students will answer yes.)

- *Why is reaction time important when you play these games?* (Students realize that speed of response is part of what makes a video game interesting.)

- *Some video games have different levels of playing difficulty. Do you think reaction time is part of what defines a level of difficulty? Why do you think this?* (Reaction time, or speed of response, can be one of the things that vary across difficulty levels.)

- *Today, you are going to compare students' fastest and slowest reaction times. Then you will make a recommendation about cutoff times for reaction times for Levels 1 (easy), 2 (medium), and 3 (hard) to Willa, the video game designer.*

Have students work in teams of two.

Here are two possible ways to proceed at this point:

1. Have students make all their own graphs by hand. You will need a copy of the data (fastest and slowest times) from Problem 3.3 for each pair of students working together.

2. Use Labsheets 3.4A–B that have the needed graphs for exploring the problem.

Explore 3.4

Students compare the fastest and slowest reaction times of all 40 students. They need to use graphs that have the same scale. When they are making their comparisons, it may help to focus on "read the data," "read between the data," and "read beyond the data" statements.

Students are still comparing equal-size groups. However, with this comparison, it is easier to see the differences as one set of data is *shifted* to the right (slowest times).

The problem questions are a way to focus their discussions; they do NOT have to approach ideas about comparing the data using the structure of read the data, read between the data, or read beyond the data. However, if this is a useful strategy, here are some examples:

Read the Data

- The slowest times include two possible outliers, one at 2.1 seconds and one at 2.48 seconds.

Read Between the Data

- The distribution of slowest times is shifted to the right; all but two of the slowest times or about 100% of the times are greater than 0.9 second. For the fastest times, about 30% of the times are greater than 0.9.

Read Beyond the Data

- The mean and median for the slowest times are about 1.5 times the mean and median for the fastest times.

In Question D, students use all this information to make a recommendation.

Question A

Discuss the need to have the scales of the graphs be the same. Then, have students share ways they compared the two distributions.

Question B

Suggested Questions You can use graphs to help focus the discussion.

- *How do the means in each distribution compare?* [The mean for the fastest reaction time is about $\frac{2}{3}$ the mean for the slowest reaction times (i.e., $\frac{2}{3}$ of 1.3 is about 0.9).]

- *How do the medians in each distribution compare?* [The medians have a similar relationship to the means. The median for the fastest reaction time is about $\frac{2}{3}$ the median for the slowest reaction times (i.e., $\frac{2}{3}$ of 1.2 is 0.8).]

- *Describe where the data seem to cluster in each distribution and compare clusters.* (The fastest time data seem to cluster below 1.0 seconds and the slowest time data seem to cluster from 1.0 seconds to 1.5 seconds. The fastest time data seem, again, to be about

$\frac{1}{3}$ less in times than the slowest time data. The slowest times are shifted to the right in comparison to the fastest times.)

- *Is one distribution more variable than the other? How do you know?* [The spreads of the two distributions are different. The range for the fastest times is 0.6 second or about 1 second less than the range of the slowest times (at 1.6 seconds). Both distributions have few repeated values because these are measurement data. The slowest times have two values that are possible outliers.]

Question C

Below are locations for all the reference lines on each of the two graphs. Students place them one at a time. (Figure 6)

Have students offer cutoff times with reasons. See answers below for one way to do this. Students may want to put reference lines at locations different from those suggested (e.g., at 1.0, 1.3, and 1.6 seconds, or at 0.8, 1.2, and 1.6 seconds). That is also possible.

Figure 6

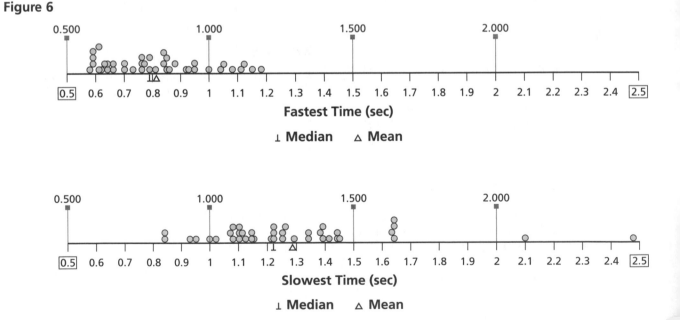

3.4 Comparing Fastest and Slowest Trials

Mathematical Goals

- Recognize that variability occurs whenever data are collected
- Use properties of distributions to describe the variability in a given data set
- Decide when to use the mean or median to describe a distribution
- Decide if a difference among data values and/or summary measures matters
- Develop and use strategies for comparing equal-sized data sets to solve problems

Launch

With the students, read the initial introduction to the problem.

- *How many play video games?*
- *Why is reaction time important when you play these games?*
- *Some video games have different levels of playing difficulty. Do you think reaction time is part of what defines a level of difficulty? Why?*
- *Today, you are going to compare students' fastest and slowest reaction times. Then you will recommend cutoff times for reaction times for Levels 1 (easy), 2 (medium), and 3 (hard) to Willa, the video game designer.*

Have students work in pairs.

For an optional approach using data analysis software, see the Teacher's Guide Appendix for Problem 3.4, beginning on page 178, and the blackline masters of student pages beginning on page A13.

Materials

All:

- Transparency of Problem 3.4 (optional)

Explore

Students compare the fastest and slowest reaction times of all 40 students. They need to use graphs so that both graphs have the same scale. When they are making their comparisons, it may help to focus on "read the data," "read between the data," and "read beyond the data" statements.

Students are still comparing equal-sized groups. However, with this comparison, it is easier to see the differences as one set of data is *shifted* to the right (slowest times).

The problem questions are a way to focus their discussions; they do NOT have to approach ideas about comparing the data using the structure of read the data, read between the data, or read beyond the data.

In Question D, students use all of this information to make a recommendation.

Materials

If not using software:

- Labsheet 3.3A–3.3K, 3.3M–3.3R, 3.4A, 3.4B (optional)

If using software:

- Computers with *TinkerPlots™* software
- *Using TinkerPlots™ with CMP Problems: Students' Guide*
- *Using TinkerPlots™ with CMP Problems: Teacher's Guide*

Question A

Discuss the need to have the scales of the graphs be the same. Then have students share ways they compared the two distributions.

Question B

You can use graphs to help focus the discussion.

- *How do the means in each distribution compare?*
- *How do the medians in each distribution compare?*

Describe where the data seem to cluster in each distribution and compare clusters.

- *Is one distribution more variable than the other? How do you know?*

Question C

In the extended TE are graphs with locations for all the reference lines on each of the two graphs. Students place them one at a time.

Have students offer cutoff times with reasons. Students may want to put reference lines at locations different from those suggested. That is also possible.

Materials
- Student notebooks
- Transparency of Problem 3.4 (optional)

ACE Assignment Guide
for Problem 3.4

Differentiated Instruction
Solutions for All Learners

Core 7, 8
Other *Connections* 23, 24; *Extensions* 25–29; unassigned choices from previous problems

Adapted For suggestions about adapting Exercise 7 and other ACE exercises, see the CMP *Special Needs Handbook*.
Connecting to Prior Units 23: *What Do You Expect?*; 24: *Data About Us*

Answers to Problem 3.4

A. The fastest time data seem to cluster below 1.0 seconds and the slowest time data seem to cluster from 1.0 seconds to 1.5 seconds. The fastest time data seem to be about $\frac{2}{3}$ of the slowest time data. The slowest times are shifted to the right in comparison to the fastest times. To make these comparisons easily, the graphs have to have the same scale.

B. 1. The mean for the fastest reaction time is about $\frac{2}{3}$ of the mean for the slowest reaction times. The medians have a similar relationship to the means. The median for

the fastest reaction time is about $\frac{2}{3}$ of the mean for the slowest reaction times.

2. The range for fastest time data (0.6 second) is about $\frac{1}{3}$ that for slowest time data (1.89 seconds).

3. See the answer to Question A.

4. The slowest time data are more variable; the range is greater and there are outliers in the data.

C. Possible answer: Most of the fastest reaction times are between 0.5 and 1 second, while most of the slowest reaction times cluster between 1 and 1.5 seconds.

D. Possible answers:
- Level 1 (easy) could be between 1.2 and 1.7 seconds (range of 0.5 seconds) or greater because about 50% of students' slowest reaction times fell in this interval.
- Level 2 (medium) could be between 0.8 and 1.2 seconds (range of 0.4 second) because about 50% of the students' fastest times fell into this interval.
- Level 3 (hard) could be between 0.5 and 0.8 second (range of 0.3 second) because about 50% of the students' fastest times fell into this interval.

Investigation 3

Comparing Distributions: Equal Numbers of Data Values

Time is a measure that is used to answer many questions.

> *What was your time running a 50-yard dash or swimming 100 meters?*
>
> *How fast is your reaction time to respond to events in a game?*
>
> *Do wood roller coaster rides last longer than steel roller coaster rides?*

You often compare times different people or groups take to complete a task. Think back to *Comparing and Scaling* and the ways you made comparisons between numbers using fractions, percents, and ratios. These ideas will help you make comparisons in data situations.

3.1 Measuring and Describing Reaction Times

When you hear, see, or touch something, a message is sent to the area of the brain that controls muscle activity. Then, a signal is sent out to muscles to respond. Sometimes it matters how quickly you react, for example:

- Swinging at a baseball with a bat or at a tennis ball with a racquet
- Swerving to miss a rock in the road while riding your bicycle
- Responding to actions in a video game

Computer programs can be used to test how quickly people react. For one such program, each trial begins with a colored circle appearing on the screen. When the circle appears, the person clicks on the circle as quickly as possible. When the trial is over, the person's time is reported.

Investigation 3 Comparing Distributions: Equal Numbers of Data Values **55**

Each student in a seventh-grade class completed five trials on a computer reaction-time game. In Problem 3.1, you will make comparisons among their reaction times.

Problem 3.1 Measuring and Describing Reaction Times

A. Write three different statements that describe the variability in Jasmine's times.

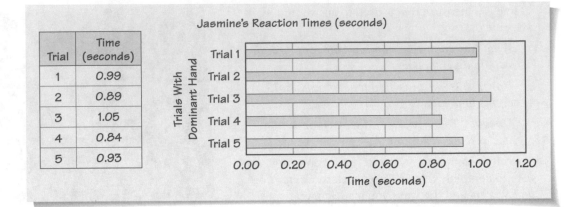

Jasmine's Reaction Times (seconds)

Trial	Time (seconds)
1	0.99
2	0.89
3	1.05
4	0.84
5	0.93

B. 1. Write three different statements that describe the variability in Nathaniel's times.

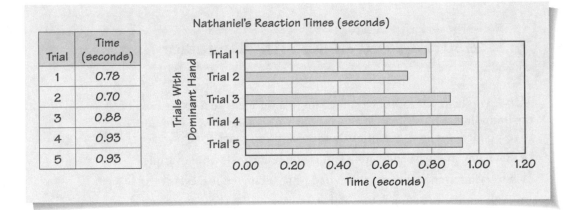

Nathaniel's Reaction Times (seconds)

Trial	Time (seconds)
1	0.78
2	0.70
3	0.88
4	0.93
5	0.93

2. How do Nathaniel's and Jasmine's results compare? Remember, you can use fractions, percents, and ratios to make comparisons.

 Homework starts on page 62.

Notes _____

_____

_____

_____

3.2 Comparing Reaction Times

The value bar graphs and data tables below show the computer game reaction times for Diana and Henry.

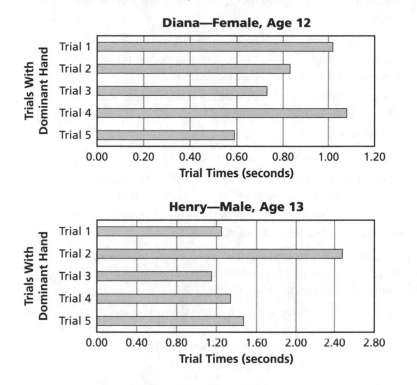

Diana—Female, Age 12

Trials With Dominant Hand: Trial 1, Trial 2, Trial 3, Trial 4, Trial 5

Trial Times (seconds): 0.00, 0.20, 0.40, 0.60, 0.80, 1.00, 1.20

Henry—Male, Age 13

Trials With Dominant Hand: Trial 1, Trial 2, Trial 3, Trial 4, Trial 5

Trial Times (seconds): 0.00, 0.40, 0.80, 1.20, 1.60, 2.00, 2.40, 2.80

Diana's Reaction Times

Trial	1	2	3	4	5
Seconds	1.02	0.83	0.73	1.08	0.59

Henry's Reaction Times

Trial	1	2	3	4	5
Seconds	1.25	2.48	1.15	1.34	1.47

Who reacted faster, Diana or Henry?

When comparing performances, you can use variability, measures of center, and fraction, percent, or ratio statements.

Investigation 3 Comparing Distributions: Equal Numbers of Data Values **57**

Notes _____

_____

_____

_____

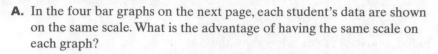
A. In the four bar graphs on the next page, each student's data are shown on the same scale. What is the advantage of having the same scale on each graph?

B. **1.** What are the minimum and maximum reaction times for each of the four students?

    2. What is the range of reaction times for each of the students?

    3. Does comparing ranges of reaction times help you decide if one student is more consistent than another student?

    4. Does comparing ranges of reaction times help you decide if one student is quicker than another student?

C. **1.** What is the median reaction time for each student?

    2. What is the mean reaction time for each student?

    3. Does comparing mean or median reaction times help you decide whether one student is more consistent than another student?

    4. Does comparing mean or median reaction times help you decide whether one student is quicker than another student?

D. Locate 1 second on each graph. Explain how comparing data below, at, or above the benchmark time of 1 second can help determine whether one student is quicker than another student.

E. Another class has challenged this class to choose one student to play the computer reaction-time game against their class champion. Would you recommend they choose Diana, Henry, Nathaniel, or Jasmine? Why?

ACE **Homework starts on page 62.**

Notes _____

_____

_____

_____

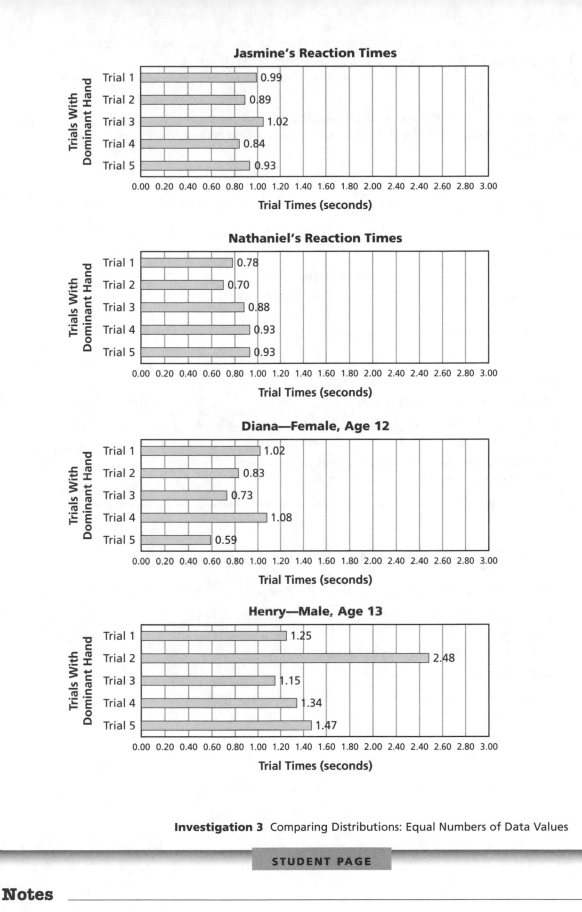

Jasmine's Reaction Times

Trials With Dominant Hand	
Trial 1	0.99
Trial 2	0.89
Trial 3	1.02
Trial 4	0.84
Trial 5	0.93

0.00 0.20 0.40 0.60 0.80 1.00 1.20 1.40 1.60 1.80 2.00 2.40 2.40 2.60 2.80 3.00

Trial Times (seconds)

Nathaniel's Reaction Times

Trials With Dominant Hand	
Trial 1	0.78
Trial 2	0.70
Trial 3	0.88
Trial 4	0.93
Trial 5	0.93

0.00 0.20 0.40 0.60 0.80 1.00 1.20 1.40 1.60 1.80 2.00 2.40 2.40 2.60 2.80 3.00

Trial Times (seconds)

Diana—Female, Age 12

Trials With Dominant Hand	
Trial 1	1.02
Trial 2	0.83
Trial 3	0.73
Trial 4	1.08
Trial 5	0.59

0.00 0.20 0.40 0.60 0.80 1.00 1.20 1.40 1.60 1.80 2.00 2.40 2.40 2.60 2.80 3.00

Trial Times (seconds)

Henry—Male, Age 13

Trials With Dominant Hand	
Trial 1	1.25
Trial 2	2.48
Trial 3	1.15
Trial 4	1.34
Trial 5	1.47

0.00 0.20 0.40 0.60 0.80 1.00 1.20 1.40 1.60 1.80 2.00 2.40 2.40 2.60 2.80 3.00

Trial Times (seconds)

Investigation 3 Comparing Distributions: Equal Numbers of Data Values **59**

Notes _____

_____

_____

_____

Comparing More Than a Few Students

For Problem 3.3, you will use a set of 40 case cards showing reaction times for a computer game. Copies of these cards can be found behind the Glossary.

Getting Ready for Problem 3.3

How can you locate each piece of information about a student on a case card?

Name	Trial 1 reaction time
Gender	Trial 2 reaction time
Age	Trial 3 reaction time
Fastest Time for 5 trials	Trial 4 reaction time
Slowest Time for 5 trials	Trial 5 reaction time

- Which attributes are categorical data?
- Which attributes are numerical data?
- Which attributes have values that vary from one student to another? Why do you think this is so?
- Which attributes have constant (the same) values for several or all of the students? Why do you think this is so?

Problem 3.3 Comparing Many Data Values

Use the reaction-time data to help you answer these questions.

A. Compare the distributions of the girls' fastest times and the boys' fastest times.

  1. Is one group more consistent? Explain.

  2. Is one group quicker? Explain.

B. Compare the distributions of the girls' slowest times and the boys' slowest times.

  1. Is one group more consistent? Explain.

  2. Is one group quicker? Explain.

ACE **Homework starts on page 62.**

60 Data Distributions

Notes _____

_____

_____

_____

Willa is a video-game designer. You will help her make some decisions about timing in her video game.

Problem 3.4 Comparing Larger Distributions

Use the reaction time data to help you answer these questions.

A. Compare the fastest reaction times of all the students to the slowest reaction times of all the students. What must be true about the scales of the two value bar graphs in order to make these comparisons easy to make?

B. 1. Describe how the means and the medians compare.

   2. Describe how the ranges compare.

   3. Where do the data cluster in each distribution? Describe how the locations of data clusters compare.

   4. Is one distribution more variable than the other? Explain.

C. For each distribution, look at 0.5 second, 1 second, 1.5 seconds, and 2 seconds. Compare the numbers of students at, above, or below each of these benchmark times on each distribution. What do you notice?

D. Write a recommendation to Willa. Based on your work in Questions B and C, how much time should she give a player to react in a video game? Include recommendations for easy, medium, and hard levels. Justify your recommendations.

ACE Homework starts on page 62.

Notes _____

_____

_____

_____

Applications

1. Write three different statements that describe the variability in Frank's reaction times.

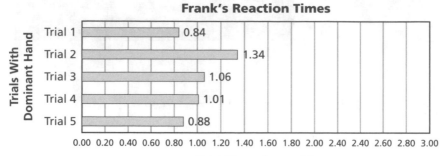

Frank's Reaction Times

2. Compare Matthew's reaction times to Frank's reaction times.

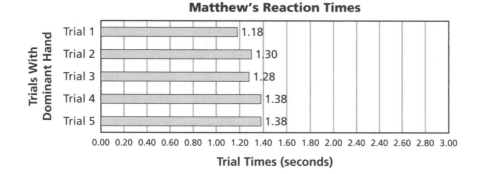

Matthew's Reaction Times

a. Determine the means, medians, minimum and maximum values, and ranges for each student.

b. Is one student quicker than the other student? Explain your reasoning.

c. Is one student more consistent than the other student? Explain.

62   Data Distributions

Notes _____

_____

_____

_____

Graph A and Graph B show the fastest reaction time on a computer reaction-time game with the non-dominant hand for each of the 40 students. Use these graphs for Exercises 3 and 4.

Graph A: Non-Dominant Hand Reaction Times

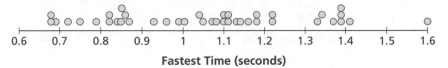

Fastest Time (seconds)

Graph B: Non-Dominant Hand Reaction Times

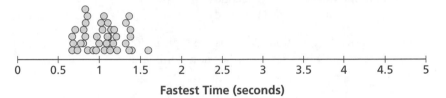

Fastest Time (seconds)

3. Tanisha says that Graph A and Graph B show the same data. Jeff says, "No way! These are not the same data." Do you agree with Jeff? Explain.

4. a. Use the statistics below and Graphs A and B above. Describe the distribution of fastest reaction times using the non-dominant hand.

Mean:	1.06 seconds
Median:	1.08 seconds
Minimum Value:	0.68 second
Maximum Value:	1.60 seconds
Range:	0.92 seconds

b. How would you answer the question, "What is the typical fastest reaction time for a student who uses his or her non-dominant hand?"

Notes _____

_____

_____

_____

5. a. Describe the distribution of the data below.

Slowest Reaction Times With Non-Dominant Hand

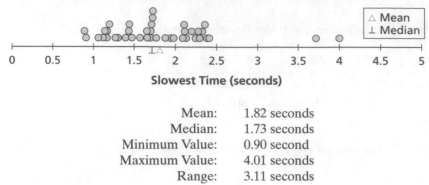

Slowest Time (seconds)

Mean:	1.82 seconds
Median:	1.73 seconds
Minimum Value:	0.90 second
Maximum Value:	4.01 seconds
Range:	3.11 seconds

b. How would you answer the question, "What is the typical slowest reaction time for a student who uses his or her non-dominant hand?" Explain.

6. Use the data in Exercise 5 and the data below to compare the fastest reaction times to the slowest reaction times for non-dominant hands. Explain your reasoning.

Fastest Reaction Times With Non-Dominant Hand

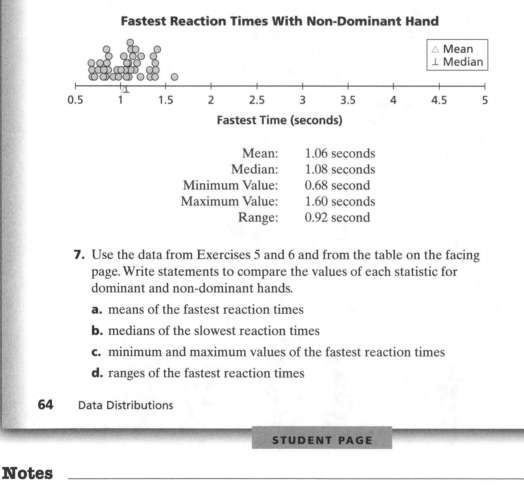

Fastest Time (seconds)

Mean:	1.06 seconds
Median:	1.08 seconds
Minimum Value:	0.68 second
Maximum Value:	1.60 seconds
Range:	0.92 second

7. Use the data from Exercises 5 and 6 and from the table on the facing page. Write statements to compare the values of each statistic for dominant and non-dominant hands.

a. means of the fastest reaction times

b. medians of the slowest reaction times

c. minimum and maximum values of the fastest reaction times

d. ranges of the fastest reaction times

STUDENT PAGE

Notes _____

_____

_____

_____

Dominant Hand Reaction Times

Statistic	Fastest Reaction Times (seconds)	Slowest Reaction Times (seconds)
Mean	0.81	1.29
Median	0.79	1.22
Minimum Value	0.58	0.84
Maximum Value	1.18	2.48
Range	0.60	1.64

8. Use the line plots and table below. How much slower are the Trial 1 reaction times for non-dominant hands than the Trial 1 reaction times for dominant hands? Explain.

Homework Help **O**nline
PHSchool.com

For: Help with Exercise 8
Web Code: ane-8308

Trial 1 Reaction Times With Dominant Hand

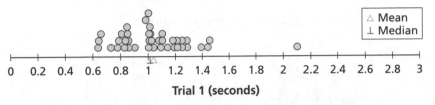

Trial 1 Reaction Times With Non-Dominant Hand

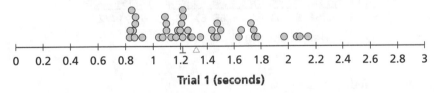

Trial 1 Reaction Times

Statistic	Dominant Hand (seconds)	Non-Dominant Hand (seconds)
Mean	1.048	1.324
Median	1.015	1.22
Minimum Value	0.64	0.83
Maximum Value	2.10	2.14
Range	1.50	1.31

Investigation 3 Comparing Distributions: Equal Numbers of Data Values **65**

Notes _____

_____

_____

_____

Connections

9. **Multiple Choice** Suppose 27 is added as a data value to the set of data: 10, 29, 15, 29, 35, and 2. Which statement is true?

   A. The mean increases by 4.   **B.** The mode decreases by 10.

   C. The median decreases by 1.   **D.** Not here

10. **Multiple Choice** The mean of six numbers is 25. If one number is 15, what is the mean of the other five numbers?

   F. 15   **G.** 25   **H.** 27   **J.** 40

For Exercises 11–13, look at the mean and median for the data. Describe how the shape of each distribution is influencing the location of the mean and the median. Explain your reasoning.

11. Mean = 62 inches, Median = 62 inches,
    Minimum and Maximum Values = 53 and 72 inches

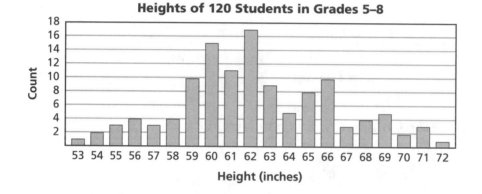

Heights of 120 Students in Grades 5–8

12. Mean = 24.7 grams, Median = 22.1 grams,
    Minimum and Maximum Values = 21.3 and 37.1 grams

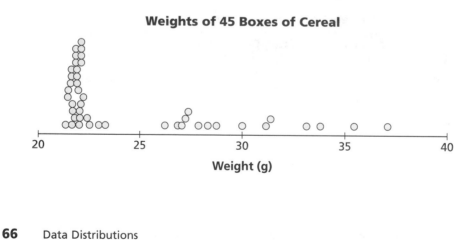

Weights of 45 Boxes of Cereal

66 Data Distributions

Notes _____

_____

_____

_____

13. Mean = 120.5 minutes, Median = 121 minutes,
Minimum and Maximum Values = 81 and 234 minutes

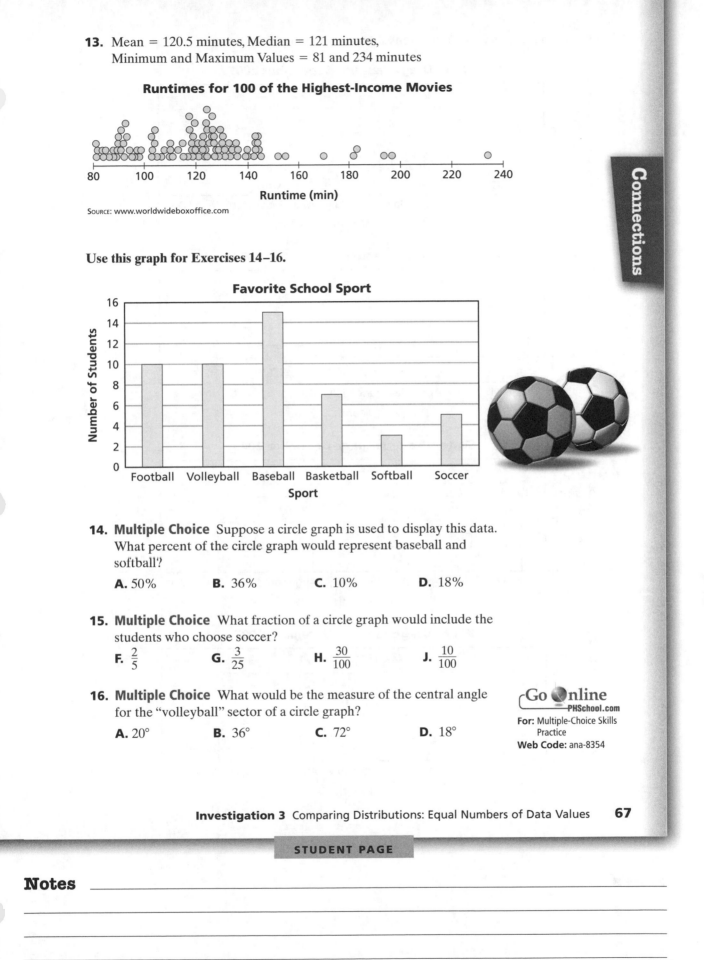

Runtimes for 100 of the Highest-Income Movies

SOURCE: www.worldwideboxoffice.com

Use this graph for Exercises 14–16.

Favorite School Sport

14. Multiple Choice Suppose a circle graph is used to display this data.
What percent of the circle graph would represent baseball and
softball?

A. 50% **B.** 36% **C.** 10% **D.** 18%

15. Multiple Choice What fraction of a circle graph would include the
students who choose soccer?

F. $\frac{2}{5}$ **G.** $\frac{3}{25}$ **H.** $\frac{30}{100}$ **J.** $\frac{10}{100}$

16. Multiple Choice What would be the measure of the central angle
for the "volleyball" sector of a circle graph?

A. 20° **B.** 36° **C.** 72° **D.** 18°

Go Online
PHSchool.com

For: Multiple-Choice Skills
Practice
Web Code: ana-8354

Investigation 3 Comparing Distributions: Equal Numbers of Data Values **67**

Notes _____

_____

_____

_____

17. Elisa receives these four graphs showing her family's water usage.

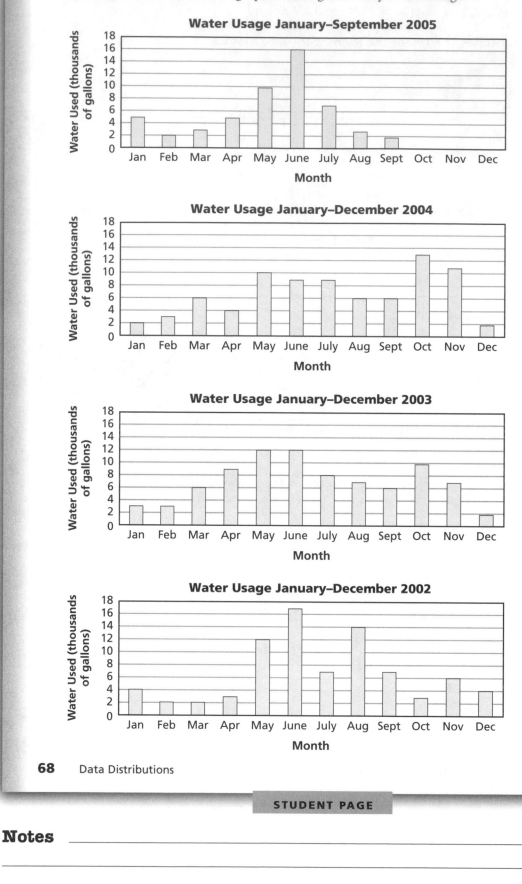

Notes

a. Describe any patterns in water usage that occur across years.

b. Use the graphs to find out how many gallons of water were used each month. Make a line plot for each of the years from 2003 to 2005 to show the distribution of the number of gallons used each month. For example, this line plot shows the data from 2002.

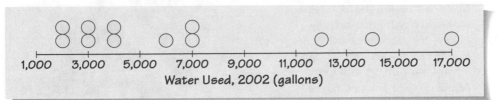

Water Used, 2002 (gallons)

c. Use the plots from part (b) to determine the mean monthly water usage for each year from 2002–2004. Mark these values on the plots. Using the mean monthly number of gallons used for each year, how does the water usage compare across the years? Explain.

d. Repeat part (c) for the median monthly water usage instead of the mean. Why should we not use the line plot for 2005 to estimate the mean or median?

e. Copy the data from your graphs in part (b) onto one line plot. You should have 45 data points. Determine the mean and the median for this new set of data. How do these two values compare? Why do you think this is so?

f. Is the median or the mean a better estimate of the typical monthly amount of water used during a year? Explain.

Investigation 3 Comparing Distributions: Equal Numbers of Data Values   **69**

Notes

For Exercises 18–22, answer each question for each statement below.

Statement A
Garter snakes are the most typical snakes in North America. Fully grown, they can be 18 – 42 inches in length. They are generally about 3 feet long with a 1-inch girth. Although their coloring can be various shades of green, blue, brown, or red, they all have a pale but conspicuous stripe along the middle of the back and a less prominent stripe along each side.

Statement B
Each man, woman, and child in America eats an average of 46 slices (23 pounds) of pizza a year.

18. How do you think the process of data analysis was carried out?

19. What kinds of data—numerical or categorical—are used?

20. What kinds of variability might there be in the original data?

21. What kinds of patterns appear to have occurred in the data?

22. What is typical about the data and what might be outliers?

23. Multiple Choice A bag contains 36 chips. Each chip is either red or black. The probability of selecting a red chip from the bag is one fourth. What is the probability of drawing a black chip?

F. $\frac{1}{4}$ **G.** $\frac{3}{5}$ **H.** $\frac{7}{8}$ **J.** $\frac{3}{4}$

Notes _____
_____
_____
_____

24. Write a title that provides the viewer with a summary snapshot of the information provided in the graph. Be clever. Do not just restate the data.

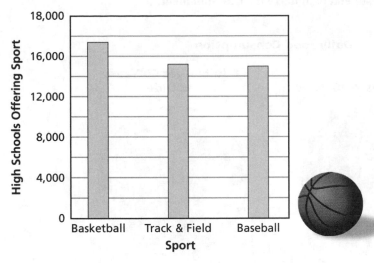

SOURCE: *National Federation of State High School Associations*

Extensions

25. The line plot below shows the median reaction times for the students in Problem 3.3. Describe the distribution of the median reaction times.

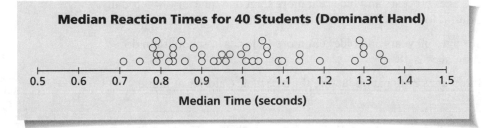

b. How do the median reaction times compare with the fastest reaction times, shown below?

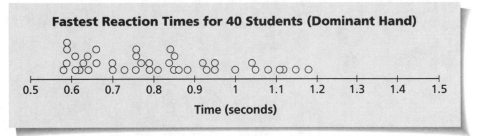

Notes _____

_____

_____

_____

Use the circle graphs to determine whether each statement in Exercises 26–29 is true. For each statement that is not true, explain how you would change the statement to make it a true statement.

Daily Food Consumption

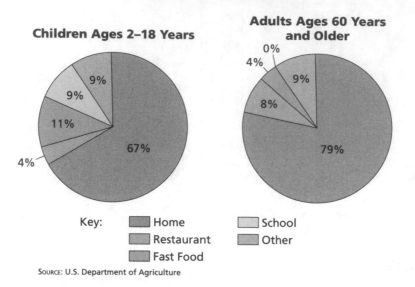

Children Ages 2–18 Years

67%
4%
11%
9%
9%

Adults Ages 60 Years and Older

0%
4%
9%
8%
79%

Key:
- ▩ Home
- ▩ Restaurant
- ▩ Fast Food
- ▩ School
- ▩ Other

Source: U.S. Department of Agriculture

26. Adults ages 60 years and older eat twice as many Calories at restaurants as do children ages 2–18.

27. Adults ages 60 years and older eat more than one quarter of their daily Calories at locations that are not their homes.

28. Adults ages 60 years and older eat more Calories at school than do children ages 2–18.

29. Children ages 2–18 eat about one third of their Calories at home.

Notes

Mathematical Reflections 3

In this investigation, you compared distributions of data with the same numbers of data values. These questions will help you summarize what you have learned.

Think about your answers to these questions. Discuss your ideas with other students and your teacher. Then write a summary of your findings in your notebook.

1. Sometimes you need to compare two or more distributions, each of which is shown on a different graph. Why is it helpful to make the scales of the axes the same on each graph?

2. Explain what a value bar graph and a line plot are. How are they related?

3. In several places you were asked to compare one or more students' reaction times. Use Henry's and Nathaniel's data from Problems 3.1 and 3.2. Describe how you can use fractions, percents, and ratios to make comparisons.

4. You also made comparisons among students' data to decide when one or more students were more consistent or quicker than other students.

   a. What does consistency mean when it refers to reaction times?

   b. What does quickness mean when it refers to reaction times?

   c. Identify a different situation in which you would compare consistency or quickness in performance. What does consistency or quickness mean in this situation?

Notes _____
_____
_____
_____

Answers

Applications   **Connections**   **Extensions**

Investigation 3

ACE
Assignment Choices

Differentiated Instruction
Solutions for All Learners

Problem 3.1
Core 1, 2, 9–13

Problem 3.2
Core 3, 4, 17
Other *Connections* 14–16; unassigned choices from previous problems

Problem 3.3
Core 5, 6, 18–22
Other unassigned choices from previous problems

Problem 3.4
Core 7, 8
Other *Connections* 23, 24; *Extensions* 25–29; unassigned choices from previous problems

Adapted For suggestions about adapting Exercise 7 and other ACE exercises, see the CMP *Special Needs Handbook*.
Connecting to Prior Units 9–13, 18–22, 24: *Data About Us*; 14, 15: *Bits and Pieces I*; 16: *Shapes and Designs*; 23: *What Do You Expect?*

Applications

1. Frank's minimum and maximum values are 0.84 and 1.34 seconds. Frank had his fastest time in the first trial and his slowest time in the second trial. The difference, or range, of his reaction times is 0.50 second.

2. **a.** Frank: mean: 1.026 seconds; median: 1.01 seconds; minimum and maximum values: 0.84 and 1.34 seconds; range: 0.50 second.
   Matthew: mean: 1.304 seconds; median: 1.30 seconds; minimum and maximum values: 1.18 and 1.38 seconds; range: 0.20 second.

   b. Frank is quicker. His mean and median are faster than Matthew's, and four out of five of his times are faster than Matthew's fastest time.

   c. Matthew is more consistent than Frank, with a range of times of 0.20 second, compared to Frank's range of 0.50 second.

3. Both graphs do show the same data. The scales are different but the data are the same.

4. **a.** The data values for the fastest reaction times vary from about 0.68 to 1.6 seconds. Less than half of the times are less than or equal to 1 second (16 out of 40). In Graph A where the scale goes by 0.1 second, the data do not seem to cluster at all. However, when the scale is changed to 0.5 second in Graph B, all of the data look like they clump together.

   b. Students could choose either the median or the mean as these two statistics are similar and in the middle of the distribution.

5. **a.** The data values for the slowest reaction times vary from approximately 0.9 to 4.0 seconds. The majority of times are less than 2.5 seconds; about $\frac{1}{3}$ of the times are above 2.0 seconds. The data cluster around 1.75 seconds. There are two possible outliers.

   b. Students could choose the median, the mean, or the mode as these three statistics are similar and in the middle of the distribution.

6. Answers will vary; possible comparison statements: Looking at means, the mean slowest reaction time is about 1.7 times the mean fastest reaction time. The median slowest reaction time is about 1.6 times the median fastest reaction time. Means and medians for each set of times are similar. The range for the slowest reaction times is more than three times the number of seconds as the range for the fastest reaction times. Also, the slowest time of the fastest reaction times is less than the mean and the median of the slowest reaction times.

ACE ANSWERS 3

7. Possible answers:

  a. The mean NDH fastest reaction time is about 0.25 second more than (or about $1\frac{1}{3}$ times) the mean DH fastest reaction time.

  b. The median NDH slowest reaction time is about half a second more than (or about $1\frac{2}{5}$ times) the median DH slowest reaction time.

  c. The difference between minimum values (non-dominant vs. dominant) is 0.1 sec. Meanwhile the difference between maximum values is 0.42 second. The reason the minimums are so close may be that there's a limit to how fast a person can be, no matter which hand is being used.

  d. The range for NDH fastest reaction time is about 0.30 second more than (or about $1\frac{1}{2}$ times) the range for DH fastest reaction time.

8. Answers will vary. The range is about the same for both distributions; the data are more spread out for the NDH distribution. For the DH, the data cluster from 0.6 to 1.5 seconds with a possible outlier at about 2.1 seconds. For the NDH, the data do not appear to cluster.

Connections

9. D (The mean would increase by 1, the median would increase by 5, the mode stays the same.)

10. H. 27: ($25 \times 6 = 150; 150 - 15 = 135;$ $135 \div 5 = 27$)

11. The mean and median are the same value of 62 inches; the data appear to peak in the middle of the distribution, around 62 inches.

12. The mean and median are different. About $\frac{2}{3}$ of the data falls between 21 and 24 g with another group of data more spread out between 25 and about 37 g.

13. The mean and median are almost the same but more than 90% of the data are in a wide interval of 80 minutes to about 150 minutes with no obvious peak. There are some possible outliers occurring that are greater than 160 minutes. The distribution is skewed right.

14. B

15. J (Five out of 50 is 1 out of 10 is equivalent to 10 out of 100.)

16. C (volleyball is 10 out of 50 or 20%; 20% of $360° = 72°$.)

17. a. Water use seems to peak in the summer months and again in the fall months. However, in 2005, the summer months showed a marked decrease in water use.

  b. See below.

Water Used Per Month, 2002 (gallons)

⊥ Median   △ Mean

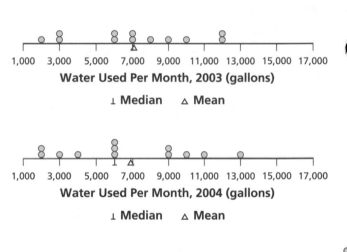

Water Used Per Month, 2003 (gallons)

⊥ Median   △ Mean

Water Used Per Month, 2004 (gallons)

⊥ Median   △ Mean

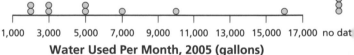

Water Used Per Month, 2005 (gallons)

  c. See means on plots above. The means are about 7,000 gallons per month in each.

d. See medians on plots in part (b). The median varies in the years, from 5,000 to 7,000 gallons. We shouldn't use the 2005 data to estimate the mean or median because there is no data for three months of 2005.

e. The median is 6,000 gallons. The mean is a bit higher at 6,600 gallons. The median is less than the mean because of the possible outliers above 15,000 gallons. (Figure 7)

f. In this case, both measures are similar—around 6,000 gallons. If there were a lot of unusual values, then the median might be a better measure.

18–22. Answers will vary. Possible answers:

18. Statement 1 Process: Scientists collected data in the field by measuring lots of garter snakes. Statement 2 Process: Some type of survey could have been conducted.

19. Statement 1: Both numerical and categorical data
Statement 2: Numerical data

20. Statement A: The spread of the length is from 18 to 42 inches or about 1.5 ft to 3.5 ft. If the typical snake is about 3 ft long, that suggests that there may be a cluster at the upper end of the range.
Statement B: There have to be people who eat little or no pizza and then people who eat a lot more than 46 slices of pizza.

21. Statement 1: We see patterns in terms of size (length and girth) and in terms of color.
Statement 2: Usually when the term *average* is used, it is the mean. As noted in Exercise 20, there may be a lot of possible outliers at either end of the distribution.

22. See Exercise 21.

23. J

24. Answers will vary. Possible answer: Boys' Hoops Leads Schools' Offerings.

Figure 7

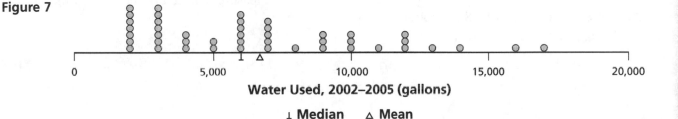

Water Used, 2002–2005 (gallons)

⊥ **Median**   △ **Mean**

Extensions

25. a. The data vary from 0.7 second to 1.35 seconds. About half of the medians are below 1 second.

   b. The median reaction times are a little slower than the fastest reaction times. The spread for the fastest reaction times is about 0.6 to 1.2 seconds; the median reaction times seem to shift right by one tenth of a second. The data for the fastest reaction times have a bit of a skew shape with the faster times below 0.9, while the data for the median times are more uniform.

26. True; adults ages 60 or older eat at restaurants 8% of the time. For children ages 2–18, it is 4%.

27. False; adults ages 60 or older eat less than $\frac{1}{4}$ of their daily food at locations away from home. Children ages 2–18 eat more than $\frac{1}{4}$ (actually about $\frac{1}{3}$) of their daily food away from home.

28. False; adults age 60 and older eat no food at school, whereas children ages 2–18 eat 9% of their daily food at school.

29. False; children ages 2–18 eat about $\frac{2}{3}$ (67%) of their daily food at home.

Possible Answers to Mathematical Reflections

1. If the axes of the scales are the same then it is much easier to make comparisons. You can visually compare the max, min, range, clusters and center when the axes have the same scale.

2. A value bar graph shows the individual data values as bars. A line plot shows the frequency of these data values.

3. Answers will vary. In comparing two or more students' reaction times, we can talk about what part of the 5 trials is below 1.0 second. The part can be represented using fractions, percents, or ratios.

4. a. A more consistent set of reaction times will have data values that are close to each other.

   b. Quickness refers to response speed.

   c. Often consistency and quickness are used in performance sports. Consistency is important because we want to be able to predict some level of performance. Not all performance tasks involve quickness but for those that do, quickness is often the measure that determines who wins.

Mathematical and Problem-Solving Goals

- Read and understand bar graphs used to display data distributions

- Understand and use counts or percents to report frequencies of occurrence of data

- Recognize that variability occurs whenever data are collected

- Use properties of distributions to describe the variability in a given data set

- Decide if a difference among data values and/or summary measures matters

- Develop and use strategies for comparing unequal-size data sets to solve problems

- Use line plots to display data distributions

- Use shape of a distribution to estimate locations of the mean and median

Summary of Problems

 Problem 4.1 **Representing Survey Data**

This problem uses the context of an ongoing, online, interactive survey of responses to questions about roller coaster rides. Students are provided survey response data from two different groups and asked to add their data to make a third group. Students find a way to represent these data in order to decide if the three groups responded in similar ways to the survey.

Problem 4.2 **Are Steel Coasters Faster Than Wood Coasters?**

This problem uses a database of 150 roller coasters (50 wood coasters and 100 steel roller coasters) to engage students in using a variety of strategies to make comparisons between speeds of wood and steel roller coasters. Students also explore relationships among variables as they consider what attributes may influence speed of a coaster.

Technology Option for Investigation 4: *TinkerPlots* Software

This Investigation has been written so that students can explore the central mathematics ideas without computer software support. However, if you have access to *TinkerPlots* software and to computers, the exploration can be greatly enhanced. The following paragraph is to help you think about your options.

If you have access to *TinkerPlots* and sufficient computers, 2 or 3 students working together on a computer is ideal. This allows all students to work on the problems at the same time. Other options are also workable but require planning. If computers are limited, it may be that students have staggered time on computers prior to discussing a problem. Another option—least desirable—is that all the computer explorations are done as demonstrations.

Ideally, you would have ways to project the software when summarizing. As students describe strategies and/or discuss findings, the actual screen they created can be re-created. Another option is for students to print out their displays and then make transparencies of the displays that you want to have the class consider prior to summarizing the problem.

Using TinkerPlots™ With CMP Problems: Students' Guide is provided as an appendix in the Teacher's Guide for students to use as they learn how to use *TinkerPlots*. There are four sections, the first is an introduction and then each section that follows is designed to accompany one of the investigations in *Data Distributions*.

	Suggested Pacing	Materials for Students	Materials for Teachers	ACE Assignments
All	$3\frac{1}{2}$ days	Calculators, student notebooks	Blank transparencies and transparency markers (optional)	
4.1	1 day		Transparencies 4.1A–4.1C, 4ACE Exercise 14	1, 8–16
4.2	2 days	If not using software: Labsheets 4.2A–4.2P (optional) 4ACE Exercise 17 If using software: Computers with *TinkerPlots™* software; *Using TinkerPlots™ With CMP Problems: Students' Guide*; Labsheet A.1 (optional)	All: Transparencies 4.2A–4.2D (optional) If using software: *Using TinkerPlots™ With CMP Problems: Teacher's Guide*	2–7, 17
MR	$\frac{1}{2}$ day			

4.1 Representing Survey Data

Goals

- Read and understand bar graphs used to display data distributions

- Understand and use counts or percents to report frequencies of occurrence of data

- Recognize that variability occurs whenever data are collected

- Use properties of distributions to describe the variability in a given data set

- Decide if a difference among data values and/or summary measures matters

- Develop and use strategies for comparing unequal-size data sets to solve problems

Launch 4.1

Introduce the survey to students; collect and tally the total responses from the class to each question. Add class data in column "Votes from your class(es)" on Transparency 4.1A. Pose this situation to students (This is Question A of the problem):

- *You are able to go to a Web site, respond to a survey, and then see a set of graphs dynamically updated to show the latest results of the survey once you have responded.*

Suggested Questions Ask:

- *What kind of graph would be the easiest to use?* (Answers will vary; bar graphs would be a reasonable choice.)

- *How would you set up the graphs?* (Answers will vary; it is important that the students consider the fact that there are different numbers of data in each group. Students encountered this situation in Problem 1.1 with the M&M candies. Students need to decide whether to use counts or percents to record frequencies. Percents (as proportions) make it possible to compare different-size groups.)

- *We have results of the survey from three different groups. What might we do to compare these results to see if each group responded to the survey in a similar way?* (Answers will vary; make graphs of each group's data so we can compare these data.)

Explore 4.1

Teachers have completed this activity in two ways: One way is to use Transparencies 4.1B and 4.1C and work through the making of the graphs as a class. This means that the activity takes a short amount of time. It also takes away the opportunity for students to decide, one more time, if percents or counts are the better way to represent this data.

Another way is to organize students in teams of two or three. Students may prepare their solutions on chart paper so that they can both present and then post their solutions. The class then discusses the variety of solutions. As you visit groups, focus on using the same frequency scales for different graphs and on displaying frequencies using percents vs. counts.

Summarize 4.1

With the students, look at the three different bar graphs for the first question of the survey. Specifically, consider why using percent frequencies vs. count frequencies is needed in order to make the data sets appear as if they are each the same size. (Each data set is redefined as "out of 100;" it is as if each survey had been given to exactly 100 people in that survey group: 100 responses from the survey respondents, 100 responses from seventh graders; 100 responses from students at your school.)

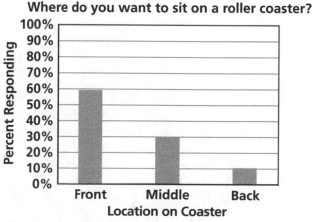

Survey Respondents
(165 original people)(100 people—100%)
Where do you want to sit on a roller coaster?

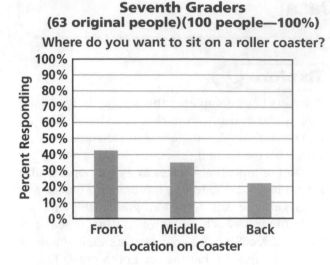

Seventh Graders
(63 original people)(100 people—100%)
Where do you want to sit on a roller coaster?

You can have a similar conversation about the second survey question.

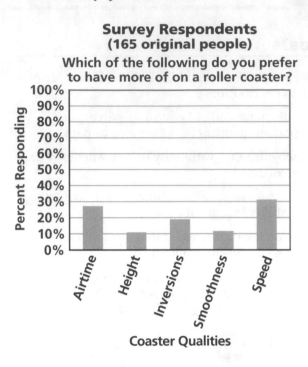

Survey Respondents
(165 original people)
Which of the following do you prefer to have more of on a roller coaster?

Suggested Questions Ask students:

- *What percent of the survey respondents like to ride up front in a roller coaster? How does this percent compare with that of the seventh graders?* (60% of survey respondents; it is 20% more than the seventh graders.)

- *How do the other seat locations compare for the two groups?* (About 30% of the survey respondents vs. 35% of the seventh graders like to sit in the middle location; about 10% of the survey respondents, vs. about 22% of the seventh graders, like the back of the roller coaster ride.)

- *How does the data from our class compare to these two distributions?* (Answers will vary.)

- *What can we say about people's preferences on location to sit in a roller coaster?* (For these two data situations, "up front" is the preference.)

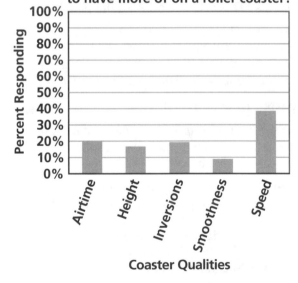

Seventh Graders
(63 original people)
Which of the following do you prefer to have more of on a roller coaster?

Labsheet 4ACE Exercise 14 is provided if

4.1 Representing Survey Data

Mathematical Goals

- Read and understand bar graphs used to display data distributions
- Understand and use counts or percents to report frequencies of occurrence of data
- Recognize that variability occurs whenever data are collected
- Use properties of distributions to describe the variability in a given data set
- Decide if a difference among data values and/or summary measures matters
- Develop and use strategies for comparing unequal-size data sets to solve problems

Launch

Introduce the survey to students; collect and tally the total responses from the class to each question. Add class data in column "Votes from your class(es)" on Transparency Problem 4.1 Survey. Pose this situation to students:

> You are able to go to a Web site, respond to a survey, and then see a set of graphs dynamically updated to show the latest results of the survey once you have responded.

- *What kinds of graphs would be the easiest to use?*
- *How would you set them up?*

Materials
- Transparency 4.1A

Explore

Have student groups each present their proposals. As a class, discuss the advantages and disadvantages of each proposal.

Materials
- Calculators
- Transparencies 4.1B, 4.1C

Summarize

Talk about students' findings and their reasoning. Ask students:

- *What percent of the survey respondents like to ride up front in a roller coaster? How does this percent compare with that of the seventh graders?*
- *How do the other preferences for seat locations compare for the two groups? How does our class data about preferences compare?*
- *What can we say about people's preferences on location to sit in a roller coaster?*

You can have a similar conversation about the second survey question.

Materials
- Student notebooks

ACE Assignment Guide
for Problem 4.1

Differentiated
Instruction
Solutions for All Learners

Core ACE 1, 8–11

Other ACE *Connections* 12–16; unassigned choices
from previous problems

Adapted For suggestions about adapting ACE
exercises, see the CMP *Special Needs Handbook*.

Connecting to Prior Units 8–12: *Data About Us*;
12: *Bits and Pieces I*

Labsheet 4ACE Exercise 14 is provided if
Exercise 14 is assigned.

Answers to Problem 4.1

A. Answers will vary as collecting class data.

B. See summary and below.

Bar graphs showing percent frequencies of
categories of responses are probably the
better way to represent these data. Using
percent frequencies treats each category of
responses as a part–whole situation expressed
as a percent. Using counts for frequencies
makes comparisons difficult.

C. These comparison statements concern the
survey respondents and the original set of
seventh graders as we do not have data from
your class to view here. Possible statements
include:

- For question 1, both groups had "front" as
  their first choice and "back" as their last
  choice.

- The survey respondents had a stronger
  preference for the front (about 60%) than
  did the seventh graders (about 40%).

- For question 2, both groups indicated a
  preference for "airtime" and "speed" when
  riding a roller coaster.

- Again, the survey respondents had stronger
  preferences for each of these choices when
  compared to the seventh graders.

- We might think that the survey respondents
  are avid coaster riders; they can choose to
  respond, and it's likely that responses to a
  Web survey would attract those who like to
  ride coasters.

4.2 Are Steel Coasters Faster Than Wood Coasters?

Goals

- Use line plots to display data distributions

- Recognize that variability occurs whenever data are collected

- Use properties of distributions to describe the variability in a given data set

- Decide if a difference among data values and/or summary measures matters

- Use shape of a distribution to estimate locations of the mean and median

- Develop and use strategies for unequal-size data sets to solve problems

   This problem uses a database of 150 roller coasters (50 wood coasters and 100 steel roller coasters) to engage students in using a variety of strategies to make comparisons between speeds of wood and steel roller coasters. Students also explore relationships among variables as they consider what attributes may influence speed of a coaster.

Technology Option For an optional approach using *TinkerPlots*™ software, see the Teacher's Guide Appendix for Problem 4.2, beginning on page 181. Blackline masters of student pages for use with this investigation begin on page A27.

Launch 4.2

Continue discussing roller coasters. Have students examine the data shown in Transparency 4.2A. Have a discussion on how to read this table and what information can be obtained from the table.

Suggested Questions Ask:

- *Is there any information in this table that surprises you? Why or why not?* (Answers will vary.)

Brainstorm with the class about what kinds of information they might collect about roller coasters.

- *What kinds of information might we collect about roller coasters?* (how fast a coaster can travel, park and state location, number of people who can ride it, tallest height, and so on)

- *How might you go about collecting this information about several coasters?* (From theme parks or amusement parks where coasters are located; from Web sites on the Internet)

Once students have done this, select some roller coasters with which your students may be familiar. Display the data about these roller coasters, or use Transparencies 4.2B and 4.2C.

- *Let's look at some examples of both steel and wood roller coasters. These are a few of the coasters that are found in a database of 150 coasters. We will examine some of the attributes of roller coasters.*

Each example is one case of a roller coaster. A case is the named data item and its related data for each of the attributes of interest. There are two cases of wood coasters and two cases of steel coasters.

As you display each case, discuss the data that are listed, highlighting the attributes used. Also make comparisons between attributes for wood coasters and for steel coasters (e.g., speeds, heights). Take time to help students link their knowledge of other contexts to understand data about the coasters. For example, what does driving in a car at 35 mi/h or 55 mi/h or 65 mi/h feel like? Which is faster? Can you describe what "faster" means in this context? Or, ask students to estimate the height of the classroom and then ask how many classrooms stacked on top of each other would you need to reach the height of a given roller coaster. It is important to connect the students with the data by relating to experiences that make sense to them.

   Next show Transparency 4.2D. This transparency introduces one format for how these data might appear in a computer database. The case cards are taken from the software program, *TinkerPlots*. They match two of the four coasters in Transparencies 4.2B and 4.2C. These case cards highlight the attributes that will be considered in this problem.

   This preliminary work has been designed to help students get familiar with the data set they will be using. They are now ready to move into the explore phase.

Hand out to teams of 2 or 3 students who will work together: copy of the Roller Coaster Database and copies of graphs that they can use to complete each part of the problem. It is recommended that you give the students the Roller Coaster Database first. When they are ready, they can request the graphs as needed for each of Questions B, C, and D. Part of their work on this problem will be to become familiar with each of the provided representations so they can use these tools to solve the problem.

Have students work in teams of 2 or 3 students to complete Questions A–C. You will probably want to stop and do a summary for this part of the problem and then have students work later on Question D. If students finish early, they can begin work on Question D.

Explore 4.2

Question A of the problem helps students get familiar with the Roller Coaster Database. It is meant to be exploratory in nature; the written paragraph helps students summarize what they found out.

Question B helps students focus specifically on the attribute of Top Speed. Teachers have found that it is important for students to think about what might be considered a fast speed for a roller coaster before analyzing these data. We suggest that students do this with their partners in order NOT to create a whole class definition of what is fast initially. That is why the prompt is part of the problem. Students don't necessarily have a good notion of speed. This question provides some opportunities for them to wrestle with this idea.

The second part of the question helps them think about whether they use speed as a criterion when choosing a roller coaster. Again, it is designed to get the students more familiar with the data set being explored.

Students will need time to explore the data in Question C. You can offer suggestions about actions to take. For example, students have speeds displayed in two different graphs, one for wood coasters and one for steel coasters (see example on the next page). This graph uses a scale of 10 for the x-axis. Graphs with scales of 5 could also be used.

Students can identify where the mean and median are located in each distribution. Interestingly, the measures of center for these data are similar, and there is not much difference between the means and medians of each distribution. This is an opportunity for students to consider that a mean of 53.18 mi/h for wood coasters and a mean of 53.08 mi/h for steel coasters may be different numerical data values, but the differences are not important in this context. Similarly, for the medians of 50 mi/h and 55 mi/h, the difference numerically is 5 mi/h. In terms of experiences of speed, this difference is not enough to use to claim that wood coasters are faster than steel coasters. (Figure 1 and Figure 2, next page)

Students will find it useful to partition or divide the distributions in order to compare parts of distributions. They can do this using benchmark speeds.

One way to partition the data is to identify benchmark speeds and then separate the data based on these benchmarks. For example, below, a *reference line* has been drawn at 50 mi/h; students can look at both the number and the percent of

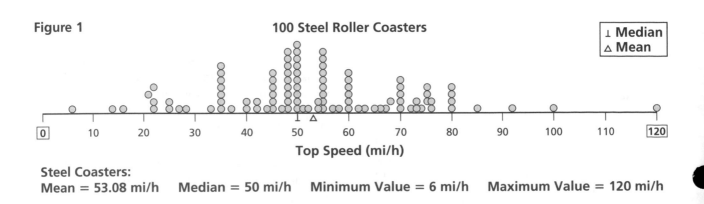

Figure 1

100 Steel Roller Coasters

⊥ Median
△ Mean

Top Speed (mi/h)

Steel Coasters:
Mean = 53.08 mi/h   Median = 50 mi/h   Minimum Value = 6 mi/h   Maximum Value = 120 mi/h

coasters of each kind that have speeds ≥ 50 mi/h. You will want to discuss with students why the decision to use percents is necessary: the two data sets are not the same size so in order to look at them as though they were the same size, it is necessary to express each as a percentage. In this case, there is a tension created because the percent of wood coasters with speeds at or above 50 mi/h is greater than the percent of steel coasters at or above 50 mi/h. (Figure 2)

Students can experiment with using different speeds to partition the distribution and then determine the percent below or at and above the benchmark speed. What students will find is that there is a benchmark speed at and above which steel coasters are faster than wood coasters. The interesting aspect of this analysis is that, for many benchmark speeds, the percent of coasters at and above these speeds of each kind are similar. (Figures 3 and 4)

Figure 2

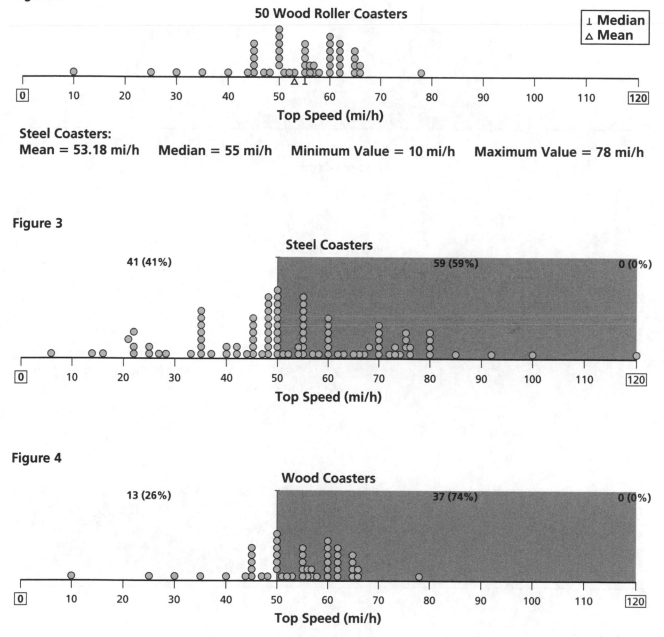

Steel Coasters:
Mean = 53.18 mi/h   Median = 55 mi/h   Minimum Value = 10 mi/h   Maximum Value = 78 mi/h

Figure 3

Figure 4

As another example, below the data have been partitioned into three sections; students can make some comments about percent of coasters of each kind with speeds in the interval of 30 mi/h ≤ speed ≤ 60 mi/h and having speeds > 60 mi/h or < 30 mi/h. (Figures 5 and 6)

In Question D, students explore the relationships between other attributes and speed. For example, a team might decide that maximum drop of a roller coaster has something to do with speed. See the

Summarize section for possible graphs and related discussions.

Summarize 4.2

Suggested Question Have students discuss their answers to the question:

* *Are wood coasters faster than steel roller coasters?*

Figure 5

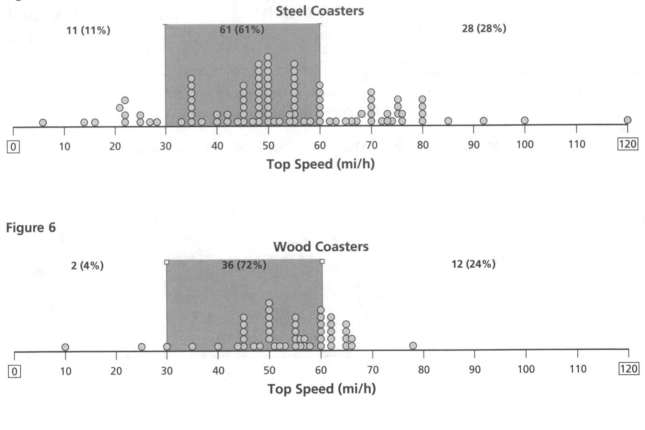

Figure 6

Figure 7

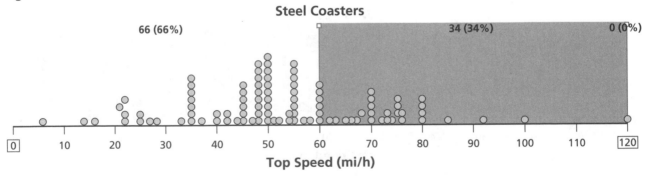

It is not possible to give a simple yes or no answer to this question. In examining the data, if coasters with speeds ≥ 60 mi/h are considered, we see that there is about the same percent of wood coasters and steel coasters in this category. (Figure 7, previous page, and Figure 8)

However, if the benchmark is changed to 65 mi/h, then we see that there are more steel coasters with speeds ≥ 65 mi/h than wood coasters; i.e., steel coasters are faster than wood coasters here. (Figures 9 and 10)

Figure 8

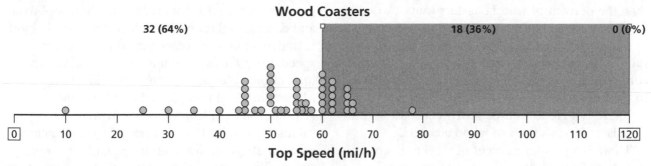

Figure 9

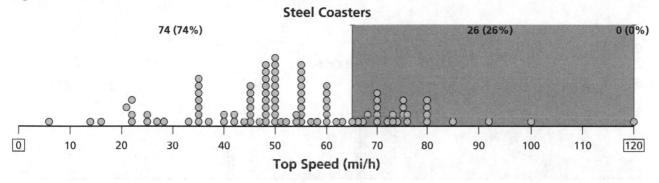

Figure 10

Similarly, if we look at the numbers of coasters with speeds ≤ 30 mi/h, there is a greater percent of steel coasters than wood coasters. (Figures 11 and 12)

Students struggle with visually seeing that actual counts (the actual count of steel coasters is more than the actual count of wood coasters in a section) that are translated to percents (the percent of steel coasters [out of 100 total] may be less than the percent of wood coasters [out of wood total] in a section). They are comparing data sets that have different numbers of data values; using relative frequencies is necessary in order to make comparisons. Here's what might be said in answer to the question:

There is a greater percent of steel coasters with speeds ≥ 65 mi/h than of wood coasters.

There is a greater percent of steel coasters with speeds ≤ 30 mi/h than wood coasters.

About 60% of the steel coasters and 70% of the wood coasters have speeds that are 30 ≤ speed ≤ 60 mi/h.

In discussing the relationships with other attributes and speed, both *maximum height* and *maximum drop* seem to be related to speed. *Track length* seems a little less related. *Duration* of ride and *Year Opened* both appear not to be related strongly. See the graphs that follow.

Each graph is considered to be a modified scatter plot, that is, the data for the y-axis attribute are partially separated but not fully separated. This permits students to visually look at chunks of data and consider relationships. It is particularly helpful if students put a reference line at a particular speed, say 50 mi/h or 60 mi/h or 65 mi/h, and then look at the slices of data on either side. In the Maximum Height and Speed graph, when a reference line is placed at 65 mi/h, there is a "stair-step effect" that is noticeable; this indicates some relationship between speed and maximum height. The same is noticeable with maximum drop and speed. This is less obvious when considering the other attributes and their relationships with speed. (Figures 13–18, next three pages)

Figure 11

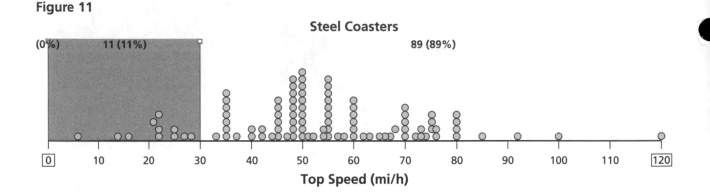

Figure 12

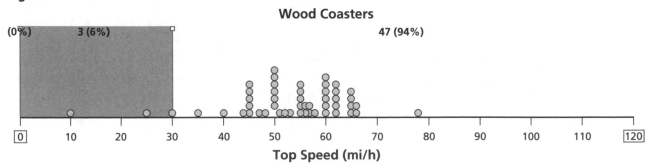

Figure 13

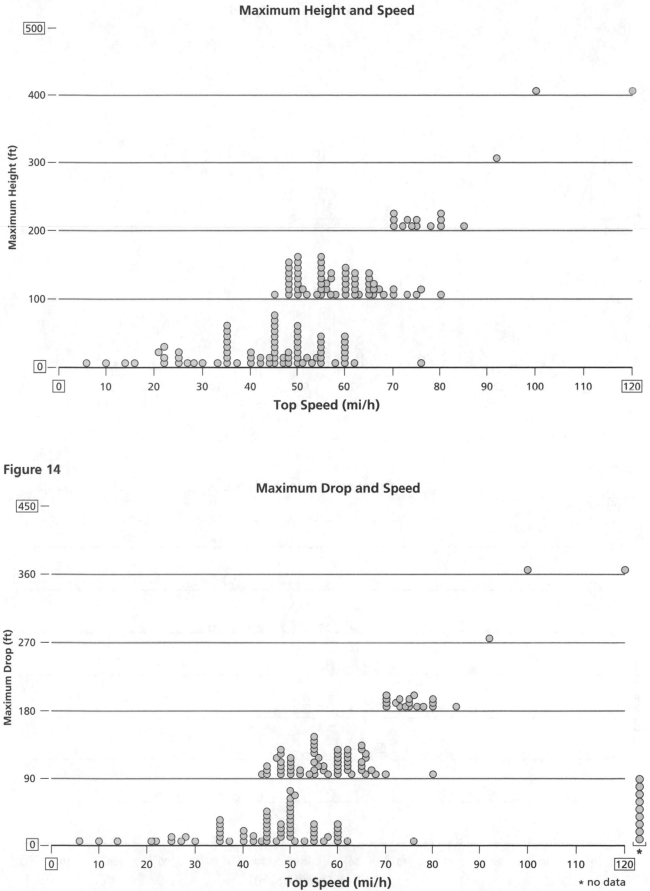

Figure 15

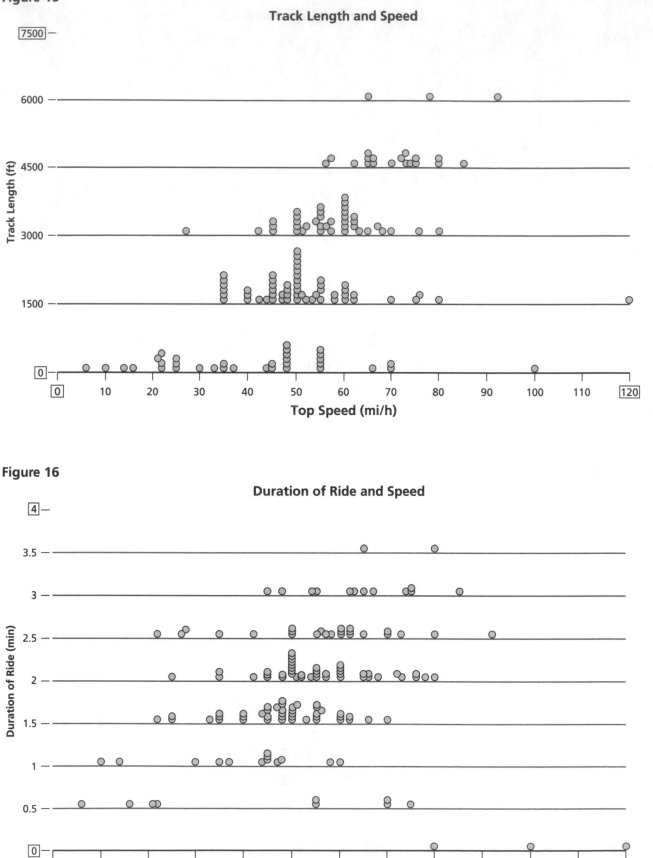

Track Length and Speed

Duration of Ride and Speed

Figure 16

Figure 17

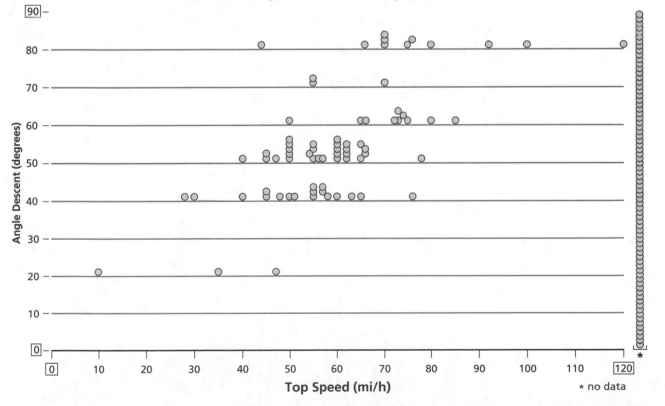

Year Opened and Speed

Figure 18

Angle of Descent and Speed

* no data

4.2 Are Steel Roller Coasters Faster than Wooden Coasters?

At a Glance

PACING 2 days

Mathematical Goals

- Use line plots to display data distributions
- Recognize that variability occurs whenever data are collected
- Use properties of distributions to describe the variability in a given data set
- Decide if a difference among data values and/or summary measures matters
- Use the shape of a distribution to estimate locations of the mean and median
- Develop and use strategies for unequal-size data sets to solve problems

Launch

Continue discussing roller coasters. Have students examine the data shown in Transparency 4.2A. Have a discussion on how to read this table and what information can be obtained from the table.

- *Is there any information in this table that surprises you? Why or why not?*

Brainstorm the kinds of information students might collect about roller coasters. Select some coasters with which your students may be familiar. Display the data about these coasters, or use Transparencies 4.2B and 4.2C.

Each example is *one case* of a roller coaster. There are two cases each of wooden coasters and steel coasters. Discuss the data that are listed. Compare attributes for wood coasters and for steel coasters (e.g., speeds, heights). Help students link their knowledge of other contexts to the coasters. For example, what does driving in a car at 35 mi/h or 55 mi/h or 65 mi/h feel like? Can you tell the difference? Or, ask students to estimate the height of the classroom, and then ask how many classrooms stacked on top of each other would reach the height of a given roller coaster. It is important to connect the students with the data by relating to experiences that make sense to them. Pose Question A for discussion. It will help students think about why roller coaster speed is or is not attractive for them. Some students many not have ridden roller coasters or don't like to ride them. Let these students participate in this discussion in ways that make sense to them; they may relate to speeds of cars on highways when you talk about speeds of coasters.

- *You have to choose between which of two roller coasters to ride. Would knowing top speed for two coasters help you make a decision about which coaster to ride? Explain why or why not.*

Finally, use Transparency 4.2D to show what the data look like when entered in on data cards. There is an example of one steel coaster and one wood coaster. Ask the students:

- *If we wanted to compare the speeds of wooden roller coasters with steel roller coasters, how can we make this comparison?*

For an optional approach using data analysis software, see the Teacher's Guide Appendix for Problem 4.2, beginning on page 181, and the blackline masters of student pages beginning on page A27.

Materials
- Transparencies 4.2A–4.2D
- Calculators

Students will need time to explore the data in Questions B and C. You can offer suggestions about actions to take. In Question D, students explore the relationships between other attributes and speed. See the extended Explore section for examples.

Materials

If not using software:
- Labsheets 4.2A–4.2P (optional)

If using software:
- Computers with *TinkerPlots™* software
- *Using TinkerPlots™ With CMP Problems: Students' Guide*
- *Using TinkerPlots™ With CMP Problems: Teacher's Guide*
- Labsheet A.1 (optional)

Summarize

Have students discuss their answers to the question:

- *Are wooden coasters faster than steel roller coasters?*

It is not possible to answer yes or no to this question. Students struggle with looking at counts vs. percentages. They are comparing data sets that have different numbers of data values; using relative frequencies is necessary. However, students can still see the actual counts even when percents are reported. Here is a sample answer to the question:

There is a greater percent of steel coasters with speeds of at least 65 mi/h. There is a greater percent of steel coasters with speeds less than 30 mi/h. About 60% of the steel coasters and 70% of the wood coasters have speeds that are 30 mi/h ≤ speed ≤ 60 mi/h.

Maximum Height and Maximum Drop seem to be related to speed. Track Length seems less related. Duration of Ride and Year Opened seem to not be related. See the extended Summarize section for fully separated plots.

Materials
- Student notebooks

ACE Assignment Guide for Problem 4.2

Core ACE 2–7
Other ACE *Extensions* 17; unassigned choices from previous problems

Labsheet 4ACE Exercise 17 is provided if Exercise 17 is assigned.

Adapted For suggestions about adapting Exercise 2 and other ACE exercises, see the CMP *Special Needs Handbook*.

Answers to Problem 4.2

A. Answers will vary.

B. 1. Answers will vary.

    2. Possible answer: If you enjoy a fast roller coaster ride, then knowing the top speed may help you make a decision.

C. 1. Possible answer: Steel roller coasters are faster because steel may provide more stability in the structure and, therefore, engineers may design them to go at faster speeds.

    2, 3. See the extended Explore and Summarize sections.

D. 1. Answers are provided as part of the discussions in the extended Explore and Summarize sections. Yes, there appears to be a relationship between *speed* and *maximum drop*—as *speed* increases so does the *maximum drop*.

    2. Both *maximum height* and *maximum drop* seem to be related to speed. *Track length* seems a little less related. *Duration of Ride* and *Year Opened* both appear to not be related strongly. See partially separated plots in the extended Summarize section.

The student edition pages for this investigation begin on the next page.

Notes _____
_____
_____
_____

Investigation 4

Comparing Distributions: Unequal Numbers of Data Values

Many people love to ride roller coasters. There are different types of roller coasters, and people have preferences about the roller coasters they ride. In this investigation, you will look at data about roller coasters, and compare wood roller coasters with steel roller coasters.

4.1 Representing Survey Data

These two questions were asked in a survey.

1. Where do you like to sit on a roller coaster (choose one)?

___ Front ___ Middle ___ Back

2. Which of the following do you prefer to have on a roller coaster (may choose more than one)?

___ Airtime ___ Height ___ Inversions ___ Smooth Ride ___ Speed

74 Data Distributions

STUDENT PAGE

Notes _____

_____

_____

_____

STUDENT PAGE

The table below summarizes results from the survey and from three classes of seventh-grade students.

Roller Coaster Seating Preferences

Preference	Votes From Survey	Votes From Three Seventh-Grade Classes
Front	97	27
Middle	50	22
Back	18	14
Total Votes	165	63

Preferences for Roller Coaster Characteristics

Preference	Votes From Survey	Votes From Three Seventh-Grade Classes
Airtime	88	31
Height	36	24
Inversions	59	29
Smoothness	39	12
Speed	105	57
Total Votes	327	153

Problem 4.1 Representing Survey Data

A. Copy the tables above. Have the members of your class answer the two roller coaster questions. Add a column to each table for your class data.

B. Make bar graphs for each of the three data sets: the survey data, the data from the three classes, and the data from your class. Your bar graphs should allow you to compare the results from the three groups. You may use counts or percents to report frequencies.

C. Write three or more statements that make comparisons among the sets of data.

ACE Homework starts on page 78.

Notes _____

_____

_____

_____

Roller-coaster enthusiasts have preferences about the coasters they like to ride. There are Web sites devoted to wood roller coasters. Other people prefer to ride steel coasters.

Have you ever wondered how many roller coasters there are in the world? The table below shows roller coaster counts.

Roller Coaster Census (2005)

Continent	Total	Wood	Steel	Some of the Types of Steel Coasters			
				Inverted	Stand Up	Suspended	Sit Down
Africa	23	0	23	3	0	0	20
Asia	489	8	481	17	5	8	441
Australia	23	3	20	2	0	0	18
Europe	581	34	547	24	1	7	506
North America	748	131	617	50	11	10	531
South America	65	1	64	2	0	0	62
Total	**1,929**	**177**	**1,752**	**98**	**17**	**25**	**1,578**

SOURCE: Roller Coaster DataBase. Go to www.PHSchool.com for a data update. Web Code: ang-9041

How do you think these data were collected?

In Problem 4.2, you will use a roller coaster database that contains data on 50 wood coasters and 100 steel coasters.

Problem 4.2 Comparing Speed

Use the Roller Coaster Database to help you answer these questions.

A. Choose an attribute about roller coasters that interests you, such as Year Opened, Maximum Drop, or Top Speed. Explore this attribute in the database. Write a short paragraph about what you find.

B. 1. What do you consider to be a fast speed for a roller coaster? Discuss your idea with a partner.

   2. Suppose you have to choose which of two roller coasters to ride. Does knowing the top speed for each coaster help you make the decision? Explain.

Notes

_____

_____

_____

_____

C. 1. Are wood roller coasters faster than steel roller coasters? Scan the *top speed* data to predict an answer to the question. Explain your reasoning.

2. Now, look at the distributions of speeds of wood roller coasters and of steel roller coasters. Use strategies that make sense to you.

   a. Identify and compare minimum and maximum values, ranges, medians, and means for each type of roller coaster.

   b. Draw a reference line on each distribution at a particular speed. Look at the percents of each type of roller coaster at and above or below this speed.

3. Compare your prediction from part (1) with your analysis of the distributions from part (2). How would you now answer the question, "Are wood roller coasters faster than steel roller coasters?" Explain.

D. Why do some roller coasters go faster than other roller coasters? To help answer this question, look at the top speed in relation to other attributes. Do you think there is some relationship between *top speed and maximum drop*? Between *top speed and maximum height*? Between *top speed and year opened, duration, track length, or angle of descent*? Explore these questions. Be prepared to share your reasoning.

active math
online
For: Stat Tools
Visit: PHSchool.com
Web Code: and–8402

ACE Homework starts on page 78.

STUDENT PAGE

Notes _____

_____

_____

_____

Applications

1. This question was asked in a survey:

What is your favorite kind of amusement-park ride?

___ Roller Coaster ___ Log Ride ___ Ferris Wheel ___ Other

The table below summarizes results from this survey and from a survey of seventh-grade students at East Junior High and West Junior High.

Homework Help Online
PHSchool.com
For: Help with Exercise 1
Web Code: ane-8401

Favorite Amusement Park Rides

Favorite Ride	Votes From Survey	Votes From East Junior High	Votes From West Junior High
Roller Coaster	84	45	36
Log Ride	36	31	14
Ferris Wheel	17	3	6
Other	18	1	4
Total Votes	**155**	**80**	**60**

a. Make bar graphs for each of the three data sets: the survey data, the data from East Junior High, and the data from West Junior High. Your bar graphs should allow you to compare the results from the three groups. Use percents to report frequencies.

b. Write three or more statements that make comparisons among the sets of data.

Notes _____

_____

_____

_____

2. The three pairs of line plots below display data about 50 wood roller coasters. Means and medians are marked on each graph.

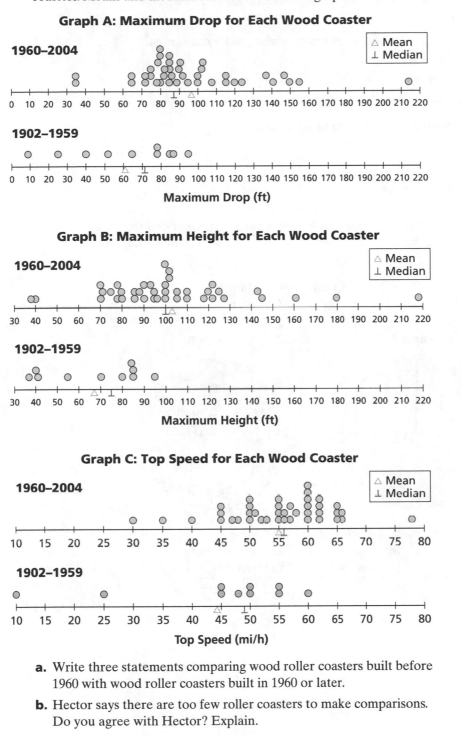

Graph A: Maximum Drop for Each Wood Coaster

1960–2004

△ Mean
⊥ Median

0 10 20 30 40 50 60 70 80 90 100 110 120 130 140 150 160 170 180 190 200 210 220

1902–1959

0 10 20 30 40 50 60 70 80 90 100 110 120 130 140 150 160 170 180 190 200 210 220

Maximum Drop (ft)

Graph B: Maximum Height for Each Wood Coaster

1960–2004

△ Mean
⊥ Median

30 40 50 60 70 80 90 100 110 120 130 140 150 160 170 180 190 200 210 220

1902–1959

30 40 50 60 70 80 90 100 110 120 130 140 150 160 170 180 190 200 210 220

Maximum Height (ft)

Graph C: Top Speed for Each Wood Coaster

1960–2004

△ Mean
⊥ Median

10   15   20   25   30   35   40   45   50   55   60   65   70   75   80

1902–1959

10   15   20   25   30   35   40   45   50   55   60   65   70   75   80

Top Speed (mi/h)

a. Write three statements comparing wood roller coasters built before 1960 with wood roller coasters built in 1960 or later.

b. Hector says there are too few roller coasters to make comparisons. Do you agree with Hector? Explain.

Investigation 4 Comparing Distributions: Unequal Numbers of Data Values   **79**

Notes _____

_____

_____

_____

3. For every one wood roller coaster there are about ■ steel roller coasters.

4. North America has about ■ times as many roller coasters as South America.

5. Asia has about ■ as many roller coasters as North America.

6. North America has ■% of all the wood roller coasters in the world.

7. Write two of your own comparison statements.

Connections

8. The titles of the two circle graphs below have been separated from the graphs. Use the data from Exercises 3–7 to determine which title goes with which graph. Explain your reasoning.

Title 1: Wood Roller Coasters by Continent
Title 2: Steel Roller Coasters by Continent

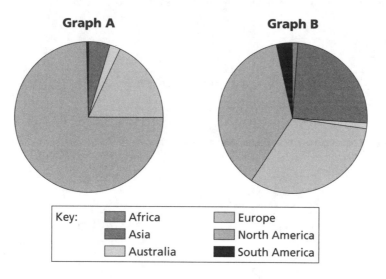

Graph A   **Graph B**

Key: Africa   Europe
      Asia   North America
      Australia   South America

Notes

9. **Multiple Choice** Jasper's test scores for eight exams are shown.

   84   72   88   84   92   94   78 x

   If the median for his scores is 86, what is a possible value for x?

   A. 68   **B.** 84   **C.** 86   **D.** 95

10. **Multiple Choice** In Mr. Ramirez's math class, there are three times as many girls as boys. The girls' mean grade on a quiz is 90 and the boys' mean grade is 86. What is the mean grade for the class altogether?

    F. 88   **G.** 44   **H.** 89   **J.** 95

11. People in the movie business track box-office profits and compare gains and losses each week. The graph below compares box-office income for consecutive weekends in the fall of 2005. Did box-office profits increase or decrease? Explain your reasoning.

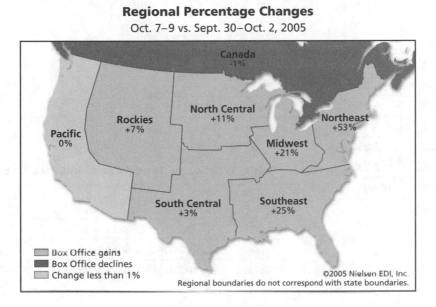

Regional Percentage Changes
Oct. 7–9 vs. Sept. 30–Oct. 2, 2005

Notes _____

12. In a large survey of nearly 15,000 children ages 5 to 15, 80% of the children were from the United States. Use the data below for parts (a)–(f).

Table 1: Years Lived in Current Home

Years	Children	Percent
<1	639	7.9%
1	776	9.6%
2	733	9.0%
3	735	■
4	587	7.3%
5	612	7.5%
6	487	6.0%
7	431	5.3%
8	442	5.5%
9	412	5.1%
10	492	6.0%
11	520	6.5%
12	508	6.3%
13	339	4.1%
14	225	2.8%
15	176	2.2%
Total	**8,114**	**100.0%**

Source: National Geographic

Table 2: Apartments or Houses Lived in Since Birth

Number of Apartments or Houses	Children	Percent
1	1,645	20.7%
2	1,957	24.7%
3	1,331	16.8%
4	968	■
5	661	8.3%
6	487	6.1%
7	291	3.7%
8	184	2.3%
9	80	1.0%
10	330	4.2%
Total	**7,934**	**100.0%**

Source: National Geographic

Table 3: Cities or Towns Lived in Since Birth

Number of Cities or Towns	Boys	Girls	Ages 5–12	Ages 13–15
1	■	42.2%	42.1%	40.9%
>1	58.9%	57.8%	■	59.1%
Total	**100%**	**100%**	**100%**	**100%**

Source: National Geographic

a. Find the missing percents in the tables above. Explain how you determined your answers.

b. Make a bar graph displaying the information in the third column of Table 2.

c. Write a summary paragraph about Table 2.

d. What percent of children have lived in the same home for 10 or more years? Justify your answer.

e. What percent of the children have lived in only one home since they were born? Justify your answer.

f. About what fraction of the boys have lived in the same city or town all their lives? Explain.

The graph below shows the amount of sugar per serving in the 47 cereals. Use the graph for Exercises 13 and 14.

Amount of Sugar per Serving

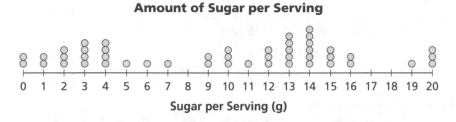

Sugar per Serving (g)

13. Describe the variability in the distribution of the amount of sugar per serving.

14. Estimate the locations of the mean and the median. How does the shape of the distribution influence your estimates?

The next graph shows the serving sizes of the 47 cereals in the graph above.

Serving Sizes of Cereals

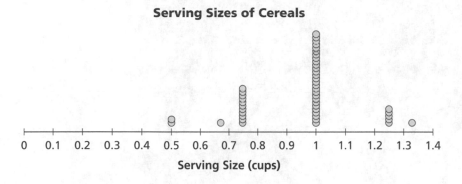

Serving Size (cups)

15. Describe the distribution of serving sizes.

16. Estimate the locations of the mean and the median. How does the shape of the distribution influence your estimates?

Investigation 4 Comparing Distributions: Unequal Numbers of Data Values **83**

Notes _____

_____

_____

_____

Extensions

17. a. Copy the scatter plot below. Locate the point $(443, 6)$ and circle it.

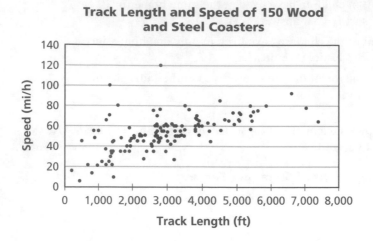

Track Length and Speed of 150 Wood and Steel Coasters

b. Locate the point $(6595, 92)$ and circle it.

c. Draw a line that connects these two points.

d. What is true about the points representing coasters that are on this line? That are above this line? That are below this line?

e. Using these two points, write an equation for the line in the form $y = mx$.

Notes _____

_____

_____

_____

Mathematical Reflections 4

In this investigation, you developed strategies to compare two or more distributions with unequal amounts of data. These questions will help you summarize what you have learned.

Think about your answers to these questions. Discuss your ideas with other students and your teacher. Then write a summary of your findings in your notebook.

1. You can use different strategies to compare two or more data sets. Some strategies are listed below. Describe how each strategy helps you compare data sets. Add other strategies you would use to the list.

   a. Use the range for each distribution.

   b. Use the mean and median for each distribution.

   c. Use benchmarks to help you compare sections of distributions.

2. In Investigations 3 and 4, you compared groups by using counts to report actual frequencies or by using percents to report relative frequencies. How is your choice to use counts or percents affected by whether you are comparing distributions with equal numbers of data values or distributions with unequal numbers of data values? Explain.

Investigation 4 Comparing Distributions: Unequal Numbers of Data Values **85**

Notes _____

_____

_____

_____

Looking Back and Looking Ahead

While working on the problems in this unit, you explored distributions of data, measures of center, and comparing groups. You explored ways to describe and make sense of the variability that is in all data.

You often need to compare two or more groups of data. Sometimes you can compare actual counts. Other times you need to use percents. In this unit, you looked at ways to compare both kinds of distributions.

Go Online
PHSchool.com
For: Vocabulary Review Puzzle
Web Code: anj-8051

Use Your Understanding: Statistical Reasoning

How do frozen pizzas compare with the real thing? The table on the next page displays some information about frozen pizza ratings.

1. Make a graph showing the number of Calories in one slice of each frozen pizza.

   a. What is the typical number of Calories per slice of pizza?

   b. Describe the variability in the number of Calories per slice of frozen pizza.

   c. Now, show separate distributions for cheese pizzas and for pepperoni pizzas. Compare the Calories in a slice of cheese pizza to those in a slice of pepperoni pizza. Do cheese pizzas have more Calories than pepperoni pizzas? Explain.

2. Make a graph showing the cost per slice of each frozen pizza.

   a. What is the typical cost per slice of pizza?

   b. Describe the variability in the cost per slice of frozen pizza.

   c. Now, show separate distributions for cheese pizzas and for pepperoni pizzas. Compare the cost of a slice of cheese pizza to that of a slice of pepperoni pizza. Do pepperoni pizzas cost more than cheese pizzas? Explain.

3. a. Make two scatter plots, one for (*fat grams, Calories*) data and one for (*cost, Calories*) data.

   b. What do you notice about the relationship between fat grams and Calories?

Notes _____

_____

_____

_____

c. What do you notice about the relationship between cost and Calories?

d. Compare the relationships in parts (b) and (c). Which one seems "stronger"? Can you make predictions about the value of one variable if you know the value for another? Explain.

Frozen Pizza Ratings

Product	Overall Rating	Cost per Slice	Calories per Slice	Fat (g)
Cheese Pizza A	VG	$0.98	364	15
Cheese Pizza B	VG	$1.23	334	11
Cheese Pizza C	VG	$0.94	332	12
Cheese Pizza D	VG	$1.92	341	14
Cheese Pizza E	VG	$0.84	307	9
Cheese Pizza F	VG	$0.96	335	12
Cheese Pizza G	VG	$0.80	292	9
Cheese Pizza H	VG	$0.96	364	18
Cheese Pizza J	VG	$0.91	384	20
Cheese Pizza K	VG	$0.89	333	12
Cheese Pizza L	G	$0.94	328	14
Cheese Pizza M	G	$1.02	367	13
Cheese Pizza N	G	$0.92	325	13
Cheese Pizza P	G	$1.17	346	17
Cheese Pizza Q	F	$0.54	299	9
Cheese Pizza R	F	$1.28	394	19
Cheese Pizza S	F	$0.67	322	14
Pepperoni Pizza A	VG	$0.96	385	18
Pepperoni Pizza B	VG	$0.88	369	16
Pepperoni Pizza C	VG	$0.90	400	22
Pepperoni Pizza D	VG	$0.88	378	20
Pepperoni Pizza E	G	$0.89	400	23
Pepperoni Pizza F	G	$0.87	410	26
Pepperoni Pizza G	G	$1.28	412	25
Pepperoni Pizza H	F	$1.26	343	14
Pepperoni Pizza J	F	$1.51	283	6
Pepperoni Pizza K	F	$0.74	372	20
Pepperoni Pizza L	F	$0.64	367	20
Pepperoni Pizza M	F	$1.62	280	4

SOURCE: Consumer Reports

STUDENT PAGE

Notes _____

_____

_____

_____

Explain Your Reasoning

When you describe a collection of data, you look for the shape of the distribution of the data. You can often visualize data patterns using graphs.

4. Explain how you would describe the variability in a distribution of data.

5. Describe how the location of the mean and the median are related to the shape of the distribution.

6. Describe strategies you can use to compare two groups of data that have equal numbers of data values.

7. Describe strategies you can use to compare two groups of data that have unequal numbers of data values.

8. What does it mean to say that the speed of a roller coaster *is related to* the maximum drop, or that the roller coaster rating *is related to* the speed of a roller coaster?

Look Ahead

You will use and extend ideas about data analysis in a variety of future *Connected Mathematics* units. In *Samples and Populations,* you will explore sampling, comparing samples, and comparing different variables in a sample. You will also find statistical plots and data summaries in everyday news reports as well as in the technical work of science, business, and government.

Notes _____

_____

_____

_____

Investigation ④

ACE
Assignment Choices

Differentiated Instruction — Solutions for All Learners

Problem 4.1

Core 1, 8–11
Other *Connections* 12–16; unassigned choices from previous problems

Problem 4.2

Core 2–7
Other *Extensions* 17; unassigned choices from previous problems

Adapted For suggestions about adapting Exercise 2 and other ACE exercises, see the CMP *Special Needs Handbook*.
Connecting to Prior Units 8–12: *Data About Us*; 12: *Bits and Pieces I*

Applications

1. a. Note: Students may draw a triple bar graph or three individual bar graphs.

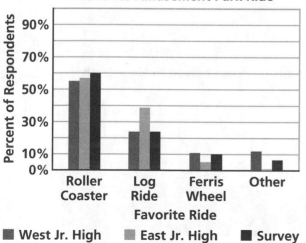

Favorite Amusement Park Ride

Legend: ■ West Jr. High ■ East Jr. High ■ Survey

b. Possible answers: Students from East Jr. High did not prefer the ferris wheel as often as West Jr. High or the Web site. Students from East Jr. High preferred the log ride more commonly than the people from the Web site. The West Jr. High students preferred roller coasters more than any other group of people.

2. a. Answers will vary; possible statements: Roller coasters built in 1960 or later were taller and had greater maximum drops. You can see this by (1) comparing the means and medians and (2) by the general shift to the right in the distributions after 1959. It looks like the distributions of maximum heights and maximum drops are similar in shape and location. This probably means that there is a relationship here. The speeds of coasters built before 1960 are not as variable as those of coasters built after 1959; it looks like roller coasters were able to go faster (greater than 60 mi/h) after 1959.

b. Answers will vary; sample size is addressed in the eighth grade unit, *Samples and Populations*, but it certainly is appropriate for students to note that the sample size of coasters built before 1950 is small. One question might be whether there are others that could be included. If students want to pursue this, they can visit the Web site that has the census table about kinds of coasters for more data.

3. For every one wood roller coaster, there are about 10 steel roller coasters. (177 to 1752)

4. North America has about 12 times as many roller coasters as South America.

5. Asia has about two thirds as many roller coasters as North America.

6. North America has about 74% of all wood coasters.

7. Answers will vary.

Connections

8. Graph A: Wood Roller Coasters by Continent
   Graph B: Steel Roller Coasters by Continent

9. D

10. H; Computation: $[(3 \times 90) + 86] \div 4 = 89$.

11. Answers will vary; graph shows the change from the week of Oct. 7–9 to Sept. 30–Oct. 2 showed box office declines everywhere (negative percentages).

12. **a.** Table 1: 9% (735 ÷ 8,114; students can also check by adding percents and subtracting total from 100%. This result will be 8.9.)
    Table 2: 12.2% (968 ÷ 7,934; students can also check by adding percents and subtracting total from 100%. This result will be 12.2.)
    Table 3, Boys: 41.1% (100% − 58.9%)
    Table 3, Ages 5–12: 57.9% (100% − 42.1%)

    b. (Figure 19)

    c. Most children have lived in 1–3 apartments or houses (about 60%). The data peak at two apartments or houses (the mode) and then seem to taper off.

    d. Use data from Table 1: 6% + 6.5% + 6.3% + 4.1% + 2.8% + 2.2% = 27.9% (Could also add all the counts and then divide this sum by 8,114.)

    e. Use data from Table 2: 20.7% have lived only in one home (taken directly from question).

    f. About $\frac{2}{5}$ of the boys have lived in the same city or town all their lives; 41.1% is close to 40%.

13. The shape appears to be clumped in two clusters, one from 0–4 g and the other from 12–15 g. The sugar per serving (g) has a range from 0 to 20.

14. Based on the shape, one can estimate that the mean and median are about 10–12 grams of sugar.

15. About one-half of the cereals have serving sizes of 1 cup; only a few have larger serving sizes and the rest have serving sizes of three-fourths cup, two-thirds cup, or one-half cup.

16. The mean is less than 1 cup and median is 1 cup serving size; the median has to be in this group at 1 cup, but there are more values below 1 that are a greater distance below 1 cup than the values above 1 cup, so the mean is less than 1 cup.

Figure 19

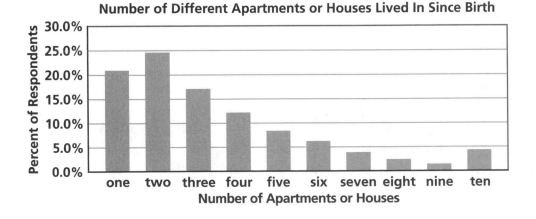

Number of Different Apartments or Houses Lived In Since Birth

Extensions

17. a–c.

Track Length and Speed of 150 Wood and Steel Coasters

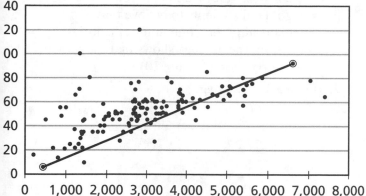

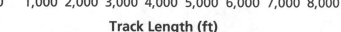

Track Length (ft)

d. Points on the line exhibit the relationship that speed = 0.014 times the track length.

Points above the line are faster roller coasters than those on the line.

Points below the line are slower roller coasters than those on the line.

e. Finding slope using two points.
Step One: Identify two points on the line. In this example we are given two points, $(6,595, 92)$ and $(443, 6)$, on a straight line.

Step Two: Select one to be (x_1, y_1) and the other to be (x_2, y_2).
It does not matter which we choose, so let's take $(6,595, 92)$ to be (x_2, y_2). Let's take the point $(443, 6)$ to be the point (x_1, y_1).
Step Three: Use the equation to calculate slope.

$$\frac{(y_2 - y_1)}{(x_2 - x_1)} = \frac{(92 - 6)}{(6,595 - 443)} = \frac{86}{6,152} =$$

$$0.014 = \frac{14}{1,000}$$

$$y = 0.014x \text{ or } \frac{14}{1,000}x$$

Possible Answers to Mathematical Reflections

1. a. The range describes how spread out data are. In comparing two distributions, if one has a larger range than the other, this suggests that the latter has more variation. However, the range is affected by outliers; one abnormally high value may make the range very large, whereas the rest of the data may be clustered together.

b. The mean and median help compare what might be considered typical values in two sets of data. It is helpful to notice if the mean/median for each distribution are similar and then to compare each between distributions. It is important to take into account the context for the data in order to decide if any differences matter. For example, with the roller coasters, the mean speed might be 53 mi/h and the median speed 55 mi/h. These statistics have different values but, given the context of speed, 53 mi/h and 55 mi/h are not really different, so the two measures are providing similar information.

c. Benchmarks are helpful to divide distributions into two or more parts and compare counts or percents by parts. Generally, benchmarks are selected with some rationale. For example, with roller coaster speeds, it might be helpful to divide the distribution of speeds by marking 35 mi/h or 55 mi/h or 65 mi/h (common driving speeds) and see what percent of coasters are above, below, or in between the marked speeds.

2. Relative frequencies are useful when you want to compare two data sets in which there are different numbers of data values. Answers may vary.

Answers to Looking Back and Looking Ahead

1. (Figure 20)

Calories per Slice

```
28 | 0 3
29 | 2 9
30 | 7
31 |
32 | 2 5 8
33 | 2 3 4 5
34 | 1 3 6
35 |
36 | 4 4 7 7 9
37 | 2 8
38 | 4 5
39 | 4
40 | 0 0
41 | 0 2
```
Key: 40 | 0 means 400 calories

a. The mean calories per slice of pizza is 350.552 and the median is 346. There is a cluster around the 340 calories and another around 370 calories. So, the typical number of calories could be reported as a band of values, 340–370.

b. The data ranges from 280 calories per slice to 412 calories per slice. The data seems to cluster about 320 to 350 and also around 360 to 390.

c. Cheese pizzas seem to contain fewer calories than pepperoni pizzas. The mean calories for cheese pizzas is about 339, while the mean calories for a pepperoni pizza is about 367 calories; however, the two lowest values are pepperoni pizza. This might lead students to believe that pepperoni pizzas contain fewer calories; however, the average shows that they do in fact carry more. (Figure 20)

2. (Figure 21, next page)

Calories per Slice

```
 5 | 4
 6 | 4 7
 7 | 4
 8 | 0 4 7 8 8 9 9
 9 | 0 1 2 4 4 6 6 6 8
10 | 2
11 | 7
12 | 3 6 8 8
13 |
14 |
15 | 1
16 | 2
17 |
18 |
19 | 2
```
Key: 10 | 2 means $1.02

Figure 20

Calories per Slice

118 Data Distributions

a. The mean cost of a slice of pizza is about $1.01, while the median cost is $0.94.

b. The data varies between $0.54 and $1.92. It has a large cluster between $0.85 and $1.00; however, it also contains many outliers, which skew the value of the mean.

c. The data is not conclusive one way or the other. Pepperoni pizzas have a higher mean cost with $1.03 compared to $1.00 for cheese. However, the median cost of a slice of pepperoni pizza is $0.90, while the median for a slice of cheese pizza is $0.94. If one only used either the mean or the median an argument could be made in favor of one type; however, considering both leads us to believe that there is no correlation between the type of pizza and the cost.

3. a.

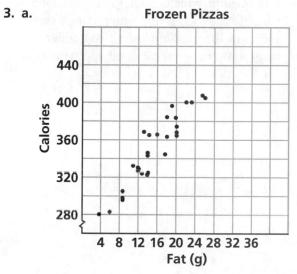

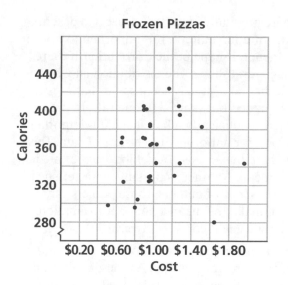

b. There seems to be a positive linear relationship between the number of calories and the amount of fat in a slice of pizza. This means that the more fat a slice has, the more calories it will have or vice versa.

c. There does not seem to be any relationship between cost and calories.

d. The calories and fat relationship is stronger. In that comparison, it is possible to make a good estimate of the value of either calories or fat given the opposite variable.

Figure 21

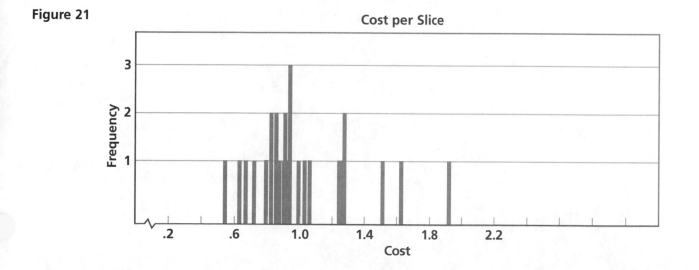

4. There are many important aspects to describing a distribution pattern. It is important to notice the general shape of the distribution, if there is a general shape. The distribution may be bell shaped or it may seem somewhat bell shaped but skewed to one side. In data that are not clearly a bell shape it is important to look for uniformity or clusters of data. This can help make sense out of locations of median and mean. Another important characteristic is the presence of outliers. These outliers can often make the mean a poor approximation of what we might consider "typical."

5. In a bell-shaped distribution the mean and median are very similar. As the distribution begins to skew to one side it will pull the mean with it faster than the median. So a skewed distribution will often have a very different mean and median score. The mean is also more likely impacted by a small number of extreme outliers, while the median may not be changed.

6. When two sets of data have an equal number of data values it is possible to make numerical comparisons. For example, if we have 10 people taste two different pizzas, it is meaningful to say that 6 people liked the first pizza and 4 people liked the second. However, if we later found out that out of 50 people only 4 liked the second pizza, the original comparison would no longer be meaningful.

7. Ratios or percentages are an excellent tool for comparing two groups of data that do not have equal numbers of data. This allows us to compare the two pizzas since $\frac{3}{5}$ people liked the first pizza, however, only 4 out of 50 liked the second pizza, which is $\frac{2}{25}$.

8. When we say something is "related to" something else, we are saying there is some relationship, which can help us determine one variable if we know the other. For example, if we know the maximum drop of a roller coaster, we can make a good approximation for the speed of the roller coaster.

A

attribute A property, quality, or characteristic of a person, place, or thing. For example, each person has attributes such as height, weight, name, gender, and eye color.

atributo Propiedad, cualidad o característica de una persona, lugar o cosa. Por ejemplo, cada persona tiene atributos, como altura, peso, nombre, género y color de ojos.

C

categorical data Data that can be placed into categories. For example, "gender" is a categorical data and the categories are "male" and "female." If you asked people in which month they were born or what their favorite class is, they would answer with names, which would be categorical data. However, if you asked them how many siblings they have, they would answer with numbers, not categories.

datos categóricos Datos que pueden ser colocados en categorías. Por ejemplo, "género" es un dato categórico y las categorías son "masculino" y "femenino." Si le preguntas a la gente en qué mes nacieron o cual es su clase favorita, responderían con nombres, lo cual es un dato categórico. Sin embargo, si le preguntas cuántos hermanos o hermanas tienen, responderán con números, no con categorías.

counts Data that give the number of occurrences (the frequency) of an attribute, for example, the number of occurrences of 3-child families.

cuentas Datos que dan el número de veces que ocurre (frecuencia) un evento, por ejemplo, el número de familias que tienen 3 niños.

D

distribution Data sets collected from observation or experiment. They can be described by measures of center and variability.

distribución Conjuntos de datos reunidos a partir de la observación o la experimentación. Pueden ser descritos con medidas de tendencia central y variabilidad.

G

graphs Any pictorial device, such as a scatter plot or bar graph, used to display categorical or numerical data.

gráficas Cualquier elemento pictórico, como una gráfica de dispersión o una gráfica de barras, usado para mostrar datos categóricos numéricos.

Notes

_____

_____

_____

_____

line plot Each data value is represented as a dot or an "x" positioned over a labeled number line. The line plot made with dots is sometimes referred to as a dot plot.

diagrama de puntos Cada valor de datos es representado como un punto o una "x" ubicada sobre una recta numérica rotulada. El diagrama de puntos hecho con puntos algunas veces se conoce como gráfica de puntos.

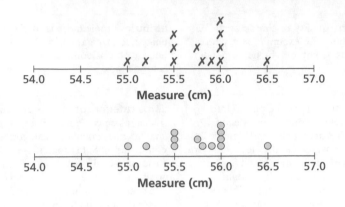

M

mean (1) The result if all of the data values are combined and then redistributed evenly among individuals so that each has the same amount. (2) The number that is the balance point in a distribution of numerical values. The mean is influenced by all of the values of the distribution, including outliers. It is often called the average, and is the sum of the numerical values divided by the number of values. For example, the mean of 1, 3, 7, 8, and 25 is 8.8 because the sum of the values, 44, is divided by the number of values, 5.

media (1) El resultado, si todos los valores de datos están combinados y luego redistribuidos uniformemente entre diferentes individuos, de modo que cada uno tenga la misma cantidad. (2) El número que es el punto de equilibrio en una distribución de valores numéricos. La media se ve afectada por todos los valores de la distribución, incluyendo los valores extremos. Por lo general se le llama promedio, es la suma de los valores numéricos dividida por el número de valores. Por ejemplo, la media de 1, 3, 7, 8 y 25 es 8.8 porque la suma de los valores, 44, se divide por el número de valores, 5.

measures Data obtained by making measurements. For example, we can measure the height of each person in a class.

medidas Datos obtenidos al hacer mediciones. Por ejemplo, podemos medir la altura de cada persona en una clase.

measures of center See *mean, median,* and *mode.*

medidas de tendencia central Ver *mean, median* y *mode.*

Notes _____

_____

_____

_____

median The median is the number that is the midpoint of an ordered set of numerical data. This means that at least half of the data values lie at or above the median and at least half lie at or below it. For example, the median of 1, 3, 7, 8, and 25 is 7 because that number is third in the list of five data values. The median of 2, 3, 4, 4, 4, 5, 6, 12, and 13 is 4 because that number is fifth in the list of nine data values.

When a distribution contains an even number of data values, the median is computed by finding the average of the two middle data values in an ordered list of the data values. For example, the median of 1, 3, 7, 8, 25, and 30 is 7.5 because the data values 7 and 8 are third and fourth in the list of six data values.

mediana La mediana es el número que es el punto medio de un conjunto ordenado de datos numéricos. Esto significa que al menos la mitad de los valores de datos están en o sobre la mediana y al menos la mitad están en o bajo la mediana. Por ejemplo, la mediana de 1, 3, 7, 8 y 25 es 7, porque éste es tercer número en la lista de cinco valores de datos. La mediana de 2, 3, 4, 4, 4, 5, 6, 12 y 13 es 4, porque éste número es el quinto en la lista de nueve valores de datos.

Cuando una distribución contiene, un número par de valores de datos, la mediana se obtiene averiguando el promedio de los dos valores medios en una lista ordenada de valores de datos. Por ejemplo, la mediana de 1, 3, 7, 8, 25 y 30 es 7.5, porque los valores de datos 7 y 8 son tercero y cuarto en la lista de seis valores de datos.

mode The data value or category occurring with the greatest frequency. For example, the mode of 3, 4, 7, 11, 11, 11, 3, and 4 is 11.

moda El valor de dato o categoría que sucede con la mayor frecuencia. Por ejemplo, la moda de 3, 4, 7, 11, 11, 11, 3 y 4 es 11.

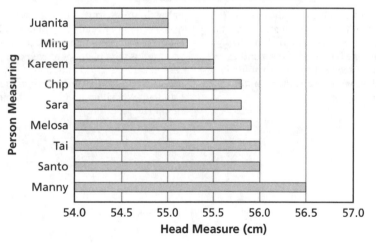

N

numerical data Data consisting of numbers, not categories, such as the heights of students.

dato numérico Dato que consiste en números, no categorías, tales como la altura de los estudiantes.

O

ordered value bar graph A value bar graph in which data values are arranged in increasing (or decreasing) order of length.

gráfica de barras con valores ordenados Gráfica de barras de valores en la cual los valores de los datos están ordenado en orden creciente (o decreciente).

Measures of Jasmine's Head

(Horizontal bar graph — Person Measuring vs. Head Measure (cm), axis from 54.0 to 57.0)

Juanita, Ming, Kareem, Chip, Sara, Melosa, Tai, Santo, Manny

Notes

outliers Unusually high or low data values in a distribution.

valores extremos o atípicos Valores de datos excepcionalmente altos o bajos en una distribución.

R

range A number found by subtracting the minimum value from the maximum value. If you know the range of the data is 12 grams of sugar per serving, you know that the difference between the minimum and maximum values is 12 grams.

rango Número que se halla al restar el valor mínimo del valor máximo. Si se sabe que el rango de los datos es 12 gramos de azúcar por porción, entonces se sabe que la diferencia entre el valor mínimo y el máximo es 12 gramos.

S

scatter plot A coordinate graph showing the relationship, if any, between two variables, for example, roller coaster track length and speed.

diagrama de dispersión Gráfica de coordenadas que muestra la relación, si la hay, entre dos variables, por ejemplo, largo de las vías de una montaña rusa y la velocidad.

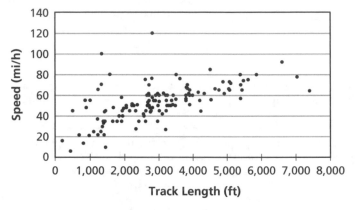

Track Length and Speed of 150 Wood and Steel Coasters

V

value of an attribute Values are the data that occur for each individual case of an attribute—that is, the number of red candies recorded for the attribute red from one bag of M&M™ candies or the time in seconds recorded for the attribute fastest time for one student who played the computer reaction-time game.

valor de un atributo Los valores son los datos que suceden para cada *caso* independiente de un atributo, o sea, el número de caramelos rojos registrados para el atributo *rojo* de una bolsa de caramelos M&M™ o el tiempo en segundos registrado para el atributo *tiempo más rápido* de un estudiante que jugó un juego de computadora de tiempo de reacción.

92 Data Distributions

Notes

value bar graph Each data value is represented by a separate bar whose relative length corresponds to the magnitude of that data value.

gráfica de barras de valores Cada valor de dato se representa por una barra independiente, cuya longitud relativa corresponde con la magnitud de ese valor de dato. Por ejemplo, si hay 12 caramelos rojos en una bolsa de M&Ms, entonces la barra para los caramelos rojos llega hasta el 12.

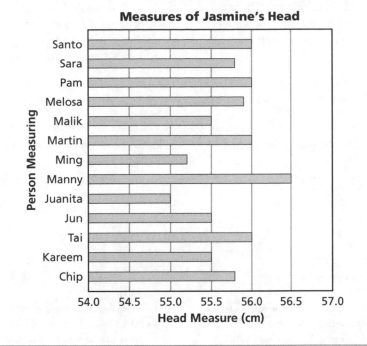

Measures of Jasmine's Head

variability of a set of numerical data An indication of how widely spread or closely clustered the data values are. Range, minimum and maximum values, and clusters in the distribution give some indication of variability.

variabilidad de un conjunto de datos numéricos Indicación de cuán dispersos o conglomerados están los valores de datos. El rango, los valores mínimo y máximo, y las conglomeraciones en la distribución dan cierta indicación de variabilidad.

English/Spanish Glossary **93**

Notes

Academic Vocabulary

Academic vocabulary words are words that you see in textbooks and on tests. These are not math vocabulary terms, but knowing them will help you succeed in mathematics.

Las palabras de vocabulario académico son palabras que ves en los libros de texto y en las pruebas. Éstos no son términos de vocabulario de matemáticas, pero conocerlos te ayudará a tener éxito en matemáticas.

C

compare To tell or show how two things are alike and different.
related terms: analyze, relate

Sample: How do the mean and the median of this data compare?

Item	Number Sold
Pencil	100
Pen	20
Mouse Pad	10
Dictionary	5
Notebook	52

The mean of this data is 37.4. The median is 20. The mean is much greater than the median because the number of pencils sold is an outlier for this data.

comparar Decir o mostrar en qué se parecen o en qué se diferencian dos cosas.
términos relacionados: analizar, relacionar

Ejemplo: ¿Cómo se comparan la media y la mediana de estos datos?

Útil	Número vendido
Lápiz	100
Bolígrafo	20
Almohadilla para ratón	10
Diccionario	5
Cuaderno	52

La media de estos datos es 37.4. La mediana es 20. La media es mucho mayor que la mediana porque el número de lápices vendidos es un valor extremo de estos datos.

D

determine To use the given information and any related facts to find a value or make a decision.
related terms: decide, find, calculate, conclude

Sample: What can you determine about the variability of the data?

Pumpkin	1	2	3	4	5
Weight (lbs)	17	25	32	16	19

The range of the data is 32 − 16 = 16 pounds. However, three of the weights are clustered in the teens: 16, 17, and 19 pounds.

determinar Usar la información dada y cualesquiera datos relacionados para hallar un valor o tomar una decisión.
términos relacionados: decidir, hallar, calcular, concluir

Ejemplo: ¿Qué puedes determinar sobre la variabilidad de los datos?

Calabaza	1	2	3	4	5
Peso (libras)	17	25	32	16	19

El rango de los datos es 32 − 16 = 16 libras. Sin embargo, tres de los pesos están muy cerca uno de otro: 16, 17 y 19 libras.

94 Data Distributions

Notes

explain To give facts and details that make an idea easier to understand. Explaining can involve a written summary supported by a diagram, chart, table, or a combination of these.

related terms: describe, show, justify, tell, present

Sample: Explain how to determine the median of the data set: 2, 7, 8, 1, 0, 7, 4, 1.

> To find the median, order all of the data points from least to greatest.
>
> 0, 1, 1, 2, 4, 7, 7, 8
>
> The value in the middle is the median. Since there are an even number of data, find the mean of the two middle values. For this data, the median is 3; because $(2 + 4) \div 2 = 3$.

explicar Dar datos y detalles que facilitan el entendimiento de una idea. Explicar puede requerir la preparación de un informe escrito apoyado por un diagrama, una tabla, un esquema o una combinación de éstos.

términos relacionados: describir, mostrar, justificar, decir, presentar

Ejemplo: Explica cómo se determina la mediana del conjunto de datos: 2, 7, 8, 1, 0, 7, 4, 1.

> Para hallar la mediana, ordena todos los puntos de datos de menor a mayor.
>
> 0, 1, 1, 2, 4, 7, 7, 8
>
> El valor del medio es la mediana. Como el número datos es par, halla la media de los dos valores del medio. Para estos datos, la mediana es 3, porque $(2 + 4) \div 2 = 3$.

R

relate To have a connection or impact on something else.

related terms: connect, correlate

Sample: Relate the data in the table to the value bar graph.

Plant	Height (cm)
1	52
2	50
3	42
4	67
5	48

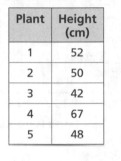

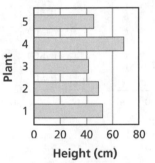

> The heights (cm) in the table are represented by the lengths of the bars in the bar graph. Each bar represents one of the plants. The plants' heights can be determined by looking at the values on the horizontal.

relacionar Haber una conexión o impacto entre una cosa y otra.

términos relacionados: unir, correlacionar

Ejemplo: Relaciona los datos de la tabla con la gráfica de barras de los valores.

Planta	Altura (cm)
1	52
2	50
3	42
4	67
5	48

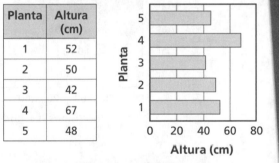

> Las alturas (cm) de la tabla están representadas por las longitudes de las barras que aparecen en la gráfica de barras. Cada barra representa una de las plantas. Las alturas de las plantas se pueden determinar observando los valores de la línea horizontal.

Academic Vocabulary **95**

Notes _____

_____

_____

_____

Reaction Time Cards

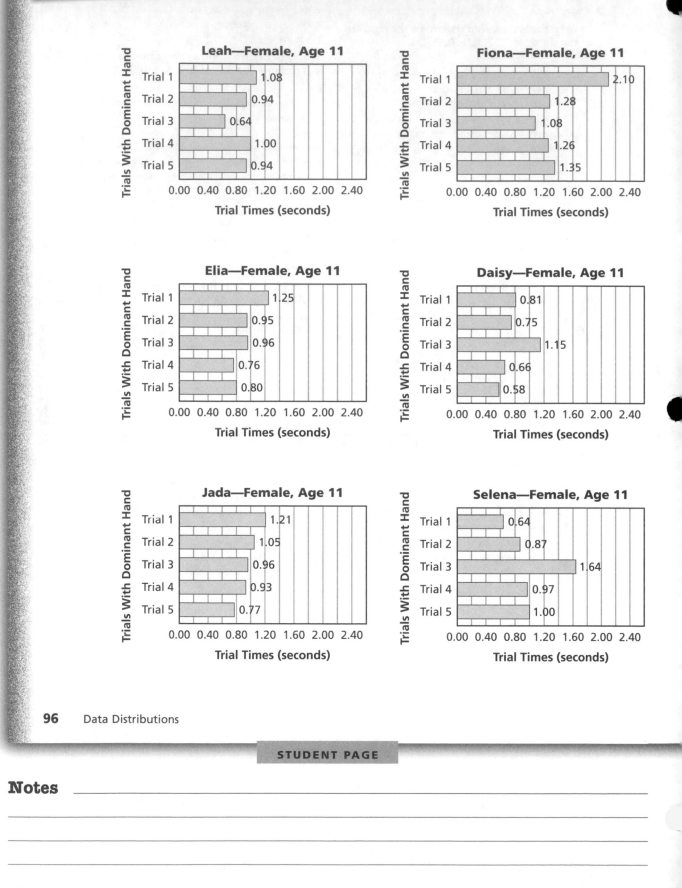

Leah—Female, Age 11

Trials With Dominant Hand

Trial	Trial Times (seconds)
Trial 1	1.08
Trial 2	0.94
Trial 3	0.64
Trial 4	1.00
Trial 5	0.94

Fiona—Female, Age 11

Trials With Dominant Hand

Trial	Trial Times (seconds)
Trial 1	2.10
Trial 2	1.28
Trial 3	1.08
Trial 4	1.26
Trial 5	1.35

Elia—Female, Age 11

Trials With Dominant Hand

Trial	Trial Times (seconds)
Trial 1	1.25
Trial 2	0.95
Trial 3	0.96
Trial 4	0.76
Trial 5	0.80

Daisy—Female, Age 11

Trials With Dominant Hand

Trial	Trial Times (seconds)
Trial 1	0.81
Trial 2	0.75
Trial 3	1.15
Trial 4	0.66
Trial 5	0.58

Jada—Female, Age 11

Trials With Dominant Hand

Trial	Trial Times (seconds)
Trial 1	1.21
Trial 2	1.05
Trial 3	0.96
Trial 4	0.93
Trial 5	0.77

Selena—Female, Age 11

Trials With Dominant Hand

Trial	Trial Times (seconds)
Trial 1	0.64
Trial 2	0.87
Trial 3	1.64
Trial 4	0.97
Trial 5	1.00

Notes

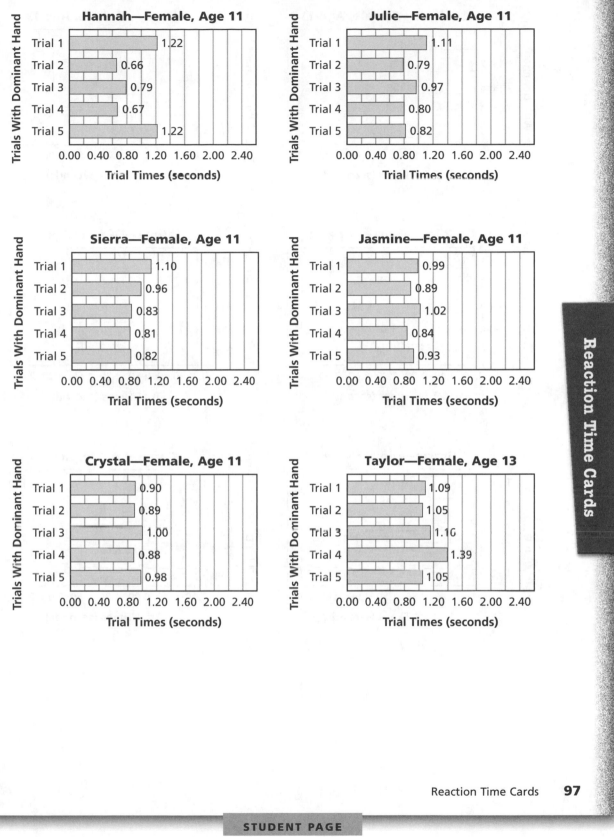

Hannah—Female, Age 11

Trials With Dominant Hand

Trial	Time
Trial 1	1.22
Trial 2	0.66
Trial 3	0.79
Trial 4	0.67
Trial 5	1.22

Trial Times (seconds)

Julie—Female, Age 11

Trials With Dominant Hand

Trial	Time
Trial 1	1.11
Trial 2	0.79
Trial 3	0.97
Trial 4	0.80
Trial 5	0.82

Trial Times (seconds)

Sierra—Female, Age 11

Trials With Dominant Hand

Trial	Time
Trial 1	1.10
Trial 2	0.96
Trial 3	0.83
Trial 4	0.81
Trial 5	0.82

Trial Times (seconds)

Jasmine—Female, Age 11

Trials With Dominant Hand

Trial	Time
Trial 1	0.99
Trial 2	0.89
Trial 3	1.02
Trial 4	0.84
Trial 5	0.93

Trial Times (seconds)

Crystal—Female, Age 11

Trials With Dominant Hand

Trial	Time
Trial 1	0.90
Trial 2	0.89
Trial 3	1.00
Trial 4	0.88
Trial 5	0.98

Trial Times (seconds)

Taylor—Female, Age 13

Trials With Dominant Hand

Trial	Time
Trial 1	1.09
Trial 2	1.05
Trial 3	1.10
Trial 4	1.39
Trial 5	1.05

Trial Times (seconds)

Reaction Time Cards **97**

Notes _____

_____

_____

_____

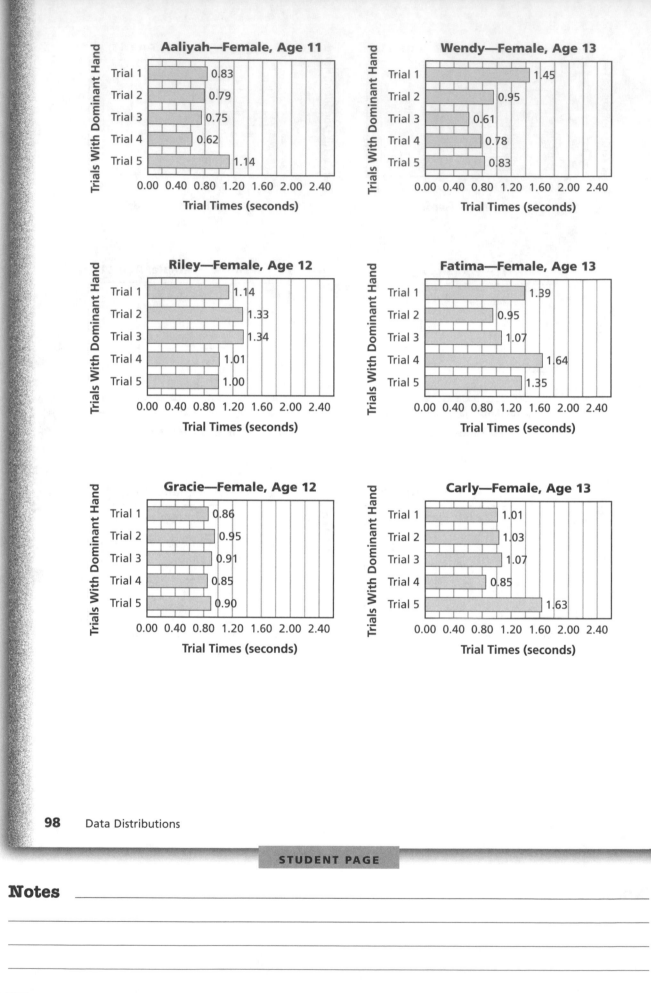

Aaliyah—Female, Age 11

Trials With Dominant Hand:
- Trial 1: 0.83
- Trial 2: 0.79
- Trial 3: 0.75
- Trial 4: 0.62
- Trial 5: 1.14

Trial Times (seconds): 0.00 0.40 0.80 1.20 1.60 2.00 2.40

Wendy—Female, Age 13

Trials With Dominant Hand:
- Trial 1: 1.45
- Trial 2: 0.95
- Trial 3: 0.61
- Trial 4: 0.78
- Trial 5: 0.83

Trial Times (seconds): 0.00 0.40 0.80 1.20 1.60 2.00 2.40

Riley—Female, Age 12

Trials With Dominant Hand:
- Trial 1: 1.14
- Trial 2: 1.33
- Trial 3: 1.34
- Trial 4: 1.01
- Trial 5: 1.00

Trial Times (seconds): 0.00 0.40 0.80 1.20 1.60 2.00 2.40

Fatima—Female, Age 13

Trials With Dominant Hand:
- Trial 1: 1.39
- Trial 2: 0.95
- Trial 3: 1.07
- Trial 4: 1.64
- Trial 5: 1.35

Trial Times (seconds): 0.00 0.40 0.80 1.20 1.60 2.00 2.40

Gracie—Female, Age 12

Trials With Dominant Hand:
- Trial 1: 0.86
- Trial 2: 0.95
- Trial 3: 0.91
- Trial 4: 0.85
- Trial 5: 0.90

Trial Times (seconds): 0.00 0.40 0.80 1.20 1.60 2.00 2.40

Carly—Female, Age 13

Trials With Dominant Hand:
- Trial 1: 1.01
- Trial 2: 1.03
- Trial 3: 1.07
- Trial 4: 0.85
- Trial 5: 1.63

Trial Times (seconds): 0.00 0.40 0.80 1.20 1.60 2.00 2.40

Notes _____

_____

_____

_____

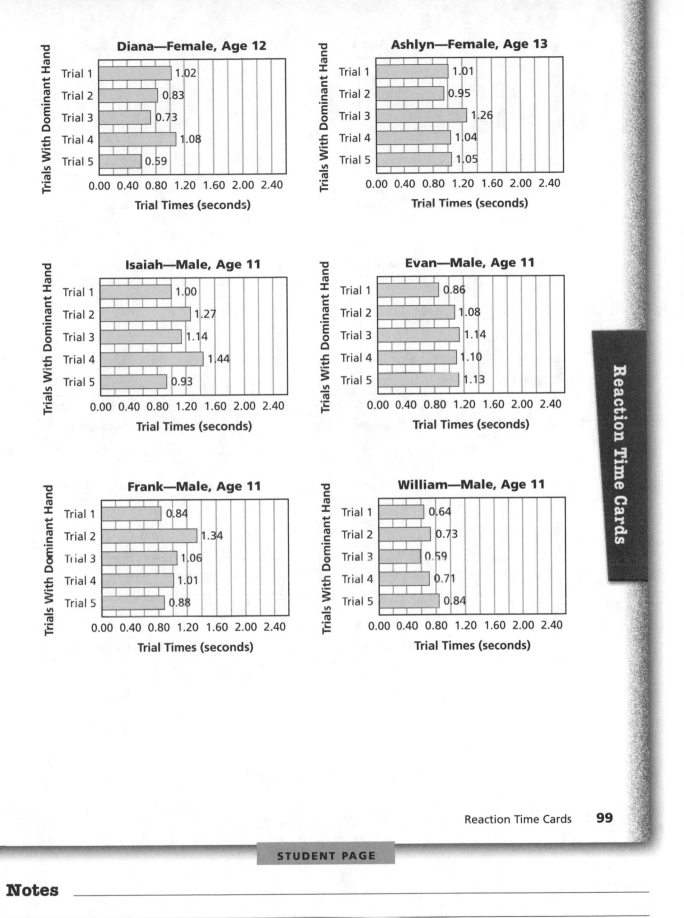

STUDENT PAGE

Reaction Time Cards   **99**

Notes _____

_____

_____

_____

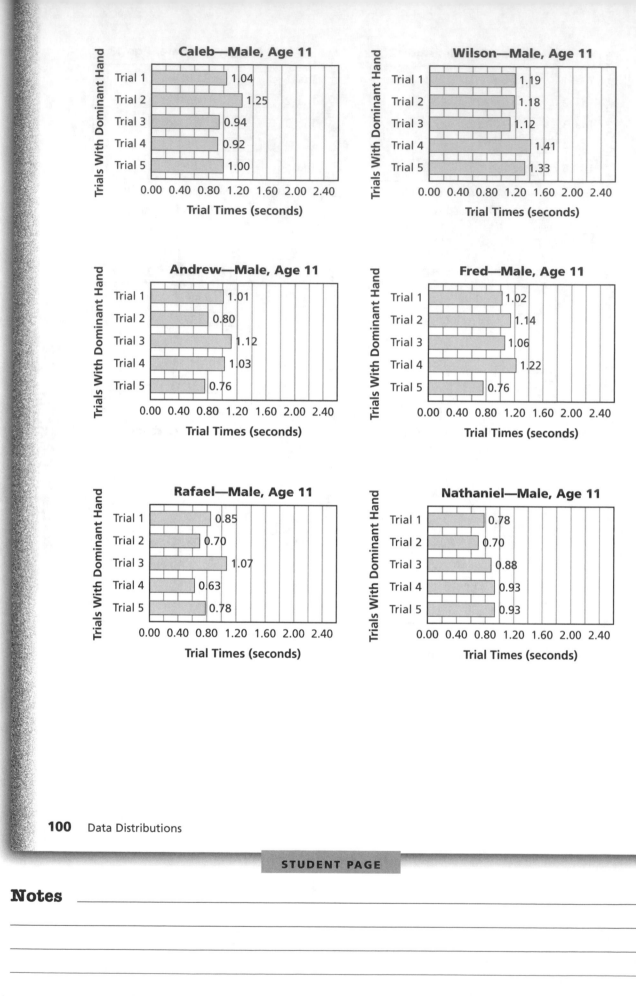

Caleb—Male, Age 11

Trials With Dominant Hand

Trial	Trial Times (seconds)
Trial 1	1.04
Trial 2	1.25
Trial 3	0.94
Trial 4	0.92
Trial 5	1.00

Wilson—Male, Age 11

Trials With Dominant Hand

Trial	Trial Times (seconds)
Trial 1	1.19
Trial 2	1.18
Trial 3	1.12
Trial 4	1.41
Trial 5	1.33

Andrew—Male, Age 11

Trials With Dominant Hand

Trial	Trial Times (seconds)
Trial 1	1.01
Trial 2	0.80
Trial 3	1.12
Trial 4	1.03
Trial 5	0.76

Fred—Male, Age 11

Trials With Dominant Hand

Trial	Trial Times (seconds)
Trial 1	1.02
Trial 2	1.14
Trial 3	1.06
Trial 4	1.22
Trial 5	0.76

Rafael—Male, Age 11

Trials With Dominant Hand

Trial	Trial Times (seconds)
Trial 1	0.85
Trial 2	0.70
Trial 3	1.07
Trial 4	0.63
Trial 5	0.78

Nathaniel—Male, Age 11

Trials With Dominant Hand

Trial	Trial Times (seconds)
Trial 1	0.78
Trial 2	0.70
Trial 3	0.88
Trial 4	0.93
Trial 5	0.93

Notes

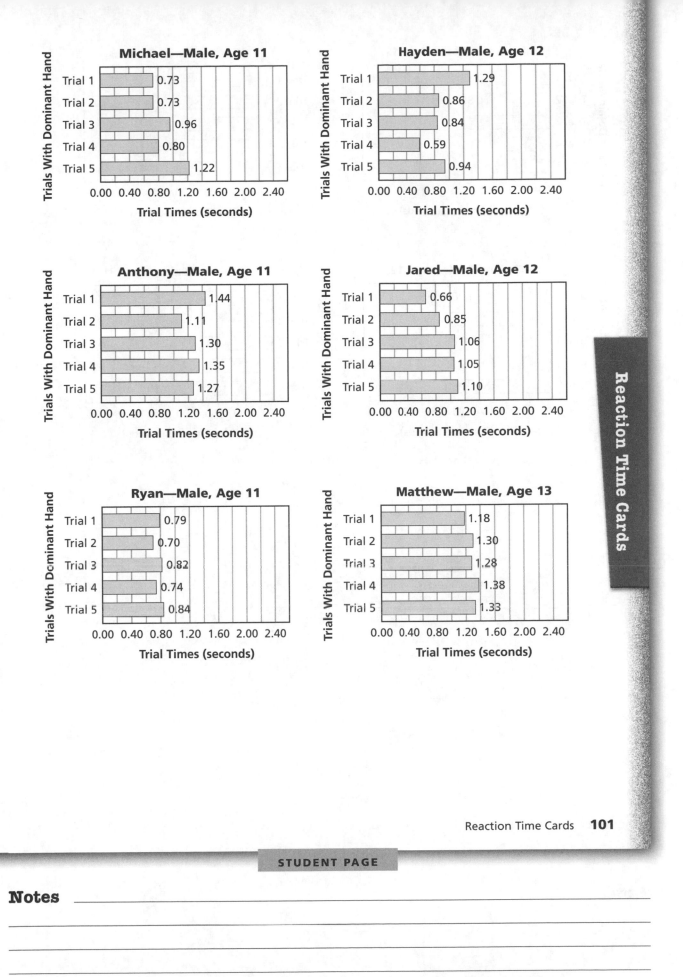

Reaction Time Cards

Michael—Male, Age 11

Trials With Dominant Hand

Trial 1	0.73
Trial 2	0.73
Trial 3	0.96
Trial 4	0.80
Trial 5	1.22

0.00 0.40 0.80 1.20 1.60 2.00 2.40
Trial Times (seconds)

Hayden—Male, Age 12

Trials With Dominant Hand

Trial 1	1.29
Trial 2	0.86
Trial 3	0.84
Trial 4	0.59
Trial 5	0.94

0.00 0.40 0.80 1.20 1.60 2.00 2.40
Trial Times (seconds)

Anthony—Male, Age 11

Trials With Dominant Hand

Trial 1	1.44
Trial 2	1.11
Trial 3	1.30
Trial 4	1.35
Trial 5	1.27

0.00 0.40 0.80 1.20 1.60 2.00 2.40
Trial Times (seconds)

Jared—Male, Age 12

Trials With Dominant Hand

Trial 1	0.66
Trial 2	0.85
Trial 3	1.06
Trial 4	1.05
Trial 5	1.10

0.00 0.40 0.80 1.20 1.60 2.00 2.40
Trial Times (seconds)

Ryan—Male, Age 11

Trials With Dominant Hand

Trial 1	0.79
Trial 2	0.70
Trial 3	0.82
Trial 4	0.74
Trial 5	0.84

0.00 0.40 0.80 1.20 1.60 2.00 2.40
Trial Times (seconds)

Matthew—Male, Age 13

Trials With Dominant Hand

Trial 1	1.18
Trial 2	1.30
Trial 3	1.28
Trial 4	1.38
Trial 5	1.33

0.00 0.40 0.80 1.20 1.60 2.00 2.40
Trial Times (seconds)

Notes

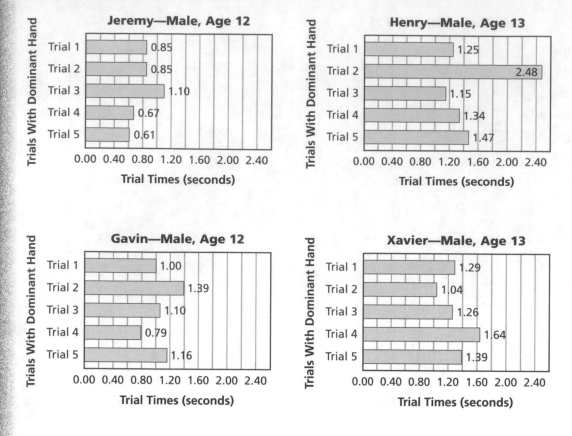

Jeremy—Male, Age 12

Trials With Dominant Hand

| | Trial Times (seconds) |
Trial 1 — 0.85
Trial 2 — 0.85
Trial 3 — 1.10
Trial 4 — 0.67
Trial 5 — 0.61

Henry—Male, Age 13

Trials With Dominant Hand

Trial 1 — 1.25
Trial 2 — 2.48
Trial 3 — 1.15
Trial 4 — 1.34
Trial 5 — 1.47

Gavin—Male, Age 12

Trials With Dominant Hand

Trial 1 — 1.00
Trial 2 — 1.39
Trial 3 — 1.10
Trial 4 — 0.79
Trial 5 — 1.16

Xavier—Male, Age 13

Trials With Dominant Hand

Trial 1 — 1.29
Trial 2 — 1.04
Trial 3 — 1.26
Trial 4 — 1.64
Trial 5 — 1.39

Notes

Index

STUDENT PAGE

STUDENT PAGE

Index

Notes

_____

_____

_____

_____

104 Data Distributions

Notes

Acknowledgments

Team Credits

The people who made up the **Connected Mathematics 2** team—representing editorial, editorial services, design services, and production services—are listed below. Bold type denotes core team members.

Leora Adler, Judith Buice, Kerry Cashman, Patrick Culleton, Sheila DeFazio, Richard Heater, **Barbara Hollingdale, Jayne Holman,** Karen Holtzman, **Etta Jacobs,** Christine Lee, Carolyn Lock, Catherine Maglio, **Dotti Marshall,** Rich McMahon, Eve Melnechuk, Kristin Mingrone, Terri Mitchell, **Marsha Novak,** Irene Rubin, Donna Russo, Robin Samper, Siri Schwartzman, **Nancy Smith,** Emily Soltanoff, **Mark Tricca,** Paula Vergith, Roberta Warshaw, Helen Young

Additional Credits

Diana Bonfilio, Mairead Reddin, Michael Torocsik, nSight, Inc.

Technical Illustration

WestWords, Inc.

Cover Design

tom white.images

Photos

2 t, Rubberball/Getty Images, Inc.; **2 m,** Gail Mooney/Masterfile; **2 b,** AP Photo/Cheryl Hatch; **3,** RNT Productions/Corbis; **5,** Chad Slattery/Getty Images, Inc.; **6,** Rubberball/Getty Images, Inc.; **11,** Jonathan Nourok/PhotoEdit; **17,** Richard Haynes; **19,** Bob Daemmrich/The Image Works; **21,** Ryan McVay/Getty Images, Inc.; **23,** David Young-Wolff/PhotoEdit; **25,** John Walmsley/Education Photos; **28,** Matthew Stockman/Getty Images, Inc.; **36,** Chris Collins/Corbis; **37,** Gail Mooney/Masterfile; **46,** Richard Haynes; **49,** Dylan Martinez/Corbis; **51,** Richard Haynes; **52,** John R. MacGregor/Peter Arnold, Inc.; **55,** Spencer Grant/PhotoEdit; **58,** MedioImages/Getty Images, Inc.; **61,** AP Photo/Cheryl Hatch; **63,** Richard Hutchings/PhotoEdit; **69,** image100/Getty Images, Inc.; **74,** Jeff Greenberg/PhotoEdit; **78,** Gail Mooney/Masterfile; **84,** Lester Lefkowitz/Getty Images, Inc.

Data Sources

Box Office Regional Access Map. Copyright © 2005 Nielsen EDI, Inc. Reproduced by permission.

The "Did You Know" information on page 6 is from *The Story of M&M's® Brand.* www.mms.com. M&M's® and "The milk chocolate melts in your mouth--not in your hand" are registered trademarks of Mars, Incorporated. Copyright © 2006 Mars, Incorporated and its Affiliates. All Rights Reserved.

Qualifying Standards for the Presidential and National Physical Fitness Award on page 24 Copyright © 2006 President's Council on Physical Fitness and Sports.

The nutritional content of ready-to-eat cereals on page 33 is from Bowes & Church's Food Values of Portions Commonly Used. 18th Edition, by Jean A. T. Pennington, PhD, RD. and Judith S. Douglass MS, RD. Copyright © 2004 Used by permission of Lippincott Williams & Wilkins. www.lww.com

Acknowledgments **105**

Notes _____

_____

_____

_____

Acknowledgments

Data Sources (continued)

Garter snake data on page 70 are from
The North Carolina Cooperative Extension,
www.ces.ncsu.edu, North Carolina State
University.

Pizza data on page 70 are from "Pizza Industry
Facts," from PACKAGED FACTS Copyright ©
Packaged Facts, New York. Reprinted with
permission of Packaged Facts.

Roller coaster data used on pages 76 and 80 are
from Roller Coaster Census Report, copyright ©
1996–2005, Duane Marden. Used by permission.

The survey information on page 82 is from
National Geographic Survey 2000. Copyright ©
1999 NGS/National Geographic Society. All
Rights Reserved. Used by permission.

Note: Every effort has been made to locate the
copyright owner of the material reprinted in this
book. Omissions brought to our attention will be
corrected in subsequent editions.

STUDENT PAGE

Notes _____

_____

_____

_____

Labsheet 1.1

Blank Graphs

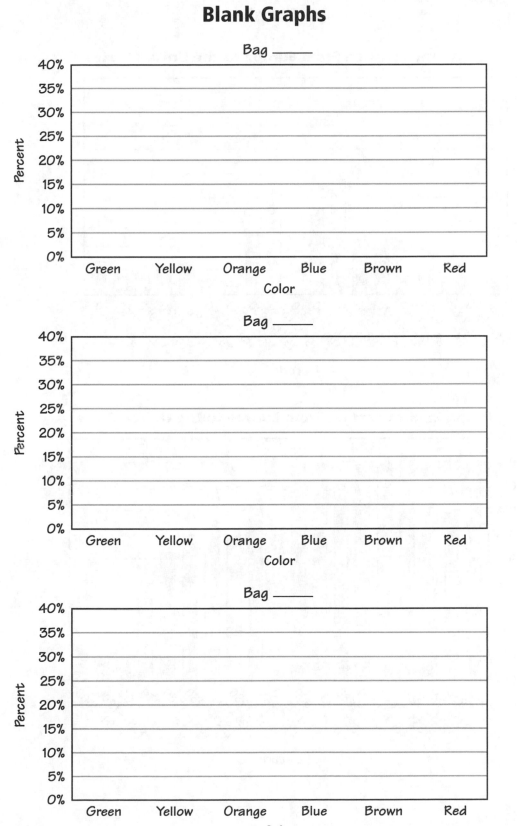

Labsheet 1.2

Graphs

Graph 1: Immigration From Europe to the United States

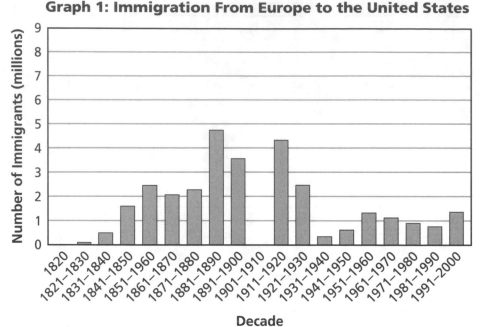

Graph 2: Immigration From Europe to the United States

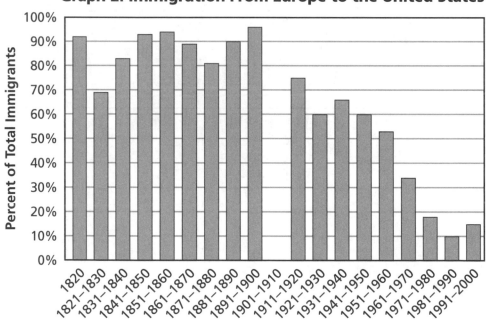

Labsheet 1ACE Exercises 8-10

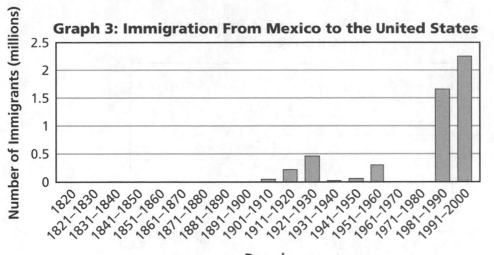

Graph 3: Immigration From Mexico to the United States

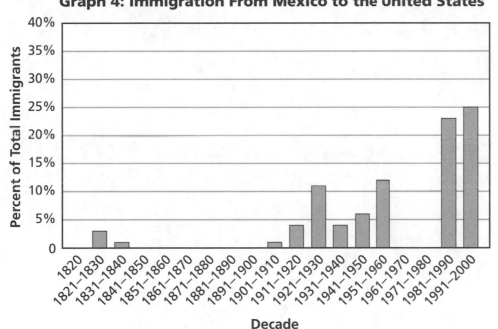

Graph 4: Immigration From Mexico to the United States

Labsheet 1ACE Exercise 22

··

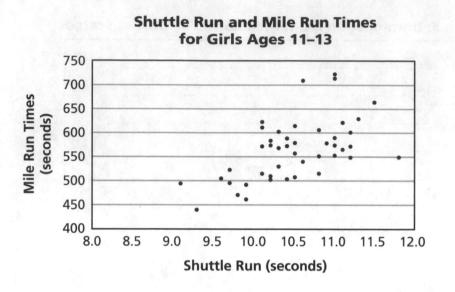

Shuttle Run and Mile Run Times
for Girls Ages 11–13

Name ______________________ Date ____________ Class ____________

Labsheet 2.1

Malaika's Project Scores

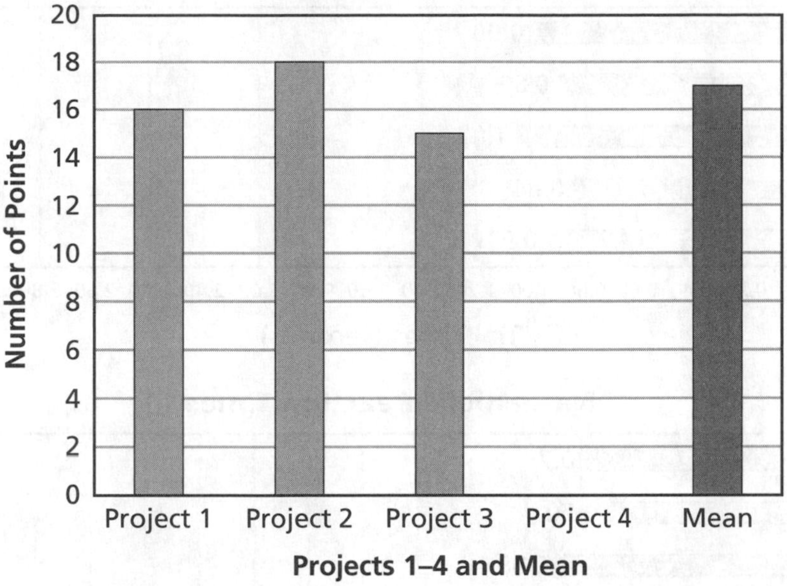
20
18
16
14
12
10
8
6
4
2
0
Number of Points
Project 1
Project 2
Project 3
Project 4
Mean
Projects 1–4 and Mean

Labsheet 3.2 Four Students

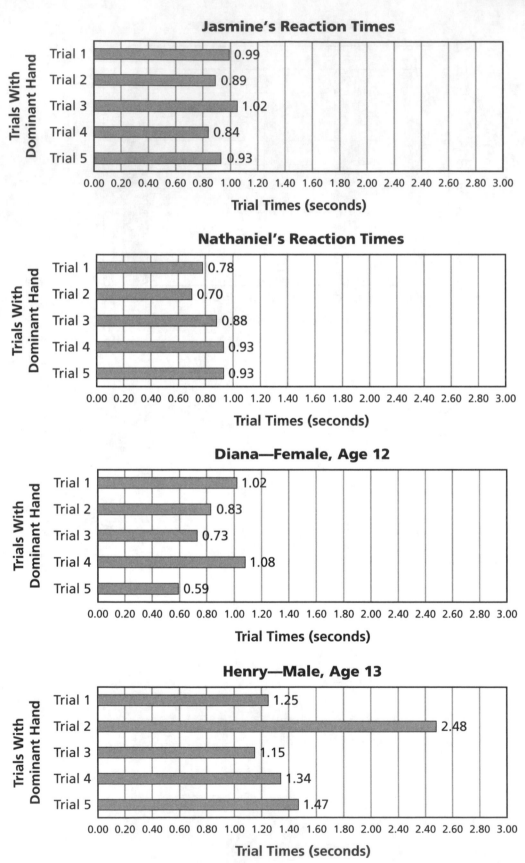

Jasmine's Reaction Times

Trial 1 — 0.99
Trial 2 — 0.89
Trial 3 — 1.02
Trial 4 — 0.84
Trial 5 — 0.93

Trials With Dominant Hand

0.00 0.20 0.40 0.60 0.80 1.00 1.20 1.40 1.60 1.80 2.00 2.40 2.40 2.60 2.80 3.00

Trial Times (seconds)

Nathaniel's Reaction Times

Trial 1 — 0.78
Trial 2 — 0.70
Trial 3 — 0.88
Trial 4 — 0.93
Trial 5 — 0.93

Trials With Dominant Hand

0.00 0.20 0.40 0.60 0.80 1.00 1.20 1.40 1.60 1.80 2.00 2.40 2.40 2.60 2.80 3.00

Trial Times (seconds)

Diana—Female, Age 12

Trial 1 — 1.02
Trial 2 — 0.83
Trial 3 — 0.73
Trial 4 — 1.08
Trial 5 — 0.59

Trials With Dominant Hand

0.00 0.20 0.40 0.60 0.80 1.00 1.20 1.40 1.60 1.80 2.00 2.40 2.40 2.60 2.80 3.00

Trial Times (seconds)

Henry—Male, Age 13

Trial 1 — 1.25
Trial 2 — 2.48
Trial 3 — 1.15
Trial 4 — 1.34
Trial 5 — 1.47

Trials With Dominant Hand

0.00 0.20 0.40 0.60 0.80 1.00 1.20 1.40 1.60 1.80 2.00 2.40 2.40 2.60 2.80 3.00

Trial Times (seconds)

Labsheet 3.3A Reaction Time Cards 1–4

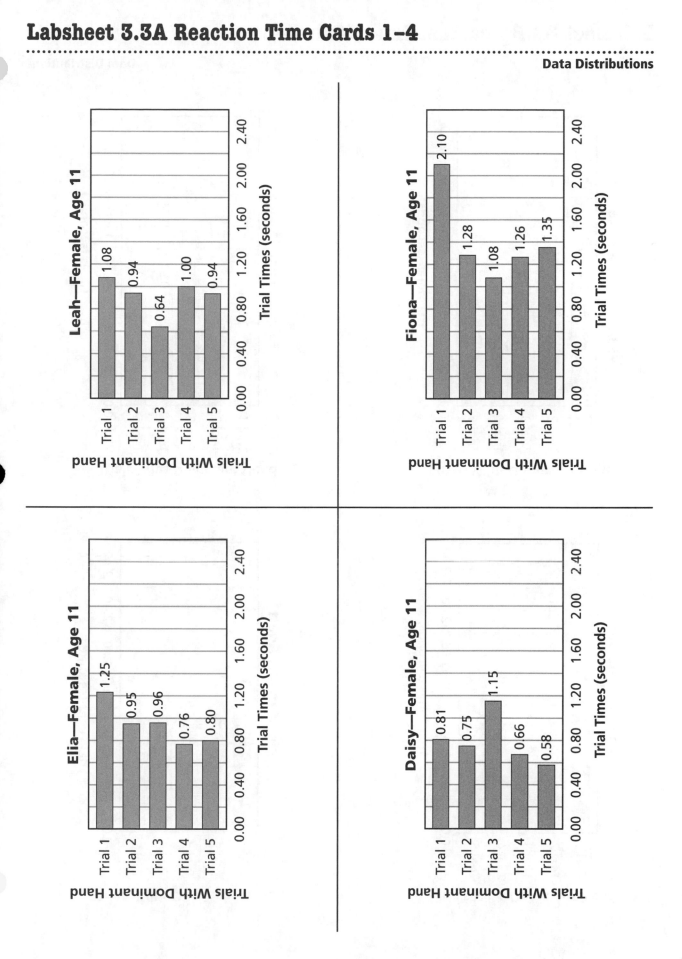

Labsheet 3.3B Reaction Time Cards 5–8

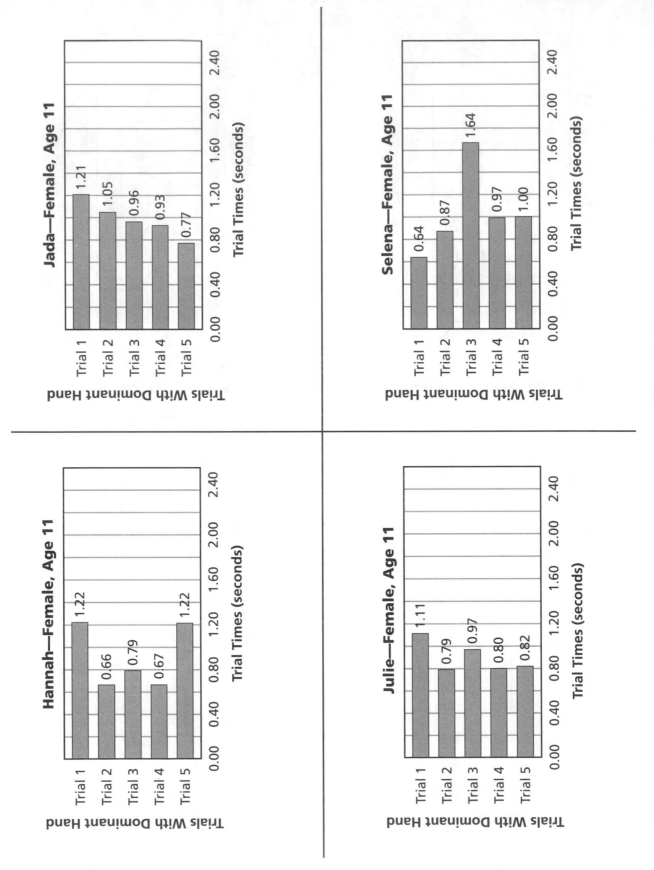

Labsheet 3.3C Reaction Time Cards 9–12

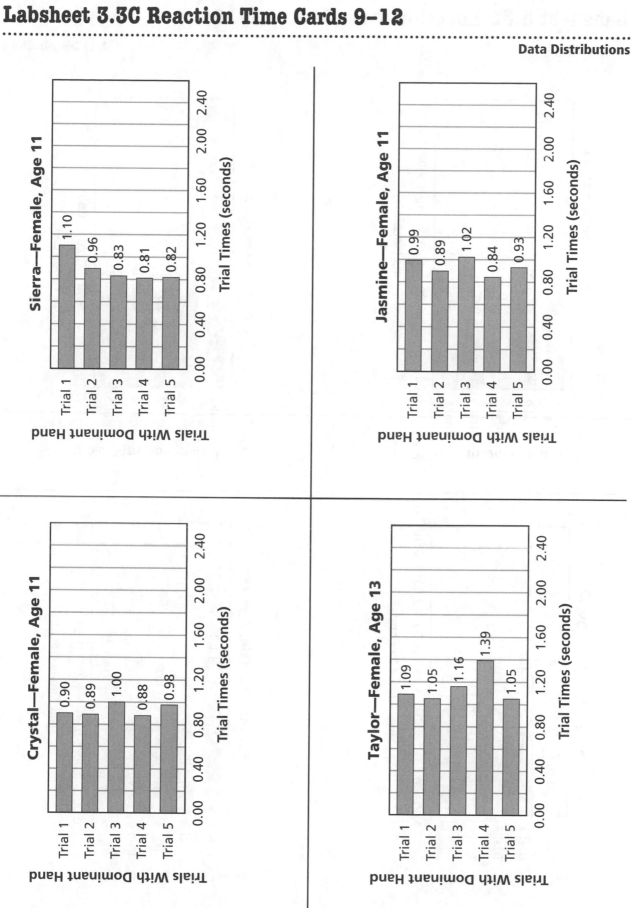

Labsheet 3.3D Reaction Time Cards 13–16

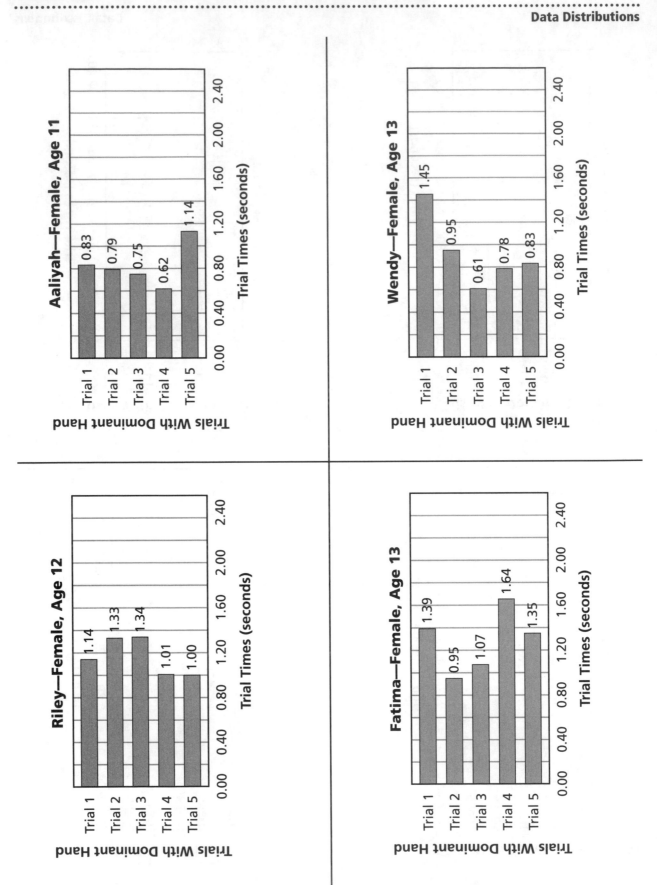

Labsheet 3.3E Reaction Time Cards 17–20

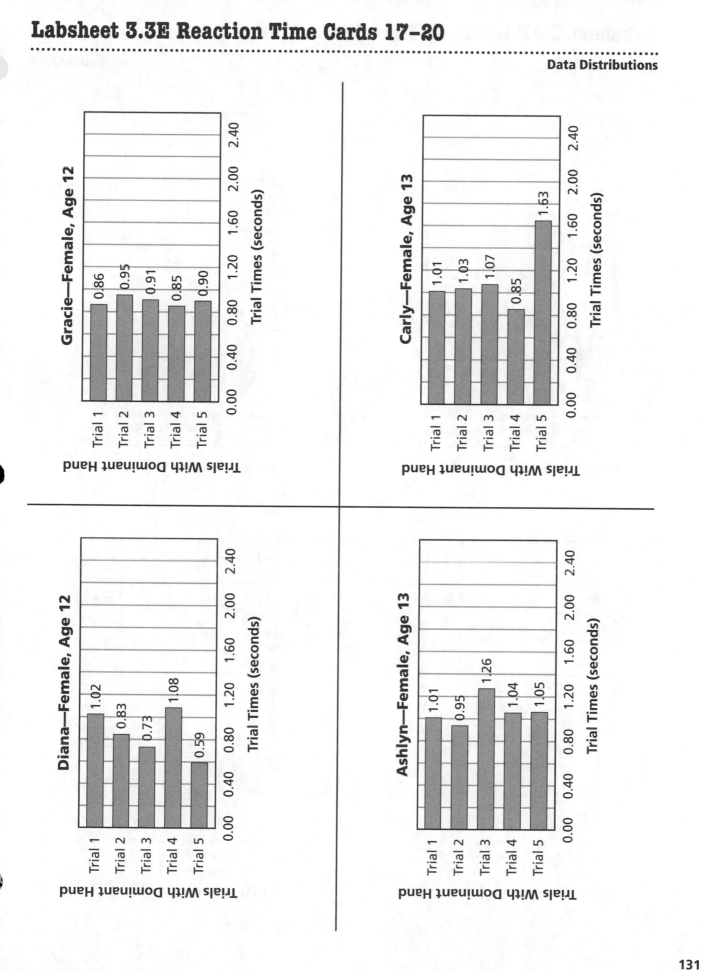

Labsheet 3.3F Reaction Time Cards 21-24

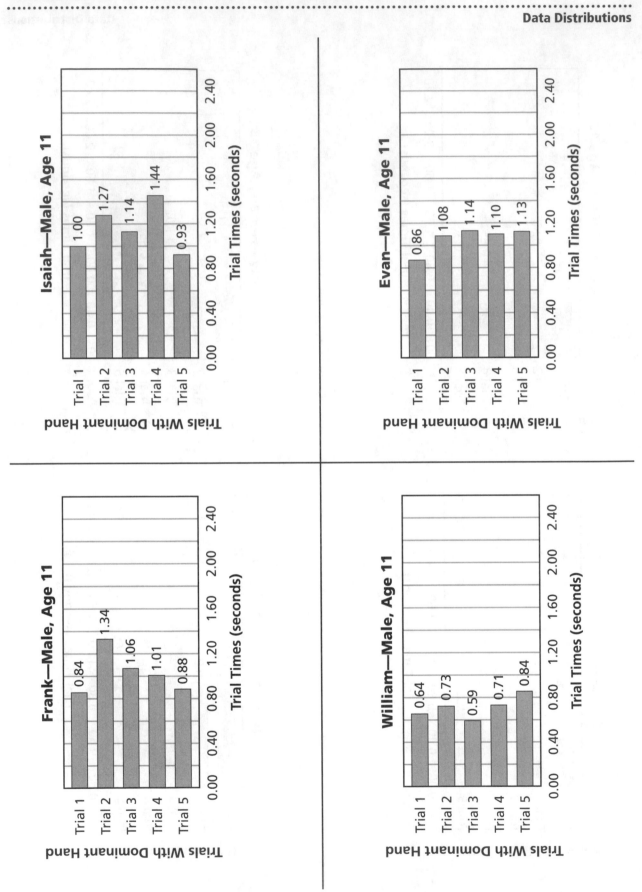

Labsheet 3.3G Reaction Time Cards 25–28

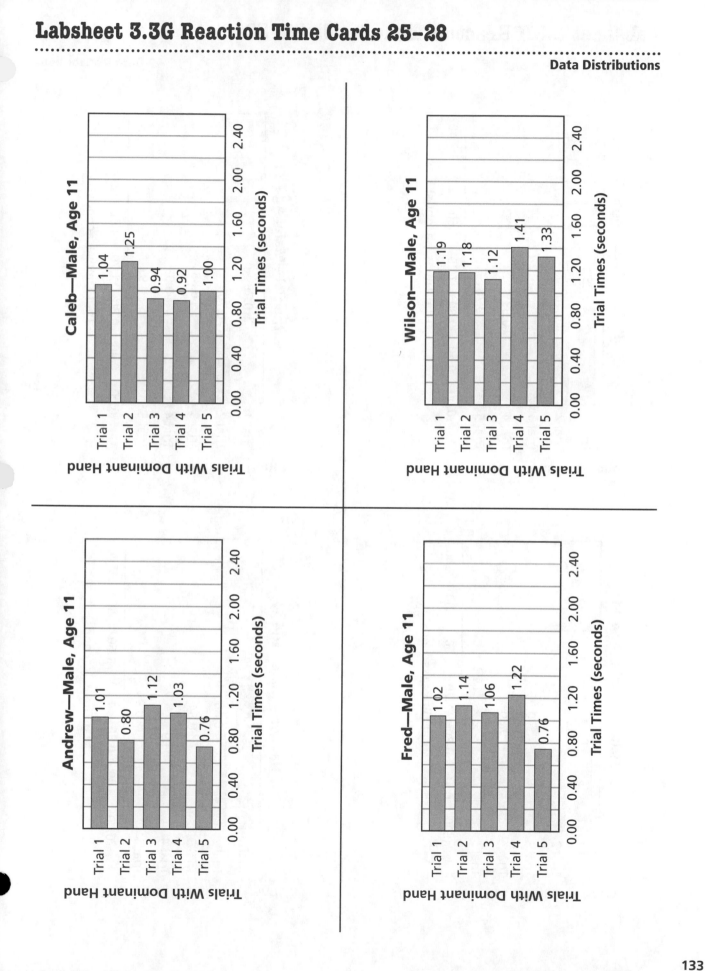

Labsheet 3.3H Reaction Time Cards 29–32

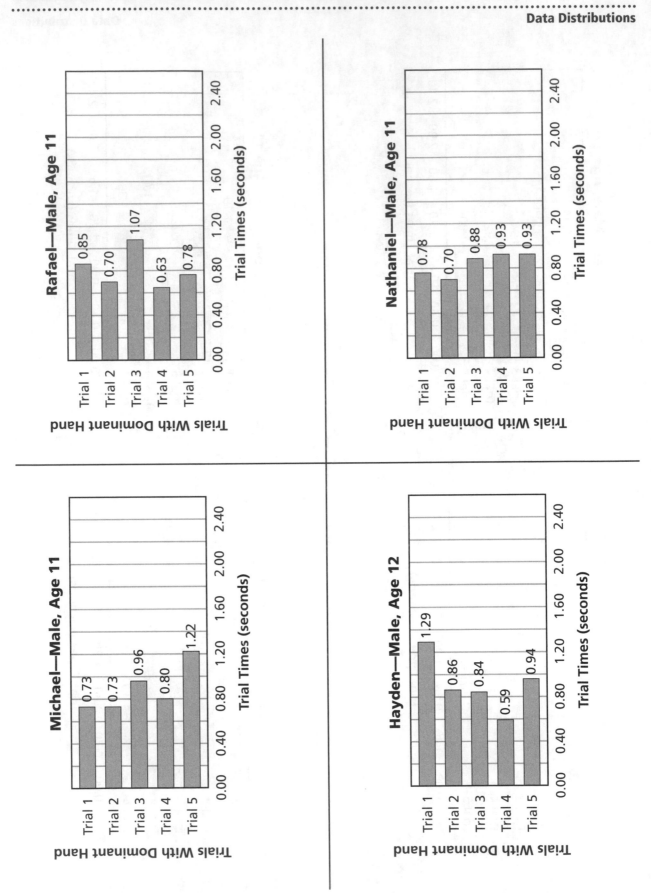

Labsheet 3.3J Reaction Time Cards 33–36

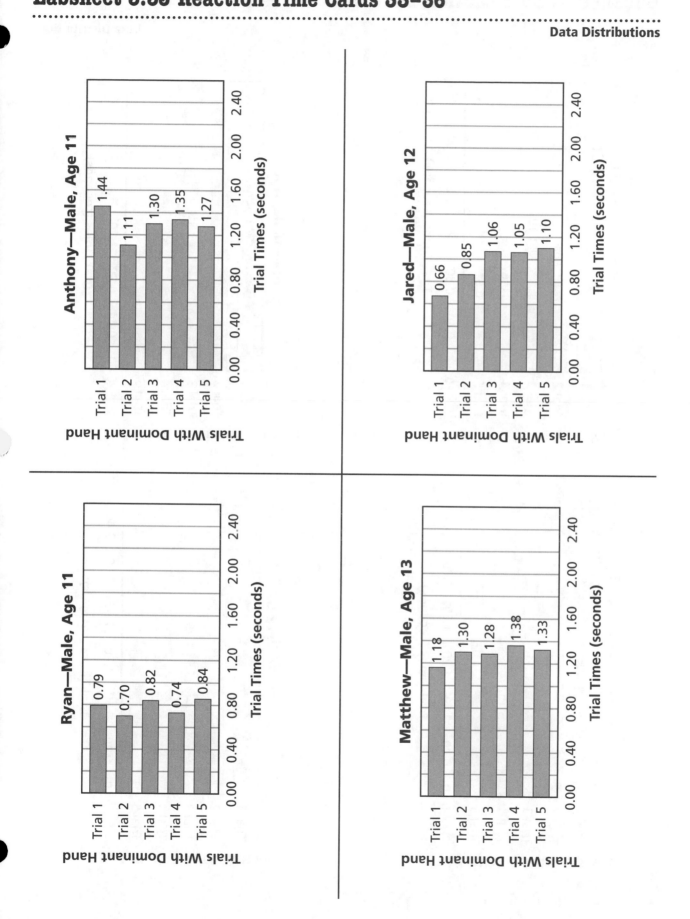

Anthony—Male, Age 11

Trials With Dominant Hand

Trial Times (seconds)

Trial 1: 1.44
Trial 2: 1.11
Trial 3: 1.30
Trial 4: 1.35
Trial 5: 1.27

Jared—Male, Age 12

Trials With Dominant Hand

Trial Times (seconds)

Trial 1: 0.66
Trial 2: 0.85
Trial 3: 1.06
Trial 4: 1.05
Trial 5: 1.10

Ryan—Male, Age 11

Trials With Dominant Hand

Trial Times (seconds)

Trial 1: 0.79
Trial 2: 0.70
Trial 3: 0.82
Trial 4: 0.74
Trial 5: 0.84

Matthew—Male, Age 13

Trials With Dominant Hand

Trial Times (seconds)

Trial 1: 1.18
Trial 2: 1.30
Trial 3: 1.28
Trial 4: 1.38
Trial 5: 1.33

Labsheet 3.3K Reaction Time Cards 37–40

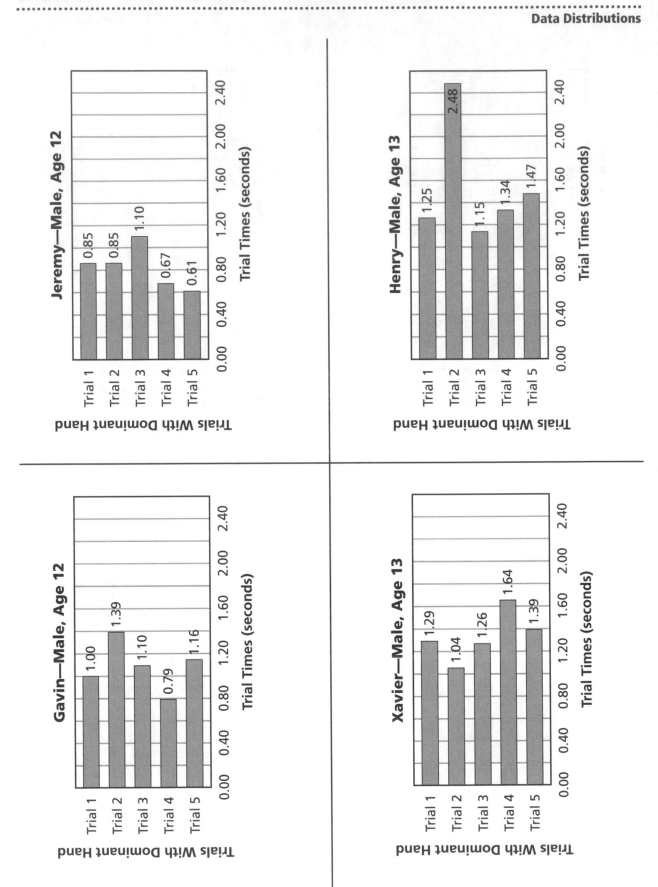

Jeremy—Male, Age 12

Trials With Dominant Hand

Trial 1: 0.85
Trial 2: 0.85
Trial 3: 1.10
Trial 4: 0.67
Trial 5: 0.61

Trial Times (seconds)

Henry—Male, Age 13

Trials With Dominant Hand

Trial 1: 1.25
Trial 2: 2.48
Trial 3: 1.15
Trial 4: 1.34
Trial 5: 1.47

Trial Times (seconds)

Gavin—Male, Age 12

Trials With Dominant Hand

Trial 1: 1.00
Trial 2: 1.39
Trial 3: 1.10
Trial 4: 0.79
Trial 5: 1.16

Trial Times (seconds)

Xavier—Male, Age 13

Trials With Dominant Hand

Trial 1: 1.29
Trial 2: 1.04
Trial 3: 1.26
Trial 4: 1.64
Trial 5: 1.39

Trial Times (seconds)

Labsheet 3.3L

Reaction Time Data

Name	Gender	Age		
Leah	F	eleven		
Elia	F	eleven		
Jada	F	eleven		
Hannah	F	eleven		
Sierra	F	eleven		
Fiona	F	eleven		
Daisy	F	eleven		
Selena	F	eleven		
Julie	F	eleven		
Jasmine	F	eleven		
Crystal	F	eleven		
Aaliyah	F	eleven		
Riley	F	twelve		
Gracie	F	twelve		
Diana	F	twelve		
Taylor	F	thirteen		
Wendy	F	thirteen		
Fatima	F	thirteen		
Carly	F	thirteen		
Ashlyn	F	thirteen		
Isaiah	M	eleven		
Frank	M	eleven		
Caleb	M	eleven		
Andrew	M	eleven		
Rafael	M	eleven		
Evan	M	eleven		
William	M	eleven		
Wilson	M	eleven		
Fred	M	eleven		
Nathaniel	M	eleven		
Michael	M	eleven		
Anthony	M	eleven		
Ryan	M	eleven		
Jeremy	M	twelve		
Gavin	M	twelve		
Hayden	M	twelve		
Jared	M	twelve		
Matthew	M	thirteen		
Henry	M	thirteen		
Xavier	M	thirteen		

Labsheet 3.3M

Reaction Times of 40 Students Sorted by Fastest Times

Student	Gender	Age	Fastest Time (s)	Slowest Time (s)	Trial 1 (s)	Trial 2 (s)	Trial 3 (s)	Trial 4 (s)	Trial 5 (s)
Daisy	F	eleven	0.58	1.15	0.81	0.75	1.15	0.66	0.58
Diana	F	twelve	0.59	1.08	1.02	0.83	0.73	1.08	0.59
William	M	eleven	0.59	0.84	0.64	0.73	0.59	0.71	0.84
Hayden	M	twelve	0.59	1.29	1.29	0.86	0.84	0.59	0.94
Wendy	F	thirteen	0.61	1.45	1.45	0.95	0.61	0.78	0.83
Jeremy	M	twelve	0.61	1.10	0.85	0.85	1.10	0.67	0.61
Aaliyah	F	eleven	0.62	1.14	0.83	0.79	0.75	0.62	1.14
Rafael	M	eleven	0.63	1.07	0.85	0.70	1.07	0.63	0.78
Leah	F	eleven	0.64	1.08	1.08	0.94	0.64	1.00	0.94
Selena	F	eleven	0.64	1.64	0.64	0.87	1.64	0.97	1.00
Hannah	F	eleven	0.66	1.22	1.22	0.66	0.79	0.67	1.22
Jared	M	twelve	0.66	1.10	0.66	0.85	1.06	1.05	1.10
Nathaniel	M	eleven	0.70	0.93	0.78	0.70	0.88	0.93	0.93
Ryan	M	eleven	0.70	0.84	0.79	0.70	0.82	0.74	0.84
Michael	M	eleven	0.73	1.22	0.73	0.73	0.96	0.80	1.22
Elia	F	eleven	0.76	1.25	1.25	0.95	0.96	0.76	0.80
Andrew	M	eleven	0.76	1.12	1.01	0.80	1.12	1.03	0.76
Fred	M	eleven	0.76	1.22	1.02	1.14	1.06	1.22	0.76
Jada	F	eleven	0.77	1.21	1.21	1.05	0.96	0.93	0.77
Julie	F	eleven	0.79	1.11	1.11	0.79	0.97	0.80	0.82
Gavin	M	twelve	0.79	1.39	1.00	1.39	1.06	0.79	1.16
Sierra	F	eleven	0.81	1.10	1.10	0.96	0.83	0.81	0.82
Jasmine	F	eleven	0.84	1.02	0.99	0.89	1.02	0.84	0.93
Frank	M	eleven	0.84	1.34	0.84	1.34	1.06	1.01	0.88
Carly	F	thirteen	0.85	1.63	1.01	1.03	1.07	0.85	1.63
Gracie	F	twelve	0.85	0.95	0.86	0.95	0.91	0.85	0.90
Evan	M	eleven	0.86	1.14	0.86	1.08	1.14	1.10	1.13
Crystal	F	eleven	0.88	1.00	0.90	0.89	1.00	0.88	0.98
Caleb	M	eleven	0.92	1.25	1.04	1.25	0.94	0.92	1.00
Isaiah	M	eleven	0.93	1.44	1.00	1.27	1.14	1.44	0.93
Fatima	F	thirteen	0.95	1.64	1.39	0.95	1.07	1.64	1.35
Ashlyn	F	thirteen	0.95	1.26	1.01	0.95	1.26	1.04	1.05
Riley	F	twelve	1.00	1.34	1.14	1.33	1.34	1.01	1.00
Xavier	M	thirteen	1.04	1.64	1.29	1.04	1.26	1.64	1.39
Taylor	F	thirteen	1.05	1.39	1.09	1.05	1.16	1.39	1.05
Fiona	F	eleven	1.08	2.10	2.10	1.28	1.08	1.26	1.35
Anthony	M	eleven	1.11	1.44	1.44	1.11	1.30	1.35	1.27
Wilson	M	eleven	1.12	1.41	1.19	1.18	1.12	1.41	1.33
Henry	M	thirteen	1.15	2.48	1.25	2.48	1.15	1.34	1.47
Matthew	M	thirteen	1.18	1.38	1.18	1.30	1.28	1.38	1.33

Labsheet 3.3N

Reaction Times of 40 Students Sorted by Gender

Student	Gender	Age	Fastest Time (s)	Slowest Time (s)	Trial 1 (s)	Trial 2 (s)	Trial 3 (s)	Trial 4 (s)	Trial 5 (s)
Daisy	F	eleven	0.58	1.15	0.81	0.75	1.15	0.66	0.58
Diana	F	twelve	0.59	1.08	1.02	0.83	0.73	1.08	0.59
Wendy	F	thirteen	0.61	1.45	1.45	0.95	0.61	0.78	0.83
Aaliyah	F	eleven	0.62	1.14	0.83	0.79	0.75	0.62	1.14
Leah	F	eleven	0.64	1.08	1.08	0.94	0.64	1.00	0.94
Selena	F	eleven	0.64	1.64	0.64	0.87	1.64	0.97	1.00
Hannah	F	eleven	0.66	1.22	1.22	0.66	0.79	0.67	1.22
Elia	F	eleven	0.76	1.25	1.25	0.95	0.96	0.76	0.80
Jada	F	eleven	0.77	1.21	1.21	1.05	0.96	0.93	0.77
Julie	F	eleven	0.79	1.11	1.11	0.79	0.97	0.80	0.82
Sierra	F	eleven	0.81	1.10	1.10	0.96	0.83	0.81	0.82
Jasmine	F	eleven	0.84	1.02	0.99	0.89	1.02	0.84	0.93
Carly	F	thirteen	0.85	1.63	1.01	1.03	1.07	0.85	1.63
Gracie	F	twelve	0.85	0.95	0.86	0.95	0.91	0.85	0.90
Crystal	F	eleven	0.88	1.00	0.90	0.89	1.00	0.88	0.98
Fatima	F	thirteen	0.95	1.64	1.39	0.95	1.07	1.64	1.35
Ashlyn	F	thirteen	0.95	1.26	1.01	0.95	1.26	1.04	1.05
Riley	F	twelve	1.00	1.34	1.14	1.33	1.34	1.01	1.00
Taylor	F	thirteen	1.05	1.39	1.09	1.05	1.16	1.39	1.05
Fiona	F	eleven	1.08	2.10	2.10	1.28	1.08	1.26	1.35
William	M	eleven	0.59	0.84	0.64	0.73	0.59	0.71	0.84
Hayden	M	twelve	0.59	1.29	1.29	0.86	0.84	0.59	0.94
Jeremy	M	twelve	0.61	1.10	0.85	0.85	1.10	0.67	0.61
Rafael	M	eleven	0.63	1.07	0.85	0.70	1.07	0.63	0.78
Jared	M	twelve	0.66	1.10	0.66	0.85	1.06	1.05	1.10
Nathaniel	M	eleven	0.70	0.93	0.78	0.70	0.88	0.93	0.93
Ryan	M	eleven	0.70	0.84	0.79	0.70	0.82	0.74	0.84
Michael	M	eleven	0.73	1.22	0.73	0.73	0.96	0.80	1.22
Andrew	M	eleven	0.76	1.12	1.01	0.80	1.12	1.03	0.76
Fred	M	eleven	0.76	1.22	1.02	1.14	1.06	1.22	0.76
Gavin	M	twelve	0.79	1.39	1.00	1.39	1.06	0.79	1.16
Frank	M	eleven	0.84	1.34	0.84	1.34	1.06	1.01	0.88
Evan	M	eleven	0.86	1.14	0.86	1.08	1.14	1.10	1.13
Caleb	M	eleven	0.92	1.25	1.04	1.25	0.94	0.92	1.00
Isaiah	M	eleven	0.93	1.44	1.00	1.27	1.14	1.44	0.93
Xavier	M	thirteen	1.04	1.64	1.29	1.04	1.26	1.64	1.39
Anthony	M	eleven	1.11	1.44	1.44	1.11	1.30	1.35	1.27
Wilson	M	eleven	1.12	1.41	1.19	1.18	1.12	1.41	1.33
Henry	M	thirteen	1.15	2.48	1.25	2.48	1.15	1.34	1.47
Matthew	M	thirteen	1.18	1.38	1.18	1.30	1.28	1.38	1.33

Labsheet 3.3P

Reaction Times of 40 Students Sorted by Slowest Times

Student	Gender	Age	Fastest Time (s)	Slowest Time (s)	Trial 1 (s)	Trial 2 (s)	Trial 3 (s)	Trial 4 (s)	Trial 5 (s)
William	M	eleven	0.59	0.84	0.64	0.73	0.59	0.71	0.84
Ryan	M	eleven	0.70	0.84	0.79	0.70	0.82	0.74	0.84
Nathaniel	M	eleven	0.70	0.93	0.78	0.70	0.88	0.93	0.93
Gracie	F	twelve	0.85	0.95	0.86	0.95	0.91	0.85	0.90
Crystal	F	eleven	0.88	1.00	0.90	0.89	1.00	0.88	0.98
Jasmine	F	eleven	0.84	1.02	0.99	0.89	1.02	0.84	0.93
Rafael	M	eleven	0.63	1.07	0.85	0.70	1.07	0.63	0.78
Diana	F	twelve	0.59	1.08	1.02	0.83	0.73	1.08	0.59
Leah	F	eleven	0.64	1.08	1.08	0.94	0.64	1.00	0.94
Sierra	F	eleven	0.81	1.10	1.10	0.96	0.83	0.81	0.82
Jeremy	M	twelve	0.61	1.10	0.85	0.85	1.10	0.67	0.61
Jared	M	twelve	0.66	1.10	0.66	0.85	1.06	1.05	1.10
Julie	F	eleven	0.79	1.11	1.11	0.79	0.97	0.80	0.82
Andrew	M	eleven	0.76	1.12	1.01	0.80	1.12	1.03	0.76
Aaliyah	F	eleven	0.62	1.14	0.83	0.79	0.75	0.62	1.14
Evan	M	eleven	0.86	1.14	0.86	1.08	1.14	1.10	1.13
Daisy	F	eleven	0.58	1.15	0.81	0.75	1.15	0.66	0.58
Jada	F	eleven	0.77	1.21	1.21	1.05	0.96	0.93	0.77
Hannah	F	eleven	0.66	1.22	1.22	0.66	0.79	0.67	1.22
Michael	M	eleven	0.73	1.22	0.73	0.73	0.96	0.80	1.22
Fred	M	eleven	0.76	1.22	1.02	1.14	1.06	1.22	0.76
Elia	F	eleven	0.76	1.25	1.25	0.95	0.96	0.76	0.80
Caleb	M	eleven	0.92	1.25	1.04	1.25	0.94	0.92	1.00
Ashlyn	F	thirteen	0.95	1.26	1.01	0.95	1.26	1.04	1.05
Hayden	M	twelve	0.59	1.29	1.29	0.86	0.84	0.59	0.94
Riley	F	twelve	1.00	1.34	1.14	1.33	1.34	1.01	1.00
Frank	M	eleven	0.84	1.34	0.84	1.34	1.06	1.01	0.88
Matthew	M	thirteen	1.18	1.38	1.18	1.30	1.28	1.38	1.33
Taylor	F	thirteen	1.05	1.39	1.09	1.05	1.16	1.39	1.05
Gavin	M	twelve	0.79	1.39	1.00	1.39	1.06	0.79	1.16
Wilson	M	eleven	1.12	1.41	1.19	1.18	1.12	1.41	1.33
Isaiah	M	eleven	0.93	1.44	1.00	1.27	1.14	1.44	0.93
Anthony	M	eleven	1.11	1.44	1.44	1.11	1.30	1.35	1.27
Wendy	F	thirteen	0.61	1.45	1.45	0.95	0.61	0.78	0.83
Carly	F	thirteen	0.85	1.63	1.01	1.03	1.07	0.85	1.63
Selena	F	eleven	0.64	1.64	0.64	0.87	1.64	0.97	1.00
Fatima	F	thirteen	0.95	1.64	1.39	0.95	1.07	1.64	1.35
Xavier	M	thirteen	1.04	1.64	1.29	1.04	1.26	1.64	1.39
Fiona	F	eleven	1.08	2.10	2.10	1.28	1.08	1.26	1.35
Henry	M	thirteen	1.15	2.48	1.25	2.48	1.15	1.34	1.47

Labsheet 3.3Q

Fastest Times for Each Gender

Fastest Reaction Times for Girls

Fastest Time (sec)

Median = 0.796   Mean = 0.8
Minimum Value = 0.58   Maximum Value = 1.08   Range = 0.50

Fastest Reaction Times for Boys

Fastest Time (sec)

Median = 0.8335   Mean = 0.775
Minimum Value = 0.59   Maximum Value = 1.18   Range = 0.59

Labsheet 3.3R

Slowest Times for Each Gender

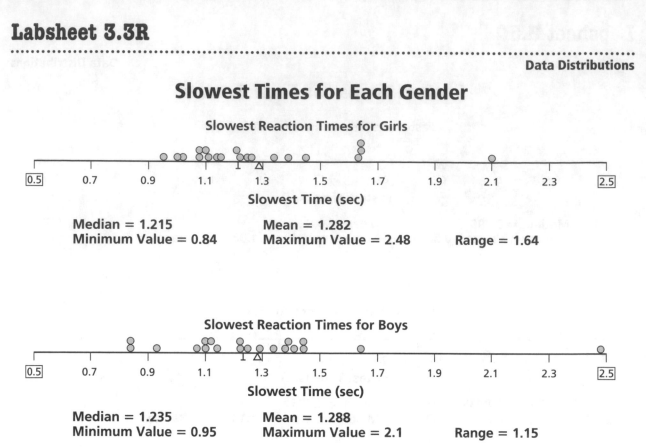

Slowest Reaction Times for Girls

Slowest Time (sec)

Median = 1.215   **Mean = 1.282**

Minimum Value = 0.84   **Maximum Value = 2.48**   **Range = 1.64**

Slowest Reaction Times for Boys

Slowest Time (sec)

Median = 1.235   **Mean = 1.288**

Minimum Value = 0.95   **Maximum Value = 2.1**   **Range = 1.15**

Labsheet 3.4A

Fastest and Slowest Reaction Times for All Students

Fastest Reaction Times for All Students

Fastest Time (sec)

Median = 0.79	**Mean = 0.81475**
Minimum Value = 0.58	**Maximum Value = 1.18** **Range = 0.60**

Slowest Reaction Times for All Students

Fastest Time (sec)

Median = 1.22	**Mean = 1.285**
Minimum Value = 0.84	**Maximum Value = 2.48** **Range = 1.64**

Labsheet 3.4B

Fastest and Slowest Reaction Times for All Students With Reference Lines

Fastest Reaction Times for All Students

Fastest Time (sec)

Median = 0.79   Mean = 0.81475

Minimum Value = 0.58   Maximum Value = 1.18   Range = 0.60

Slowest Reaction Times for All Students

Slowest Time (sec)

Median = 1.22   Mean = 1.285

Minimum Value = 0.84   Maximum Value = 2.48   Range = 1.64

Labsheet 3ACE Exercise 17

Water Use 2002–2005

Water Usage January–September 2005

Water Usage January–December 2004

Water Usage January–December 2003

Water Usage January–December 2002

Labsheet 4.2A

Roller Coaster Database (1–25)

	Name	Park	State	Year Opened	Max Drop (ft)	Max Height (ft)	Track Length (ft)	Top Speed (mi/h)	Duration (min)	Sharpest Angle of Descent (degrees)	Type
1	Hurricane	Adventureland	NY	1991	35	59	1,427	35	1.43		steel
2	Desperado	Buffalo Bill's Resort & Casino	NV	1994	225	209	5,843	80	2.72	60	steel
3	Kumba	Busch Gardens Tampa	FL	1993	135	143	3,978	60	2.90		steel
4	Loch Ness Monster	Busch Gardens Williamsburg	VA	1978	114	130	3,240	60	2.17	55	steel
5	Big Bad Wolf	Busch Gardens Williamsburg	VA	1984	80	100	2,800	48	3.00		steel
6	Wild Maus	Busch Gardens Williamsburg	VA	1995		46	1,217	22	1.50		steel
7	Alpengeist	Busch Gardens Williamsburg	VA	1997	170	195	3,828	67	3.17		steel
8	Apollo's Chariot	Busch Gardens Williamsburg	VA	1999	210	170	4,882	73	2.25	65	steel
9	Cedar Creek Mine Ride	Cedar Point	OH	1969	48	48	2,540	42	2.70		steel
10	Wildcat	Cedar Point	OH	1970	45	50	1,837	40	1.53	52	steel
11	Corkscrew	Cedar Point	OH	1976	65	85	2,050	48	2.00	45	steel
12	Gemini	Cedar Point	OH	1978	118	125	3,935	60	2.37	55	steel
13	Junior Gemini	Cedar Point	OH	1979	19	19	443	6	0.77		steel
14	Disaster Transport	Cedar Point	OH	1985	63	63	1,932	40	1.95		steel
15	Iron Dragon	Cedar Point	OH	1987	65	76	2,800	76	2.00	45	steel
16	Magnum XL-200	Cedar Point	OH	1989	194	205	5,106	72	2.00	62	steel
17	Raptor	Cedar Point	OH	1994	119	137	3,790	57	2.27	45	steel
18	Mantis	Cedar Point	OH	1996	137	145	3,900	60	2.67	52	steel
19	Woodstock's Express	Cedar Point	OH	1999	38	38	1,100	25	1.67		steel
20	Millennium Force	Cedar Point	OH	2000	300	310	6,595	92	2.75	80	steel
21	Top Thrill Dragster	Cedar Point	OH	2003	400	420	2,800	120	0.07	90	steel
22	Laser	Dorney Park and Wildwater Kingdom	PA	1986	93	93	2,200	52	2.00		steel
23	Steel Force	Dorney Park and Wildwater Kingdom	PA	1997	205	205	5,600	75	3.00	60	steel
24	Steamin' Demon	Great Escape	NY	1984	60	95	1,430	45	1.50	45	steel
25	Boomerang	Great Escape	NY	1997	125	125	875	48	1.80		steel

Labsheet 4.2B

Roller Coaster Database (26–50)

	Name	Park	State	Year Opened	Max Drop (ft)	Max Height (ft)	Track Length (ft)	Top Speed (mi/h)	Duration (min)	Sharpest Angle of Descent (degrees)	Type
26	Alpine Bobsled	Great Escape	NY	1998		65	1,650	35	1.67		steel
27	Nightmare at Crackaxle Canyon	Great Escape	NY	1999	40	45	1,772	35	1.50		steel
28	Sidewinder	Hersheypark	PA	1991	125	125	875	48	1.80		steel
29	Great Bear	Hersheypark	PA	1998	90	124	2,800	58	2.92	45	steel
30	Storm Runner	Hersheypark	PA	2004	180	150	2,600	75	0.83	90	steel
31	Incredible Hulk	Islands of Adventure	FL	1999	105	110	3,800	60	2.25		steel
32	Steel Phantom (Phantom's Revenge)	Kennywood Park	PA	1991	225	225	3,500	80	2.07		steel
33	Exterminator	Kennywood Park	PA	1999		40	1,400	22	2.50		steel
34	Whirlwind (N)	Knoebels Amusement Resort	PA	1984	48	64	1,200	37	1.37		steel
35	Jaguar!	Knott's Berry Farm	CA	1995	45	65	2,602	35	2.00	25	steel
36	Colossus the Fire Dragon	Lagoon	UT	1982	85	87	2,850	55	1.75		steel
37	Puff The Little Fire Dragon	Lagoon	UT	1985		11	198	16	0.83		steel
38	Wild Chipmunk	Lakeside Amusement Park	CO	1955	15	33	970	21	0.80		steel
39	Carolina Goldrusher	Paramount's Carowinds	NC	1973	43	43	2,397	35	2.28		steel
40	Vortex	Paramount's Carowinds	NC	1992	80	91	2,040	50	2.32		steel
41	Top Gun-The Jet Coaster	Paramount's Carowinds	NC	1999	113	113	2,956	62	2.78	50	steel
42	Demon	Paramount's Great America	CA	1976	90	95	2,130	45	1.75	54	steel
43	Greased Lightnin'	Paramount's Great America	CA	1977	135	142	849	55	0.50	70	steel
44	Green Slime Mine Car	Paramount's Great America	CA	1984		36	1,300	25	2.20		steel
45	Vortex	Paramount's Great America	CA	1991	80	91	1,920	45	2.23		steel
46	Top Gun	Paramount's Great America	CA	1993	91	100	2,260	50	2.43		steel
47	Invertigo	Paramount's Great America	CA	1998	138	138	985	55	1.50	45	steel
48	Shockwave	Paramount's Kings Dominion	VA	1986	84	95	2,231	50	2.00		steel
49	Anaconda	Paramount's Kings Dominion	VA	1991	144	144	2,700	50	2.67		steel
50	HyperSonic XLC	Paramount's Kings Dominion	VA	2001	133	165	1,560	80	0.30	90	steel

Labsheet 4.2C

Roller Coaster Database (51–75)

	Name	Park	State	Year Opened	Max Drop (ft)	Max Height (ft)	Track Length (ft)	Top Speed (mi/h)	Duration (min)	Sharpest Angle of Descent (degrees)	Type
51	King Cobra	Paramount's Kings Island	OH	1984	95	95	2,210	50	2.00	45	steel
52	Vortex	Paramount's Kings Island	OH	1987	138	148	3,800	55	2.50	55	steel
53	Adventure Express	Paramount's Kings Island	OH	1991	63	63	2,963	35	2.50		steel
54	Top Gun	Paramount's Kings Island	OH	1993	78	100	2,352	51	1.50	45	steel
55	Outer Limits: Flight of Fear	Paramount's Kings Island	OH	1996		78	2,705	54	2.40		steel
56	Two-Face: The Flip Side	Six Flags America	MD	1999	138	78	2,705	60	1.50		steel
57	Serpent	Six Flags AstroWorld	TX	1969	3	35	810	14	1.48		steel
58	Greased Lightnin'	Six Flags AstroWorld	TX	1978	138	138	849	55	0.50		steel
59	Viper	Six Flags AstroWorld	TX	1981	90	90	1,968	47	1.50	28	steel
60	XLR-8	Six Flags AstroWorld	TX	1984	52	81	3,000	45	3.00		steel
61	Ultra Twister	Six Flags AstroWorld	TX	1987	92	97	1,421	44	1.67	87	steel
62	Boomerang Coast to Coaster	Six Flags Darien Lake	NY	1998	125	125	875	48	1.80		steel
63	Superman Ride of Steel	Six Flags Darien Lake	NY	1999	205	208	5,400	70	2.50	78	steel
64	Sidewinder	Six Flags Elitch Gardens	CO	1980	47	47	502	45	1.10		steel
65	Boomerang Coast to Coaster	Six Flags Elitch Gardens	CO	1999	125	125	875	48	1.80		steel
66	Boomerang Coast to Coaster	Six Flags Fiesta Texas	TX	1999	125	125	875	48	1.80		steel
67	Great American Scream Machine	Six Flags Great Adventure	NJ	1989	155	173	3,800	68	2.37		steel
68	Batman the Ride	Six Flags Great Adventure	NJ	1993	87	100	2,693	50	2.00	50	steel
69	Viper	Six Flags Great Adventure	NJ	1995	75	89	1,670	48	2.22		steel
70	Skull Mountain	Six Flags Great Adventure	NJ	1996		41	1,377	33	1.67		steel
71	Nitro	Six Flags Great Adventure	NJ	2001	215	230	5,394	80	4.00		steel
72	Demon	Six Flags Great America	IL	1976	90	95	2,300	45	1.75	54	steel
73	Whizzer	Six Flags Great America	IL	1976	64	70	3,100	42	2.00		steel
74	Shockwave	Six Flags Great America	IL	1988	155	170	3,900	65	2.37	55	steel
75	Iron Wolf	Six Flags Great America	IL	1990	90	100	2,900	55	2.00		steel

Labsheet 4.2D

Roller Coaster Database (76–100)

	Name	Park	State	Year Opened	Max Drop (ft)	Max Height (ft)	Track Length (ft)	Top Speed (mi/h)	Duration (min)	Sharpest Angle of Descent (degrees)	Type
76	Invertigo	Six Flags Great America	IL	1998	138	138	985	55	1.50	45	steel
77	Spacely's Sprocket Rockets	Six Flags Great America	IL	1998	20	28	679	22	0.73		steel
78	Raging Bull	Six Flags Great America	IL	1999	200	208	5,057	73	2.50	65	steel
79	Chang	Six Flags Kentucky Kingdom	KY	1997	144	154	4,155	63	3.00	45	steel
80	Ninja	Six Flags Magic Mountain	CA	1988		60	2,700	55	1.50		steel
81	Viper (N)	Six Flags Magic Mountain	CA	1990	171	188	3,830	70	2.50		steel
82	Flashback	Six Flags Magic Mountain	CA	1992		86	1,900	35	2.00		steel
83	Batman the Ride	Six Flags Magic Mountain	CA	1994	87	105	2,700	50	2.00		steel
84	Superman The Escape	Six Flags Magic Mountain	CA	1997	415	415	1,315	100	0.47	90	steel
85	Goliath	Six Flags Magic Mountain	CA	2000	235	255	4,500	85	3.00	61	steel
86	Déjà vu	Six Flags Magic Mountain	CA	2001	177	192	1,204	66	1.53	90	steel
87	X	Six Flags Magic Mountain	CA	2002	200	196	3,610	76	2.00	89	steel
88	Superman Ultimate Escape	Six Flags Ohio	OH	2000	180	180	2,700	70	1.50	90	steel
89	Dahlonega Mine Train	Six Flags Over Georgia	GA	1967	47	37	2,323	28	2.85	45	steel
90	Mind Bender	Six Flags Over Georgia	GA	1978	56	80	3,253	50	2.55		steel
91	Viper	Six Flags Over Georgia	GA	1978	85	142	849	55	0.50	70	steel
92	Batman the Ride	Six Flags Over Georgia	GA	1997	87	109	2,693	50	2.00		steel
93	Georgia Scorcher	Six Flags Over Georgia	GA	1999	101	107	3,000	54	3.00	55	steel
94	Mr. Freeze	Six Flags Over Texas	TX	1998	218	218	1,300	70	0.55	90	steel
95	Mr. Freeze	Six Flags St. Louis	MO	1998	218	218	1,300	70	0.55	90	steel
96	Wild Thing	Vallyfair!	MN	1996	207	207	5,469	74	3.00	60	steel
97	Space Mountain	Walt Disney World-Magic Kingdom	FL	1975	18	90	3,196	27	2.58		steel
98	Orient Express	Worlds of Fun	MO	1980	115	117	3,470	50	2.50	55	steel
99	Mamba	Worlds of Fun	MO	1998	205	205	5,600	75	3.00		steel
100	Boomerang	Worlds of Fun	MO	2000	125	125	875	48	1.00		steel

Labsheet 4.2E

Roller Coaster Database (101–125)

	Name	Park	State	Year Opened	Max Drop (ft)	Max Height (ft)	Track Length (ft)	Top Speed (mi/h)	Duration (min)	Sharpest Angle of Descent (degrees)	Type
101	Cyclone	Astroland	NY	1927	85	85	2,640	60	1.83	59	wood
102	Blue Streak	Cedar Point	OH	1964	72	78	2,558	40	1.75	45	wood
103	Mean Streak	Cedar Point	OH	1991	155	161	5,427	65	3.22	52	wood
104	Ozark Wildcat	Celebration City	MO	2003	80	80	2,600	45	1.50		wood
105	New Mexico Rattler	Cliff's Amusement Park	NM	2002	75	80	2,750	47	1.25	52	wood
106	Thunderhawk	Dorney Park	PA	1923	65	80	2,767	45	1.30		wood
107	Wildcat	Frontier City	OK	1991	65	75	2,653	60	2.17		wood
108	Excalibur	Funtown Splashtown U.S.A.	ME	1998	82	108	2,700	62	1.97	53	wood
109	Comet	Great Escape	NY	1947	87	95	4,197	55	2.00		wood
110	Comet	Hersheypark	PA	1946	78	84	3,360	50	1.75		wood
111	Lightning Racer	Hersheypark	PA	2000	85	90	3,400	51	2.33		wood
112	Raven	Holiday World	IN	1995	85	70	2,731	48	1.67		wood
113	Jack Rabbit	Kennywood Park	PA	1920	40	40	2,132	45	1.25	45	wood
114	Thunderbolt	Kennywood Park	PA	1924	95	70	2,887	55	1.50		wood
115	Phoenix	Knoebels	PA	1985	72	78	3,200	45	2.00		wood
116	Twister	Knoebels	PA	1999	90	102	3,900	52	2.17		wood
117	Ghost Rider	Knott's Berry Farm	CA	1998	108	118	4,533	56	2.67	51	wood
118	Wildcat	Lake Compounce	CT	1927	78	85	2,746	44	1.25		wood
119	Boulder Dash	Lake Compounce	CT	2000	115	145	4,752	65	2.50		wood
120	Leap the Dips	Lakemont Park	PA	1902	9	41	1,452	10	1.00	25	wood
121	Shivering Timbers	Michigan's Adventure	MI	1998	120	122	5,383	57	2.50	53	wood
122	Great White	Morey's Piers	NJ	1996	100	110	3,300	50	2.00		wood
123	Cyclops	Mt. Olympus Theme Park	WI	1995	75	70	1,900	58	1.00		wood
124	Zeus	Mt. Olympus Theme Park	WI	1997	85	90	2,900	60	1.42		wood
125	Hurricane	Myrtle Beach Pavilion	SC	2000	100	102	3,800	55	2.00	53	wood

Labsheet 4.2F Roller Coaster Database (126–150)

Roller Coaster Database (126–150)

	Name	Park	State	Year Opened	Max Drop (ft)	Max Height (ft)	Track Length (ft)	Top Speed (mi/h)	Duration (min)	Sharpest Angle of Descent (degrees)	Type
126	Scooby-Doo's Ghoster Coaster	Paramount's Carowinds	NC	1976	35	40	1,356	35	1.67		wood
127	Rebel Yell	Paramount's Kings Dominion	VA	1975	85	86	3,368	55	2.25	50	wood
128	Beastie	Paramount's Kings Island	OH	1972	35	38	1,350	30	1.33	45	wood
129	Racer	Paramount's Kings Island	OH	1972	83	88	3,415	60	2.50	45	wood
130	Beast	Paramount's Kings Island	OH	1979	141	105	7,400	65	3.67	45	wood
131	Son of Beast	Paramount's Kings Island	OH	2000	214	218	7,032	78	2.33	55	wood
132	Coaster Thrill Ride	Puyallup Fair	WA	1935	52	55	2,650	50	1.75	63	wood
133	Tremors	Silverwood Theme Park	ID	1999	103	100	3,000	60	1.67		wood
134	Texas Cyclone	Six Flags AstroWorld	TX	1976	80	93	3,184	60	2.25	53	wood
135	Rattler	Six Flags Fiesta Texas	TX	1992	124	180	5,080	65	2.41	66	wood
136	Rolling Thunder	Six Flags Great Adventure	NJ	1979	85	96	3,200	55	3.00	45	wood
137	American Eagle	Six Flags Great America	IL	1981	147	127	4,650	66	2.38	55	wood
138	Viper	Six Flags Great America	IL	1995	80	100	3,458	50	1.75	50	wood
139	Colossus	Six Flags Magic Mountain	CA	1978	115	125	4,325	62	3.08		wood
140	Psyclone	Six Flags Magic Mountain	CA	1991	78	95	2,970	50	1.83	53	wood
141	Great American Scream Machine	Six Flags Over Georgia	GA	1973	89	105	3,800	57	2.00	45	wood
142	Georgia Cyclone	Six Flags Over Georgia	GA	1990	79	95	2,970	50	1.80	53	wood
143	Judge Roy Scream	Six Flags Over Texas	TX	1980	65	71	2,670	53	1.50		wood
144	Texas Giant	Six Flags Over Texas	TX	1990	137	143	4,920	62	2.50	53	wood
145	Screamin' Eagle	Six Flags St. Louis	MO	1976	92	110	3,872	62	2.50		wood
146	Boss	Six Flags St. Louis	MO	2000	150	122	5,051	66	2.00	52	wood
147	Rampage	VisionLand	AL	1998	102	120	3,500	56	1.65		wood
148	Comet	Waldameer Park	PA	1951	25	37	1,300	25	1.50		wood
149	Cheetah	Wild Adventures	GA	2001	91	86	3,120	62	1.63	55	wood
150	Timber Wolf	Worlds of Fun	MO	1989	95	100	4,230	45	2.22		wood

Labsheet 4.2G

Comparing Steel and Wood Coasters (1)

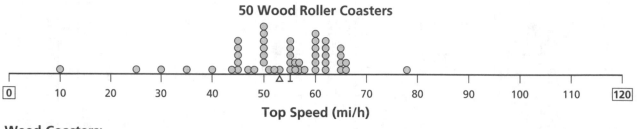

100 Steel Roller Coasters

Top Speed (mi/h)

Steel Coasters:
Mean = 53.08 mi/h   **Median = 50 mi/h**   **Minimum Value = 6 mi/h**   **Maximum Value = 120 mi/h**

50 Wood Roller Coasters

Top Speed (mi/h)

Wood Coasters:
Mean = 53.18 mi/h   **Median = 55 mi/h**   **Minimum Value = 10 mi/h**   **Maximum Value = 78 mi/h**

Labsheet 4.2H

Comparing Steel and Wood Coasters (2)

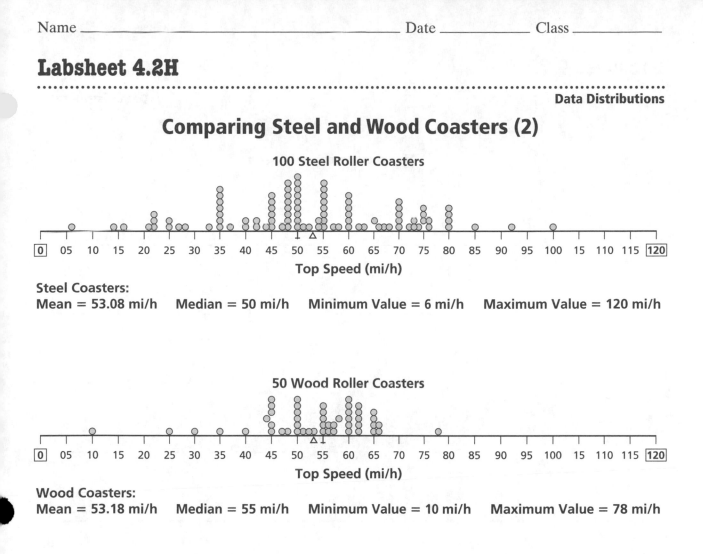

100 Steel Roller Coasters

Top Speed (mi/h)

Steel Coasters:

Mean = 53.08 mi/h   Median = 50 mi/h   Minimum Value = 6 mi/h   Maximum Value = 120 mi/h

50 Wood Roller Coasters

Top Speed (mi/h)

Wood Coasters:

Mean = 53.18 mi/h   Median = 55 mi/h   Minimum Value = 10 mi/h   Maximum Value = 78 mi/h

Labsheet 4.2J

Is Maximum Drop Related to Top Speed?

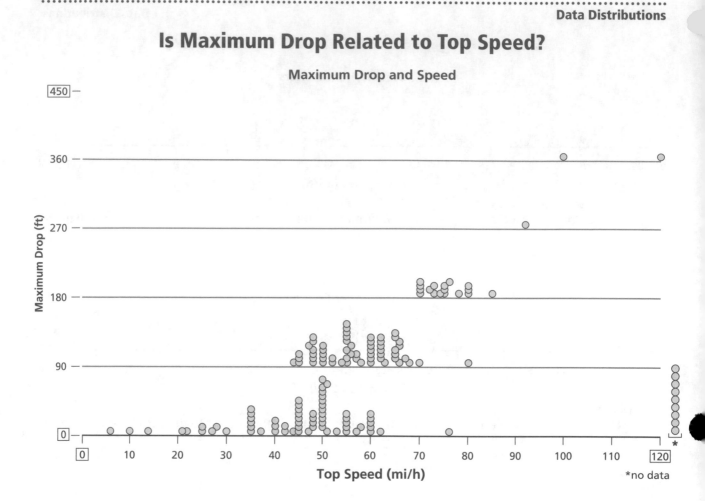

Maximum Drop and Speed

Labsheet 4.2K

Is Maximum Height Related to Top Speed?

Maximum Height and Speed

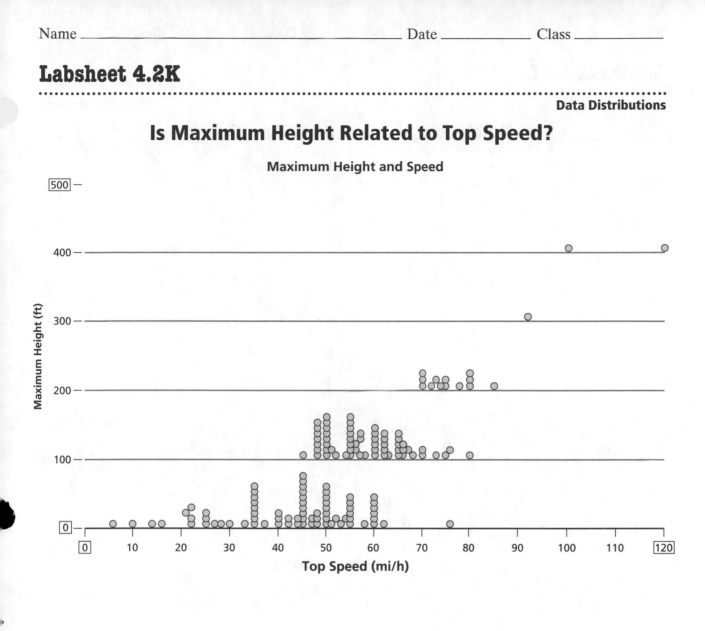

Labsheet 4.2L

Is Track Length Related to Top Speed?

Track Length and Speed

Labsheet 4.2M

Is Duration of a Ride Related to Top Speed?

Duration of Ride and Speed

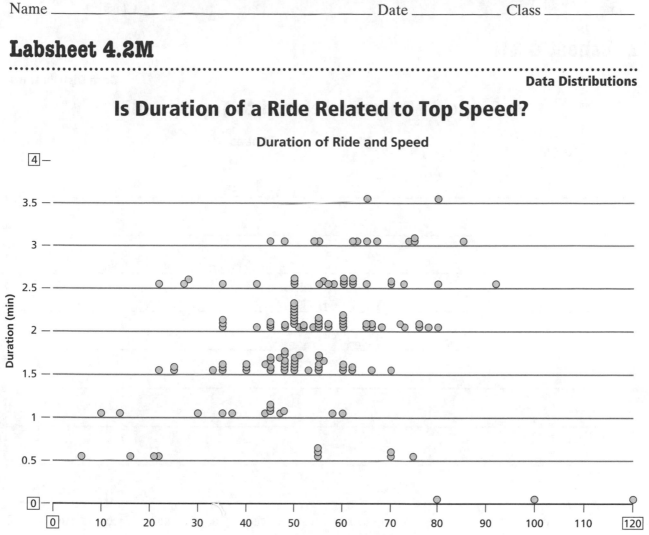

Labsheet 4.2N

Is Angle of Descent Related to Top Speed?

Angle Descent and Speed

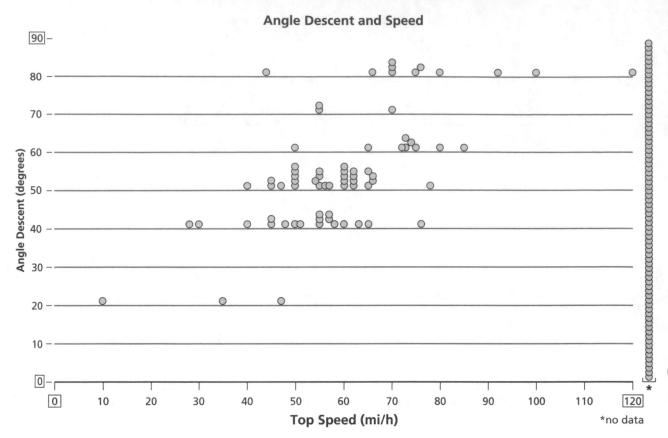

*no data

Labsheet 4.2P

Is Year Opened Related to Top Speed?

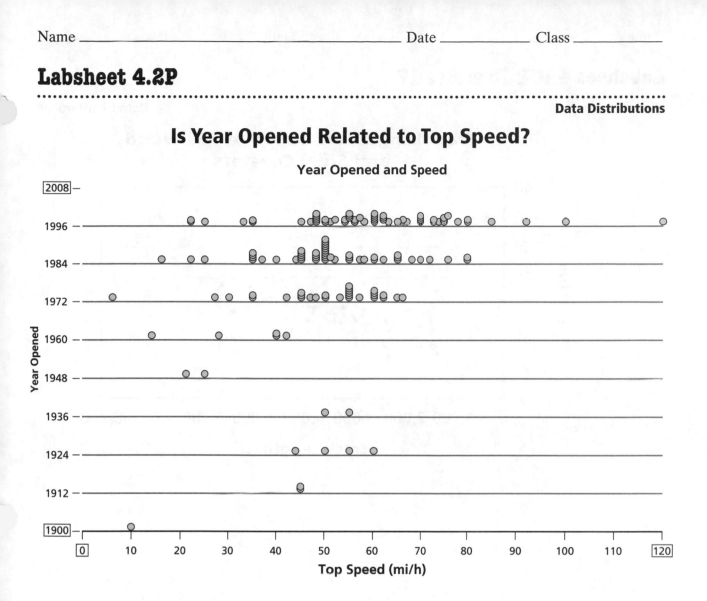

Year Opened and Speed

Labsheet 4ACE Exercise 17

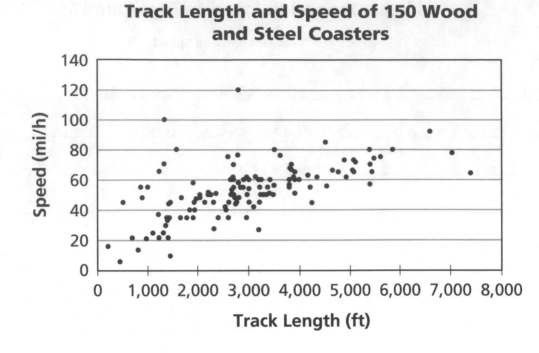

Track Length and Speed of 150 Wood and Steel Coasters

Mathematical Goals

_____

_____

_____

_____

Launch

_____

_____

_____

_____

_____

_____

_____

Materials

Explore

_____

_____

_____

_____

_____

_____

_____

Materials

Summarize

_____

_____

_____

_____

_____

_____

_____

Materials

Glossary

A

attribute A property, quality, or characteristic of a person, place, or thing. For example, each person has attributes such as height, weight, name, gender, or eye color.

C

categorical data Data that can be placed into categories. For example, "gender" is categorical data and the categories are "male" and "female." Also, if you asked people in which month they were born or what their favorite class is, they would answer with names, which would be categorical data. However, if you ask them how many siblings they have, they would answer with numbers, not categories.

counts Data that give the number of occurrences (the frequency) of an attribute, for example, the number of occurrences of 3-child families.

D

distribution Data sets collected from observation or experiment. They can be described by measures of center and variability.

G

graphs Any pictorial device, such as a scatter plot or bar graph, used to display categorical or numerical data.

L

line plot Each data value is represented as a dot or an "X" positioned over a labeled number line. The line plot made with dots is sometimes referred to as a dot plot. (Figure 1)

M

mean (1) The result if all the data values are combined and then redistributed evenly among individuals so that each has the same amount. (2) The number that is the balance point in a distribution of numerical values. The mean is influenced by all values of the distribution, including outliers. It is often called the average and is the sum of the numerical values divided by the number of values. For example, the mean of 1, 3, 7, 8, and 25 is 8.8 because the sum of the values, 44, is divided by the number of values, 5.

measures Data obtained by making measurements. For example, we can measure the height of each person in a class.

measures of center *See mean, median, and mode.*

median The median is the number that is the midpoint of an ordered set of numerical data. This means that at least half of the data values lie at or above the median and at least half lie at or below it. For example, the median of 1, 3, 7, 8, and 25 is 7 because that number is third in the list of five data values. The median of 2, 3, 4, 4, 4, 5, 6, 12, and 13 is 4 because that number is fifth in the list of nine data values.

When a distribution contains an even number of data values, the median is computed by finding the average of the two middle data values in an ordered list of the data values. For example, the median of 1, 3, 7, 8, 25, and 30 is 7.5 because the data values 7 and 8 are third and fourth in the list of six data values.

Figure 1

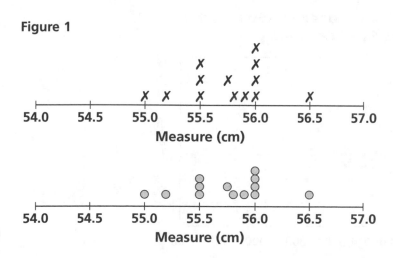

mode The data value or category occurring with the greatest frequency. For example, the mode of 3, 4, 7, 11, 11, 11, 3, and 4 is 11.

numerical data Data consisting of numbers, not categories, such as the heights of students.

ordered value bar graph A value bar graph in which data values are arranged in increasing (or decreasing) order of length. (Figure 2)

outliers Unusually high or low data values in a distribution.

range A number found by subtracting the minimum value from the maximum value. If you know the range of the data is 12 grams of sugar per serving, you know that the difference between the minimum and maximum values is 12 grams.

scatter plot A coordinate graph showing the relationship, if any, between two variables, for example, roller coaster track length and speed. (Figure 3)

Figure 2

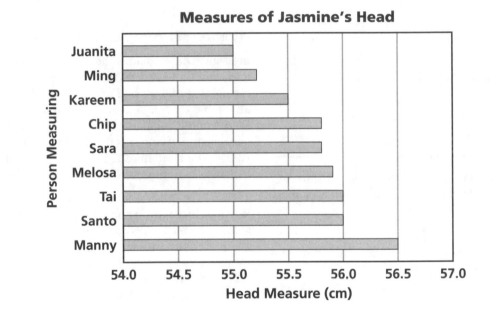

Measures of Jasmine's Head

Figure 3

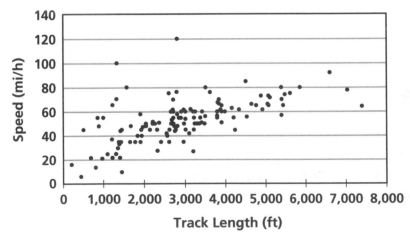

Track Length and Speed of 150 Wood and Steel Coasters

value of an attribute Values are the data that occur for each individual case of an attribute—that is, the number of red candies recorded for the attribute red from one bag of M&M candies or the time in seconds recorded for the attribute Fastest Time for one student who played the computer reaction time game.

value bar graph Each data value is represented by a separate bar whose relative length corresponds to the magnitude of that data value. (Figure 4)

variability of a set of numerical data An indication of how widely spread or closely clustered the data values are. Range, minimum and maximum values, and clusters in the distribution give some indication of variability.

Figure 4

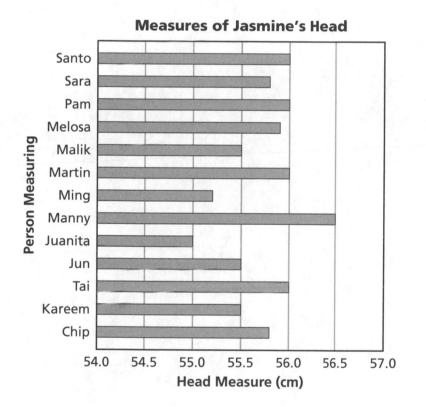

Measures of Jasmine's Head

Using *TinkerPlots*™ With CMP Problems:
Teacher's Guide

Using *TinkerPlots*™

Problems 2.4, 3.3., 3.4, and 4.2 in *Data Distributions* may be explored using *TinkerPlots*™ software.

For each problem, the discussion and any relevant Teacher Notes are worded specifically for use with *TinkerPlots*. When students are directed to make graphs, it is anticipated that they will make dot plots. Very specific directions follow for *your* use so you know at least one way to use the software to accomplish each task. We want students to experiment but the directions will help if they seem to get bogged down.

For the Teacher:
Recording and Printing Out Screens

Students can complete each part of a problem using *TinkerPlots* and then print out the *TinkerPlots* workspace. You may wish to display a transparency of Labsheet A.1 to show how to print.

Students select Page Setup from the file menu and set the screen to print in Landscape and at a scale of 80%. They can open a text box and record their answers to a part of the problem. Then, if they select Show Page Breaks from the file menu, they see where the page edges are; they can move their plot(s) and text box so that all can be printed on one page. Students can print a screen copy after each part of a problem.

Median and Mean and Shapes of Distributions

Goals

- Read and understand line plots used to display data distributions
- Recognize that variability occurs whenever data are collected
- Use properties of distributions to describe the variability in a given data set
- Understand when and how changes in data values in a distribution affect the median or the mean
- Relate the shape of a distribution to the location of its mean and median

Have students work in pairs, open *TinkerPlots*, and use Investigation 2 Getting Started With *TinkerPlots* in *Using TinkerPlots™ With CMP Problems: Student Edition* (page A5).

Launch 2.4

Introduce the problem by discussing when means and medians are similar or are different in the two cereal and shelves distributions.

Suggested Question Ask:

- *What is it about the data distribution that impacts where the mean or median might be located?*

Have students work in pairs to continue with Question A.

Explore 2.4

Students will need to set up their own distribution using *TinkerPlots* (one distribution per pair of students). Make sure that they make a prediction before they make a set of changes. For Question A, part (1), only the mean will change in value. Once students make this observation, as you visit with groups, ask:

- *Why do you think the median did not change in this situation?* (Answers will vary; students may not yet have enough information to sort this out. The median separates the data into two equal-size groups; to make a change, you will need to change a data value so that it "crosses the median.")

Have students continue with the rest of the problem, being deliberate in making a prediction, changing one data value at a time, and then making sure they see what the change created. In Question A, part (2), the median will shift when students move to part (b). Hopefully, students will be able to anticipate this change. Before part (c), their graphs should look like the graph below, where two of the three data values have been changed to 8 grams.

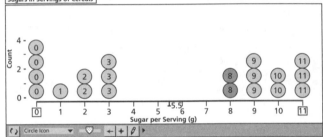

Suggested Question As you visit groups, ask:

- *Why has the median changed to 5.5?* (Because there are 10 data values before and 10 data values after this value that is halfway between 3 and 8 grams.)

After Question A, part (2c), their graphs should look like the graph below, where three data values have been changed to 8 grams.

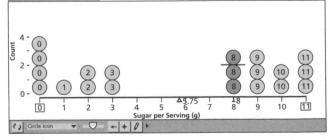

Suggested Question As you visit groups, ask:

- *Why has the median changed to 8?* (Because there are 10 data values before and 10 data values after the median of 8.)

Have students continue to explore Questions A and B. For Question B, part (2), they begin with their graph from Question A, part (2c). They can make any kinds of distributions they would like, using 20 cases (dot icons on graph), and can add cases.

Stop and do a summary of findings from these two parts once students have had time to explore.

Launch Question C by looking at the distributions in the Student Edition. Have students complete this part of the problem.

Summarize 2.4

The goal is to summarize how the mean and median behave and how easily changed a measure is or is not.

In conducting the summary when students have used *TinkerPlots*, teachers have found it helpful to go through the actions of Question A using *TinkerPlots* and, at the same time, use a strip of 20 stick-on notes, each with one of the current data values written on it. So, initially, the distribution is:

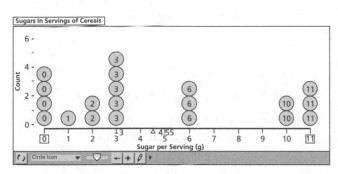

And the stick-on note display on a nearby board would look like this:

Have students locate the median and draw an arrow to indicate its location.

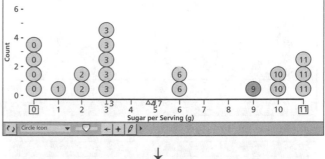

Then, as each change is made to the *TinkerPlots* graph, make the associated change to the stick-on notes display so that the students can begin to reason about when the mean is affected and when the median is affected. For example, here is the associated sequence of changes in data values for the actions carried out in Question A.

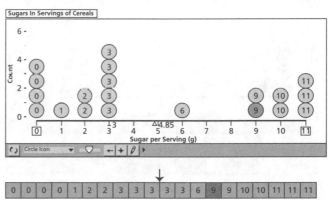

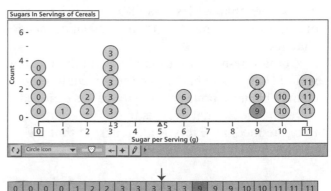

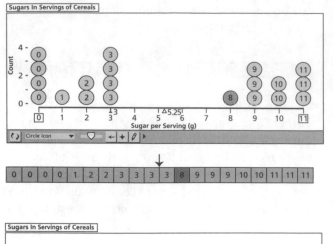

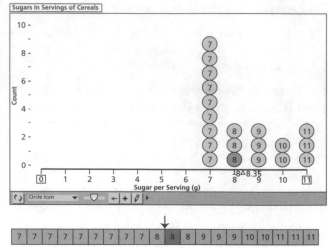

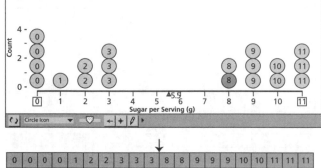

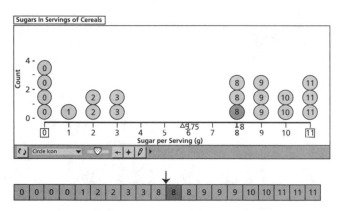

One teacher asked his students at this point, "What would happen if I changed each of the data values that are less than 8 grams to 7 grams of sugar per serving? Would the median or mean change?"

About one-half of the class thought the median would change and half argued that it could not change because none of the data values changed were changed to data values that were greater than the median. Every student agreed that the mean would change its value.

Classroom Dialogue Model

Teacher *One of the goals of this problem is to look at what happens to the median and mean when we replace data values in a data set. When you look at what we've done in this problem, what can you say about how the mean changes?*

Student 1 *The mean changed and got bigger when we replaced some of the data with larger values. It started moving to the right.*

Student 2 *Whenever we change a data value, the mean changes. Because we are making data values larger, the mean is getting larger.*

Teacher *What do you think would happen if we made data values smaller?*

Student 2 *The mean would start to get smaller.*

Teacher *Now, when we made our changes, what happened with the median?*

Student 2 *The median didn't change at first, then all of a sudden it moved and got larger.*

Teacher *Why do you think this happened?*

Student 2 *The median changed after we had moved some of the data on 3 grams.*

Teacher *You mean when we replaced some of the cereals with 3 grams of sugar with cereals with more grams of sugar?*

Student 2 *Yeah. There were 10 numbers on each side of the median so it didn't change.*

Teacher Now, what happened to the median when we removed one cereal with 3 grams and replaced it with a cereal that has 8 grams? The distribution became two cereals, each with 3 grams, and four cereals, each with 8 grams?

Student 3 Now there are 9 numbers and 11 numbers. The median changes again.

Student 2 Then there's an even number [same number of numbers] on each side of the median. If you change a 2 to a 10, it might change. If you put something on one side (move it), it might change.

Teacher So you're saying remove a cereal with 2 grams of sugar and add a cereal with 10 grams of sugar.

Student 2 Yeah.

Teacher Let's try it. We are trying to figure out what changes the median and what doesn't. Let's change a 2 to a 10 and see if it changes. Hey, look at that. The median gets larger.

Student 2 Because there is an uneven amount of numbers on each side of the median.

Teacher This was your idea to change the 2 grams to 10 grams and that worked. How do we get it to increase again? What change might we make?

Goals

- Recognize that variability occurs whenever data are collected

- Use properties of distributions to describe the variability in a given data set

- Decide when to use the mean and median to describe a distribution

- Decide if a difference among data values and/or summary measures matters

- Develop and use strategies for comparing equal-size data sets to solve problems

   Have students work in pairs, open *TinkerPlots*, and use Investigation 3: Exploring With *TinkerPlots* in *Using TinkerPlots*™ *With CMP Problems: Student Edition*. Students will use the database: **React Time DH 40 Students.tp**

Launch 3.3

Begin Problem 3.3 using the Labsheets 3.3A–3.3K to make a set of Reaction Time Cards. Make sure each group of 2 or 3 students has a card set. If not already done, students should cut the pages so that each graph is a single sheet or card that can be moved around. There are 40 cards in the card set; each card is considered a case that shows all data about one student's trials. All of the graphs have the same scales.

Suggested Questions

- *Look at the cards you have. What can you tell about the different students that are represented in the card set?* (You can tell first name, gender, age, time it took for each trial, and can compare the trials visually.)

- *We can describe the information you have as a case or one individual in the data set. Let's list the attributes that we know from looking at the cases.*

Name	Trial 2(sec)
Gender	Trial 3(sec)
Age	Trial 4(sec)
Trial 1(sec)	Trial 5(sec)

- *Can we determine any other information? Fastest trial? Slowest trial? Mean or median trials? How would you determine these values for a single case?* (All of this information can be determined; each card looks like the cards used in the previous problem.)

- *With your table partners, sort the cards in any way you want. Be prepared to describe how you sorted the cards.* (Students use a variety of methods; some like to sort by gender, others by age; let students offer their methods and things they noticed. The goal is for them to get familiar with this data set.)

- *Are there any attributes where the values for several cases are the same [constant]?* (Gender is either M or F; age is eleven, twelve, or thirteen.)

- *Which attributes have values that are categorical data?* (Gender and age are written as categorical data; age could be written as numerical data in some other situation.)

- *Which attributes have values that are numerical data?* (the trial times)

Have students look at the attribute of Fastest Trial.

- *What is the range of the values for the fastest trials?* (The data vary from 0.58 to 1.18 seconds, so the range is 0.6 second.)

- *Based on the spread, how might we make a number line so we can make a line plot to show the distribution of these data?*

Discuss the use of decimal data and setting up a scale that permits marking decimal data. For example, the entire data set of Fastest Trials varies from 0.58 to 1.18 seconds, so we might use 0.5 seconds to 1.2 seconds with ticks at every tenth of a second. Have the students look at their cards and share ten of the Fastest Trials so you can mark these times on the number line to make a line plot.

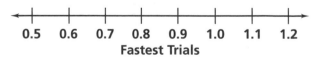

- *We are going to learn how to use software that will make graphs and do other actions on data electronically.*

Introduce students to the pictures of the four *TinkerPlots* data cards in the SE that show data about Diana, Nathaniel, Jasmine, and Henry.

- *How are the data about each student displayed using the TinkerPlots data cards?* (Have the students locate these four students' cards in the card set. The students also can look back at Problem 3.2 to see the tables used.)

Have students work in pairs.

Explore 3.3

Comparing the boys and girls on the fastest and slowest times gives students opportunities to compare equal-size data sets. Students can compare statistics both within a distribution and between distributions: mean, median, range. They can also look for clusters and use benchmarks at specific times to make comparisons.

They are focusing on two ways of characterizing reaction times: using the characteristic of "quickness" and using the characteristic of "consistency." They will need to think about what this means when comparing two groups.

Once students have been introduced to *TinkerPlots*, it is time for them to experiment.

Like any new manipulative tool, it is important to give students time to play with the software so don't be too task oriented initially. In this unit, we structure their work to follow selected routes in using the software to make your use of the software time-efficient and manageable. However, it is fine for students to do more exploring using the features of *TinkerPlots*.

Students begin with the file open in *TinkerPlots*. They will see both the *TinkerPlots* data cards and a graph window with icons displayed. Also, they can continue to use the Card Deck if they want; these cards match the data set in *TinkerPlots*.

The TinkerPlot Student Guide has ideas about working with *TinkerPlots* for students.

For A, students look at Fastest_Time.

1. Highlight the attribute Fastest_Time_sec on the data card in order to activate this attribute on the graph. (You must click on the attribute name and not on the value for the attribute to do this.)

2. Separate the data to make a fully separated dot plot showing the distribution of fastest reaction times. The scale is automatically set by the software and is based on the spread of the data.

3. Select "Stack" from the menu.

Here is one possible graph shown as fully separated. (Figure 1) ICON Size 16 is shown first, then ICON Size 8.

Figure 1

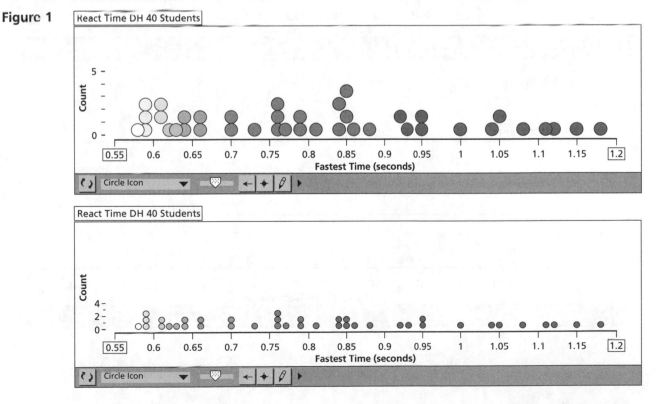

Next, separate vertically by Gender. Highlight the attribute Gender on the data card in order to activate this attribute on the graph. Drag a yellow dot upwards to separate M and F. You will see two colors. (Figure 2) Again, ICON Size 16 is shown first, then ICON Size 8.

Students can activate the mean and median locations. (Figure 3) They can also get numeric values for these locations if they need to do so (see Student Guide).

Figure 2

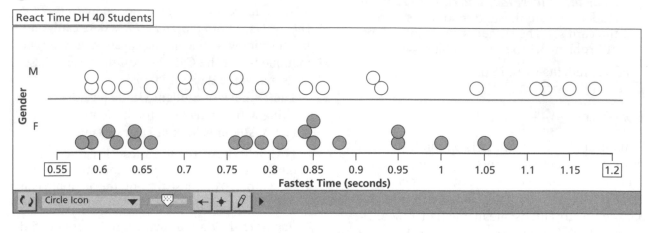

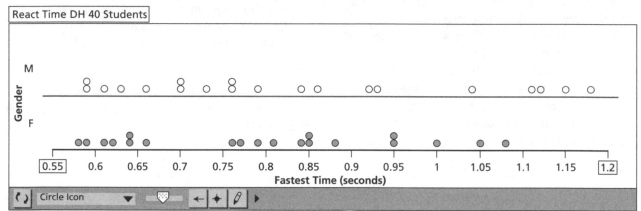

Figure 3

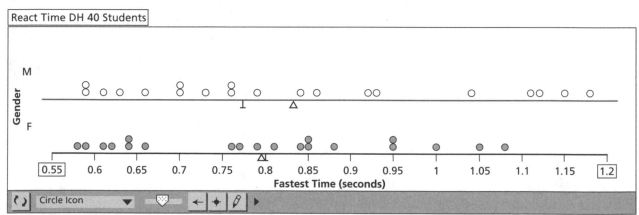

For Question B, have students look at Slowest_Time. (Figure 4)

1. Change the attribute in the graph. Highlight the attribute Slowest_Time on the data card. Then drag the attribute name of Slowest_Time from the data card to the horizontal axis.

2. Separate the data to make a dot plot showing the distribution of slowest reaction times by Gender. The scale is automatically set by the software and is based on the spread of the data.

Here is one possible graph shown as fully separated. ICON Size 16 is shown first, then ICON Size 8.

Students will print two screens, one for Question A and one for Question B.

Summarize 3.3

You can use the framework of *read the data*, *read between the data*, and *read beyond the data* to organize data analysis. The discussion that follows deals only with fully separated plots. It is possible to have a similar discussion about data represented in partially separated plots. All the statistics can be gathered from *TinkerPlots*; you can also look at the Teachers' Edition for a discussion that has the statistics provided.

Question A: Fastest Trials

Read the data

The fastest time for girls is 0.58 seconds and the slowest time is 1.08.

The fastest time for boys is 0.59 seconds and the slowest time is 1.18.

The distributions have few repeated values since measurement data are being used.

Figure 4

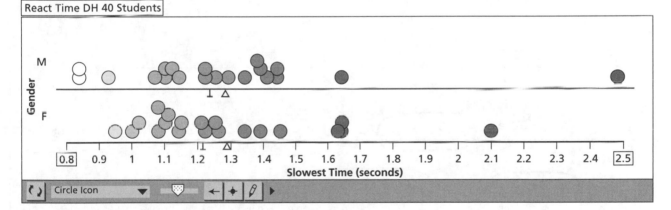

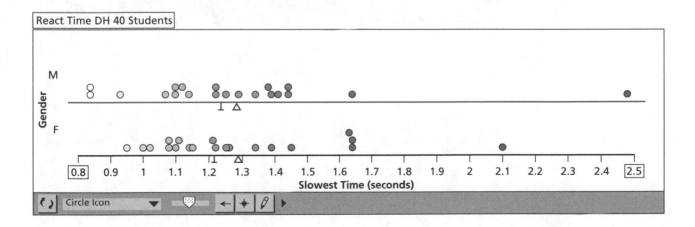

Read Between the Data

The spread for the girls is 0.58 to 1.08 seconds with a range of 0.50 second.

The spread for the boys is 0.59 to 1.18 seconds with a range of 0.59 second.

There is a difference between the two ranges of about one-tenth of a second.

The data seem to cluster in two locations for each distribution (Figure 5); the girls' data seem to be more clumped than the boys.

Read Beyond the Data

The median is 0.8 second (girls) and 0.775 second (boys) and the mean is 0.796 second (girls) and 0.8335 second (boys). The girls' mean and median are between the boys' mean and median.

The girls mean and median are almost identical values; there is a difference of 0.004 second.

The difference between the boys' mean and median is 0.037 second or about 4 hundredths of a second, which is a small difference that may not matter much in this context since it looks like there is a spread from about 0.5 to 1.2 seconds.

About 35% of the reaction times for boys and girls together are ≤ 0.7 second.

About 25% of the girls' and 35% of the boys' times are greater than 0.9 second.

The boys have some higher times than the girls: 10% of their times are > 1.10 seconds; none of the girls had times greater than 1.10 seconds.

Question B: Slowest Trials

Read the Data

The fastest time for girls is 0.95 second and the slowest time is 2.1.

The fastest time for boys is 0.84 second and the slowest time is 2.48.

The distributions have few repeated values since measurement data are being used.

Figure 5

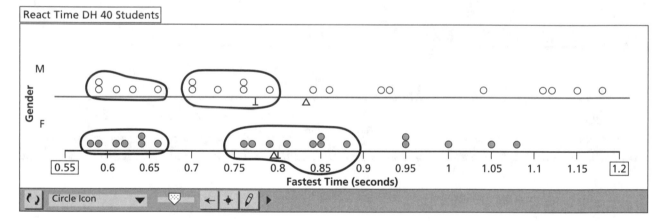

Read Between the Data

The spread for the girls is 0.95 to 2.1 seconds, with a range of 1.15 seconds.

The spread for the boys is 0.84 to 2.48 seconds, with a range of 1.64 seconds.

There is a difference between the two ranges of about half a second.

The data seem to cluster in one (similar) location for each distribution. (Figure 6)

There is a possible outlier in each distribution; without the possible outliers, the two ranges are quite similar.

Read Beyond the Data

The median is 1.215 seconds (girls) and 1.235 seconds (boys) and the mean is 1.288 seconds (girls) and 1.282 seconds (boys). The girls' mean and median are similar and the boys' mean and median are very similar.

The girls' mean and median are almost identical values; there is a difference of 0.073 second.

The boys' mean and median are almost identical values; there is a difference of 0.047 second or about 5 hundredths of a second.

About 20% of the girls' slowest reaction times and about 10% of the boys' slowest reaction times are ≥ 1.6 seconds.

Figure 6

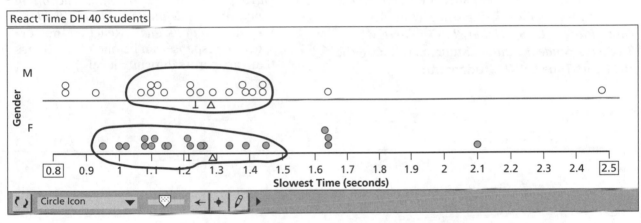

Mathematical Goals

- Recognize that variability occurs whenever data are collected

- Use properties of distributions to describe the variability in a given data set

- Decide when to use the mean or median to describe a distribution

- Decide if a difference among data values and/or summary measures matters

- Develop and use strategies for comparing equal-size data sets to solve problems

  Have students work in pairs, open *TinkerPlots* and use Investigation 3 Exploring With *TinkerPlots* in *Using TinkerPlots*™ *With CMP Problems: Student Edition*. Students will need the file: **React Time DH 40 Students.tp**

With the students, read the initial introduction to the problem.

Suggested Questions

- *How many of you play video games?* (Many students will answer yes.)

- *Why is reaction time important when you play these games?* (Students realize that speed of response is part of what makes a video game interesting.)

- *Some video games have different levels of playing difficulty. Do you think reaction time is part of what defines a level of difficulty? Why do you think this?* (Reaction time or speed of response can be one of the things that vary across difficulty levels.)

Figure 7

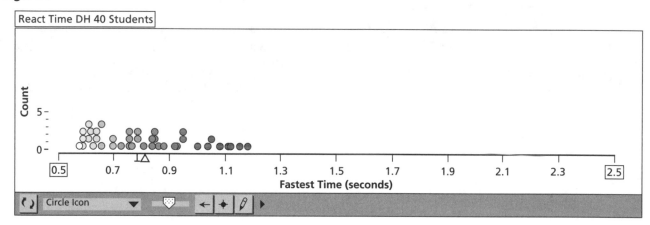

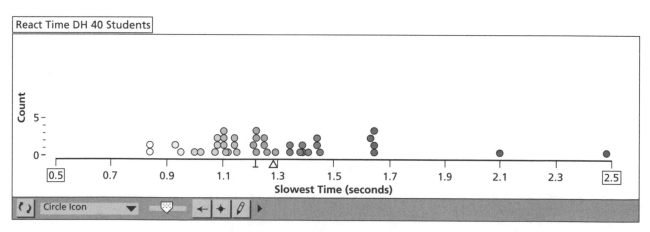

- *Today, you are going to use* TinkerPlots *to help you compare students' fastest and slowest reaction times. Then you will make a recommendation about cut off times for reaction times for Levels 1 (easy), 2 (medium), and 3 (hard) to Willa, the video game designer.*

Have students work in pairs at a computer to do Questions A and B.

Explore 3.4

Students compare the fastest and slowest reaction times of all 40 students. They need to use two graphs that both have the same scale.

In making the graphs, the endpoints are adjusted to make the scales the same. It is easier to readjust both so that the scale is from 0.5 to 2.5 seconds. (Figure 7, previous page)

When they are making their comparisons, it may help to focus on read the data, read between the data, and read beyond the data statements.

Students are still comparing equal-size groups. However, with this comparison, it is easier to see the differences as one set of data is shifted to the right (slowest times).

The problem questions are ways to focus their discussions; they do NOT have to approach ideas about comparing the data using the structure of "read the data," "read between the data," or "read beyond the data." However, if this is a useful strategy, here are some examples:

Read the Data

The slowest times include two possible outliers, one at 2.1 seconds and one at 2.48 seconds.

Read Between the Data

The distribution of slowest times is shifted to the right; all but two of the slowest times or about 100% of the times are > 0.9 second. For the fastest times, about 30% of the times are > 0.9.

Read Beyond the Data

The mean and median for the slowest times are about 1.5 times the mean and median for the fastest times.

In Question D students use all of this information to make a recommendation.

Figure 8

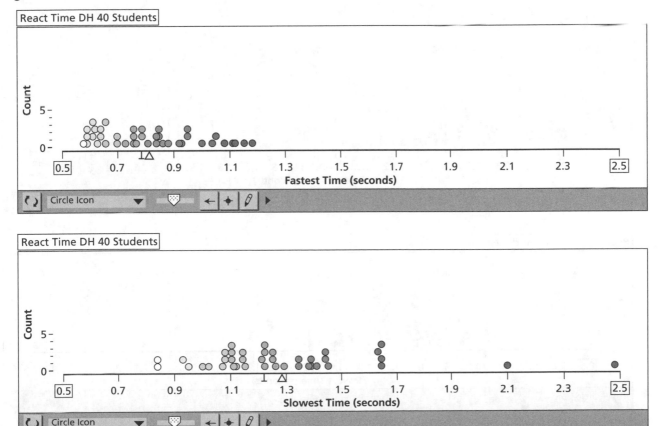

Summarize 3.4

You can use graphs to help focus the discussion. (Figure 8, on previous page)

- *How do the means in each distribution compare?* [The mean for the fastest reaction time is about $\frac{2}{3}$ the mean for the slowest reaction times (i.e., $\frac{2}{3}$ of 1.3 is about 0.9).]

- *How do the medians in each distribution compare?* [The medians have a similar relationship to the means. The median for the fastest reaction time is about $\frac{1}{3}$ smaller than the mean for the slowest reaction times (i.e., $\frac{2}{3}$ of 1.2 is 0.8).]

- *Describe where the data seem to cluster in each distribution and compare clusters.* (The fastest time data seem to cluster below 1.0 seconds and the slowest time data seem to cluster from 1.0 seconds to 1.5 seconds. The fastest time data seem, again, to be about $\frac{1}{3}$ less in times than the slowest time data. The slowest times are shifted to the right in comparison to the fastest times.)

- *Is one distribution more variable than the other? How do you know?* [The spreads of the two distributions are different. The range for the fastest times is 0.6 second, or about $\frac{2}{3}$ less than the range of the slowest times (at 1.6 seconds). Both distributions have few repeated values because these are measurement data. The slowest times have two values that are possible outliers.]

Question C

The locations for all the reference lines are shown on each of the two graphs. (Figure 9) Students place them one at a time.

Have students offer cutoff times with reasons. See answers below for one way to do this. Students may want to put reference lines at locations different from those suggested. That is also possible.

Figure 9

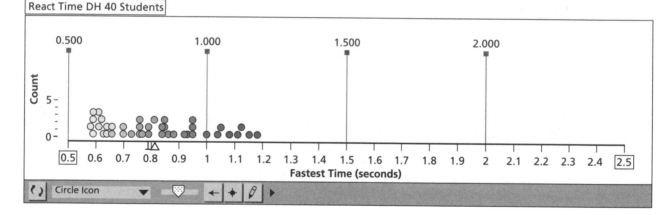

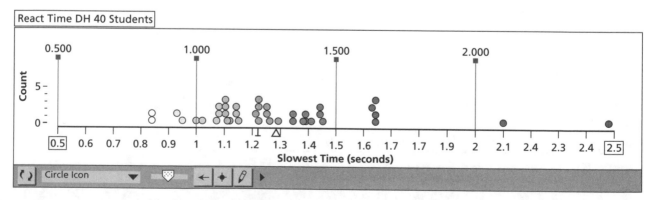

4.2 Are Steel Coasters Faster Than Wooden Coasters?

Mathematical Goals

- Use line plots to display data distributions
- Recognize that variability occurs whenever data are collected
- Use properties of distributions to describe the variability in a given data set
- Decide if a difference among data values and/or summary measures matters
- Use shape of a distribution to estimate locations of the mean and median
- Develop and use strategies for unequal-size data sets to solve problems

This problem uses a database of 150 roller coasters (50 wooden coasters and 100 steel coasters) to engage students in using a variety of strategies to make comparisons between speeds of wooden and steel roller coasters. Students also explore relationships among variables as they consider what attributes may influence speed of a coaster.

Have students work in pairs, open *TinkerPlots*, and use Investigation 4 Exploring Further With *TinkerPlots* in *Using TinkerPlots™ With CMP Problems: Student Edition*.

Launch 4.2

Continue discussing roller coasters. Have students examine the data shown in Transparency 4.2A. Have a discussion on how to read this table and what information can be obtained from the table.

Suggested Questions Ask:

- *Is there any information in this table that surprises you? Why or why not?* (Answers will vary.)

Brainstorm with the class what kinds of information they might collect about roller coasters.

- *What kinds of information might we collect about roller coasters?* (how fast a coaster can travel, park and state location, number of people who can ride it, tallest height, and so on)

- *How might you go about collecting this information about several coasters?* (from theme parks or amusement parks where coasters are located; from Web sites on the Internet)

Once students have done this, select some roller coasters with which your students may be familiar. Display the data about these roller coasters, or use Transparencies 4.2B and 4.2C.

- *Let's look at some examples of both steel and wood roller coasters. These are a few of the coasters that are found in a database of 150 coasters. We will look at the attributes that are used to name different categories of data that can be collected about roller coasters.*

Each example is *one case* of a roller coaster. A case is the named data item and its related data for each of the attributes of interest. There are two cases of wood coasters and two cases of steel coasters.

As you display each case, discuss what kinds of information can be found by looking at the picture; this information is often subjective but a visual image of a coaster helps define the coaster. Discuss the data that are listed to the right of each picture, highlighting the attributes used. Also make comparisons between attributes for wood coasters and for steel coasters (e.g., speeds, heights). Take time to help students link their knowledge of other contexts to understand data about the coasters. For example, what does driving in a car at 35 mi/h or 55 mi/h or 65 mi/h feel like? Which is faster? Can you describe what "faster" means in this context? Or, ask students to estimate the height of the classroom and then ask how many classrooms stacked on top of each other would you need to reach the height of a given roller coaster. It is important to connect the students with the data by relating to experiences that make sense to them.

Next show Transparency 4.2D to show what the data look like when entered in data cards using *TinkerPlots*. The case cards match two of the four pictures of coasters examined earlier.

This preliminary work has been designed to get students familiar with the data they will be using. They are now ready to move to the explore phase.

Take some time to talk about how to use *TinkerPlots* here. Major actions might include:

Opening the file either by selecting the file directly or by opening it from within *TinkerPlots*.

Making sure that both the data cards and a plot window are open.

Making a dot plot showing one of the attributes (e.g., top speed) of roller coasters.

Separating vertically by TYPE so both wood and steel coaster speeds can be compared.

Be sure to open a text box and record your answers to the problem questions with your plots. Students may do a text box for Questions A and B and then do a new text box for Question C and a final text box for Question D. They should print out their graphs/text box information for each of these tasks. Distribute Labsheet A.1 for helpful hints on how to successfully print material so it will be easy to see. If they cannot print it out, then have them save the files under their names for later retrieval, for example:

> Sam J. & Sally S. Questions A and B
> Sam J. & Sally S. Question C

Have students work in teams of 2 (preferably) or 3 students to complete Questions A–C; you will probably want to stop and do a summary for this part of the problem and then have students work later on Question D. If students finish early, they can begin work on Question D.

Explore 4.2

Read the Explore section in the Teacher's Guide for this Problem in addition to using the material detailed below.

Question A of the problem helps students get familiar with the Roller Coaster Database as it functions in *TinkerPlots*. Students can experiment with different actions using *TinkerPlots* and look at different attributes. This part of the problem is meant to be exploratory in nature; the written paragraph helps students summarize what they found out.

In Questions B and C, students will need time to explore these data. The *TinkerPlots* Student Guide will help, or you can offer suggestions about actions to take. For example, students have speeds displayed and separated by types of coasters. From here, they can find out how many of each kind of coaster they have, and they can estimate where they think the mean and median are located in each and then find out by selecting these markers using *TinkerPlots*. (Figure 10) Interestingly, the measures of center are about the same for each and there is not much difference between the means and medians of each distribution.

Students need to partition the distributions using dividers so that they can look at counts and percents of data at or above benchmark speeds. For example, below the data have been partitioned at 50 mi/h (Figure 11, next page); students can make some comments about percent

Figure 10

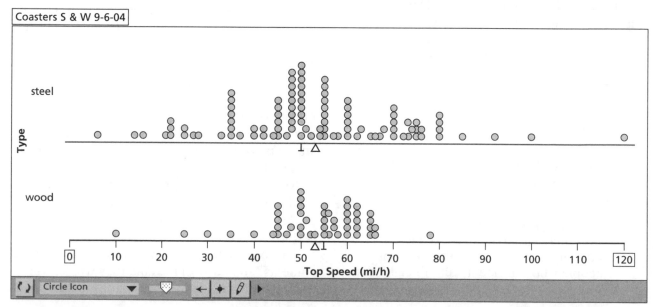

of coasters of each kind that have speeds greater than or equal to 50 mi/h. (Figure 12)

As another example, the data in Figure 13 have been partitioned into three parts; students can make some comments about percent of coasters of each kind with speeds in the interval of 30 mi/h ≤ speed ≤ 60 mi/h and having speeds greater than 60 mi/h or less than 30 mi/h.

Figure 11

Use a Reference Line to Estimate the Location of 50 mi/h

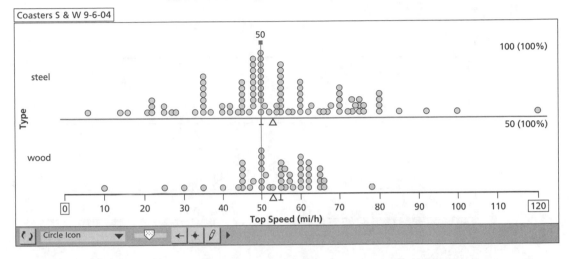

Figure 12

Use Dividers to Determine Counts/Percents

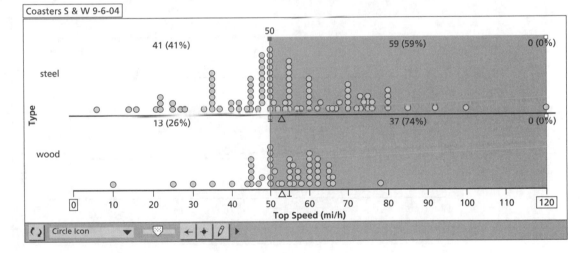

Figure 13

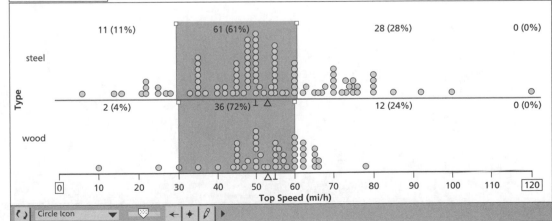

Question D

In this part, students explore the relationships between other attributes and speed. For example, a team might decide that maximum drop of a roller coaster has something to do with speed. They choose maximum drop to separate vertically and begin to separate. (Figure 14) What do they notice as they start to separate?

Figure 14

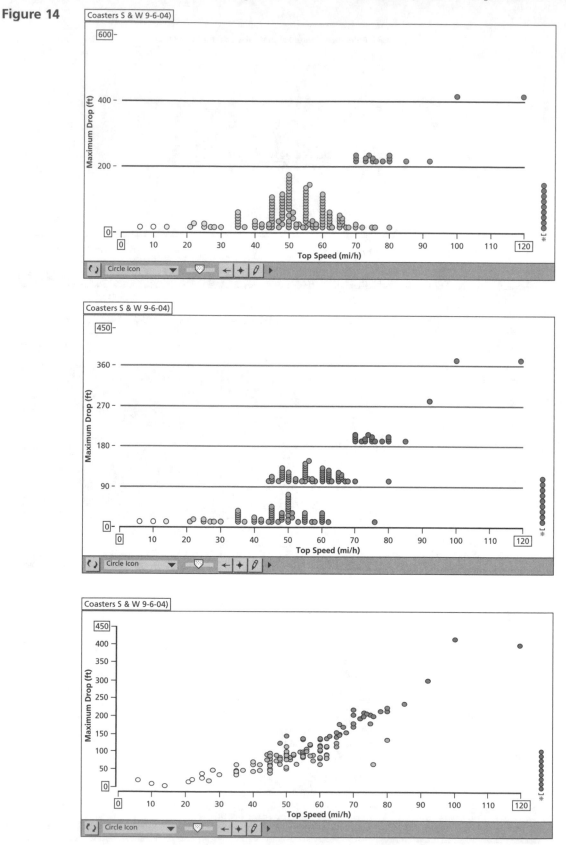

Summarize 4.2

Suggested Question Have students discuss their answers to the question:

- *Are wooden coasters faster than steel roller coasters?*

It is not possible to give a simple yes or no answer to this question. In examining the data, if coasters with speeds greater than or equal to 60 mi/h are considered, we see that there is a greater percent of wood coasters than steel coasters in this category. (Figure 15)

However, if the benchmark is changed to 65 mi/h, then we see that steel coasters with

speeds greater than or equal to 65 mi/h are faster than wood coasters. (Figure 16)

Similarly, if we look at the numbers of coasters with speeds less than 30 mi/h, there is a greater percent of steel coasters than wood coasters. (Figure 17, next page)

Students struggle with looking at counts of the actual icons vs. percentages expressing a part–whole relationship. They are comparing data sets that have different numbers of data values; using relative frequencies is necessary in order to make comparisons. However, using *TinkerPlots*, students can still see the actual counts even when percents are reported. It is fine that students are struggling with these ideas.

Figure 15

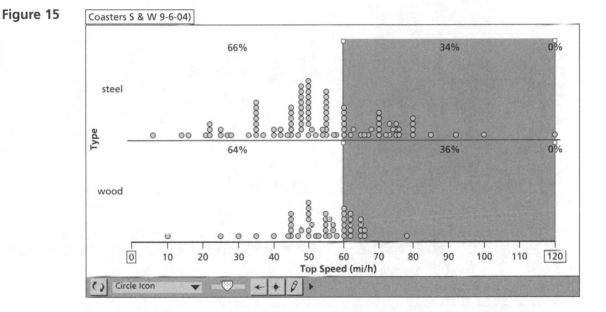

Figure 16

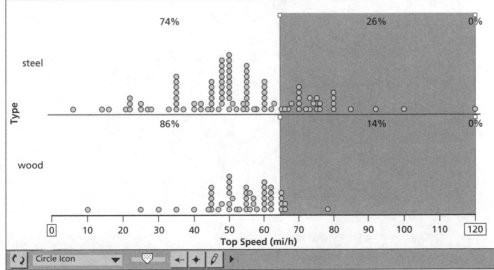

Here's what might be said in answer to the question:

- *There is a greater percent of steel coasters with speeds greater than or equal to 65 mi/h than there is of wood coasters.*
  There is a greater percent of steel coasters with speeds less than 30 mi/h.
  Approximately 60% of the steel coasters and over 70% of the wood coasters have speeds that are 30 mi/h ≤ speed ≤ 60. (Figure 18)

In discussing the relationships with other attributes and speed, both Maximum Height and Maximum Drop seem to be related to speed. Track Length seems less related. Duration of Ride and Year Opened both appear to not be related strongly. See the fully separated plots in Figures 19 and 20 (next page). Partially separated plots of the same data can be found in the Teacher's Guide discussion of Problem 4.2. Also see the following sample dialogue with students about ideas addressed in this problem.

Figure 17

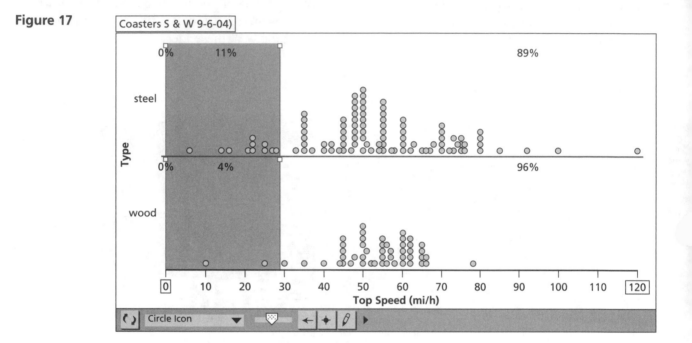

Figure 18

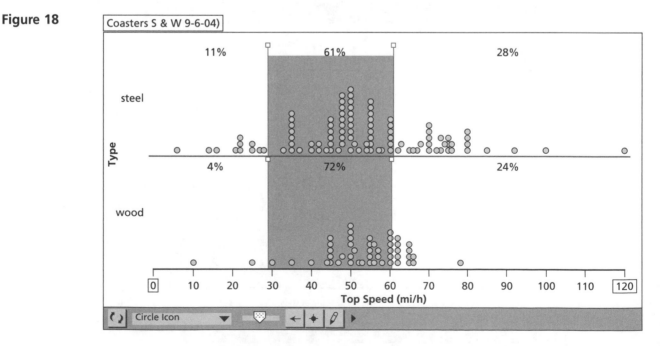

Figure 19

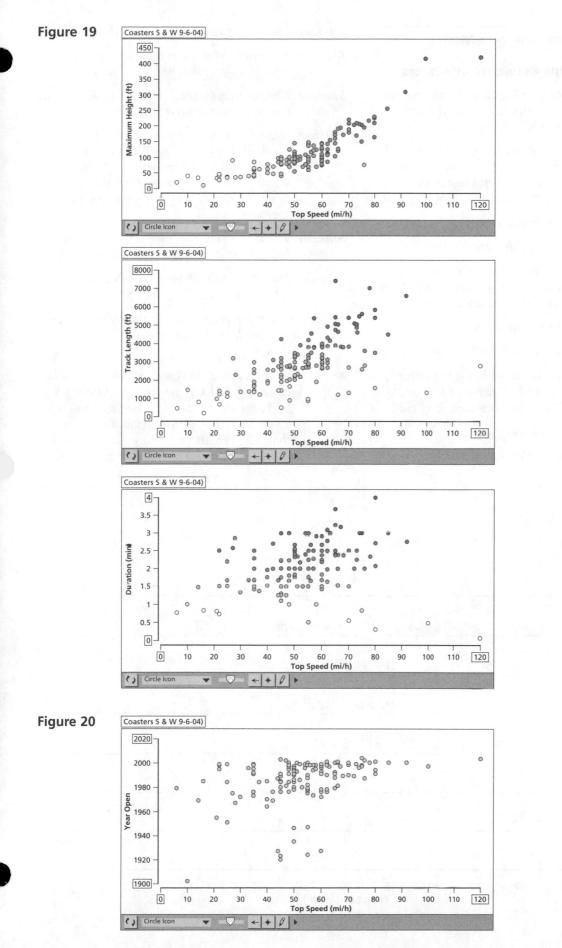

Figure 20

Classroom Dialogue Model

Relationships Between Attributes

Teacher So you have speed and how long the ride lasts. Do you think how long it lasts affects the speed? *(Figure 21)*

Student The shorter ones were fast—they would have a shorter time. The slower ones were longer—they would last 5 minutes. The beast is a long ride but not very fast.

Student It is a long ride that is fast.

Student Most of the fast rides are shorter.

Teacher Give me evidence. Show me your fast rides. Draw a reference line at 65 mi/h. So most of your fast rides are shorter.

Student Some are 2 or 3 minutes.

Teacher What do you think?

Student I don't think duration has a big difference. Some could go fast and it is over. Some could go slow but be a long ride.

Student The data varies too much.

Teacher What about angle of descent? *(Figure 22, next page)*

Student The fastest ride goes straight down.

Teacher The angle of descent relates to speed, what does that mean?

Student The more the angle, an angle of 10 would not go as fast as an angle of 80.

Teacher Here are some that have 40–60 degrees [look at that part of graph]. Is there some common speed where you think there might be a point that angle of descent might be steep enough to be related to speed?

Student The angle gets it started. And, after the hill, you still are moving from the angle.

Teacher Put Maximum Drop up. Do you think it relates to speed? *(Figure 23, next page)*

Student Yes, there is one coaster that is the fastest and the highest. About 120 mi/h is the fastest.

Student 65 mi/h is the slowest speed that could be considered fast. If you draw a line at 65 mi/h, the drops start to change more as speed increases. At speeds that are less than 65 mi/h, there is more variability in the drops without as much change in the speeds.

Figure 21

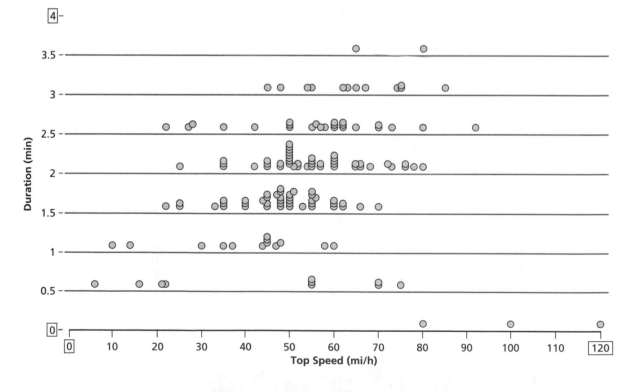

Figure 22

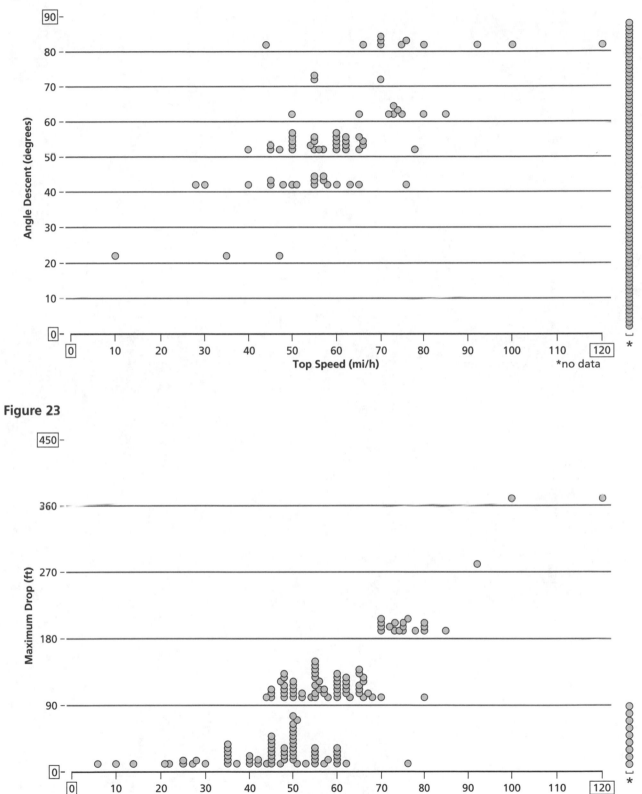

Figure 23

Labsheet A.1

Printing with *TinkerPlots*™

Under "File" in the menu:

• Choose Page Setup.

  1. Set the page orientation to "landscape."

  2. Set the scale to 75% or 80% so that the graph, text box, and data cards can fit in the same window.

• Choose Show Page Breaks.

  This will let students see where the pages will break when printing. Move the graph, text box, and data cards so that all three fit on a single page.

• Choose Print to print the screen. A sample is shown below.

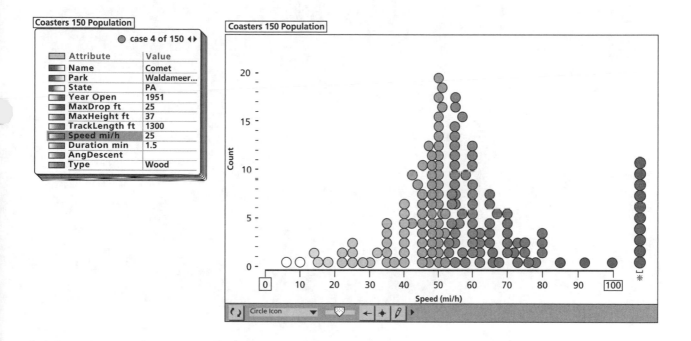

This shows how a screen might look with the text box, a plot or graph, and the data cards displayed. Right now, the graph shows the distribution of speeds of all roller coasters. The icons stacked to the right are roller coasters for which there is no data about speed available.

The dotted line to the right marks a page break. There also may be a page break shown here. If students' work is within the page boundaries, then they may not see these page break lines. They appear when the graph or text box gets too close to the edge of a page.

Using *TinkerPlots*™ With CMP Problems
Students' Guide

TinkerPlots Quick Reference Guide

TinkerPlots™
Dynamic Data Exploration

Quick Reference Card

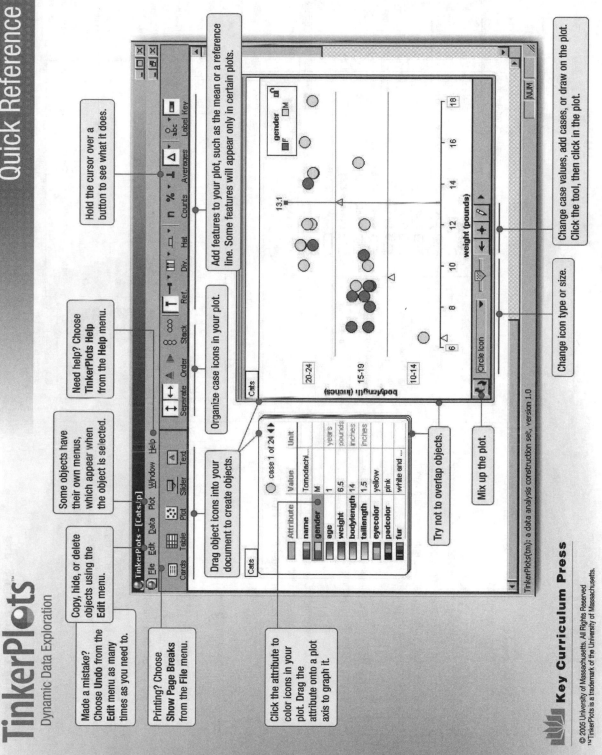

Made a mistake? Choose **Undo** from the **Edit** menu as many times as you need to.

Copy, hide, or delete objects using the **Edit** menu.

Some objects have their own menus, which appear when the object is selected.

Need help? Choose **TinkerPlots Help** from the **Help** menu.

Hold the cursor over a button to see what it does.

Printing? Choose **Show Page Breaks** from the **File** menu.

Drag object icons into your document to create objects.

Organize case icons in your plot.

Add features to your plot, such as the mean or a reference line. Some features will appear only in certain plots.

Click the attribute to color icons in your plot. Drag the attribute onto a plot axis to graph it.

Try not to overlap objects.

Mix up the plot.

Change icon type or size.

Change case values, add cases, or draw on the plot. Click the tool, then click in the plot.

TinkerPlots(tm): a data analysis construction set, version 1.0

Key Curriculum Press

TinkerPlots Quick Reference Guide *continued*

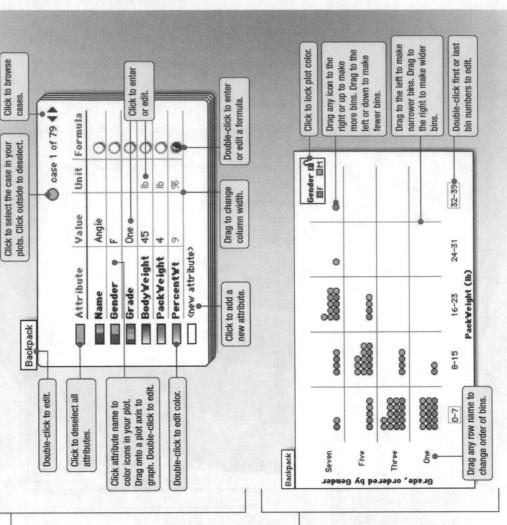

Callout labels (top card):
- Click to browse cases.
- Click to select the case in your plots. Click outside to deselect.
- Click to enter or edit.
- Double-click to enter or edit a formula.
- Double-click to edit.
- Click to deselect all attributes.
- Click attribute name to color icons in your plot. Drag onto a plot axis to graph. Double-click to edit.
- Double-click to edit color.
- Drag to change column width.
- Click to add a new attribute.

case 1 of 79

Attribute	Value	Unit	Formula
Name	Angie		
Gender	F		
Grade	One		
BodyWeight	45	lb	
PackWeight	4	lb	
PercentWt	9	%	
<new attribute>			

Backpack

Callout labels (bottom plot):
- Click to lock plot color.
- Drag any icon to the right or up to make more bins. Drag to the left or down to make fewer bins.
- Drag to the left to make narrower bins. Drag to the right to make wider bins.
- Double-click first or last bin numbers to edit.
- Drag any row name to change order of bins.

Gender: F M
Grade, ordered by Gender: Seven, Five, Three, One
PackWeight (lb): 0–7, 8–15, 16–23, 24–31, 32–39
Backpack

TinkerPlots™
Dynamic Data Exploration

Data Cards Use data cards to enter or edit data and change your plot.
Cards

Case Table Use a case table to see more than one case at a time. Cases appear as rows and attributes appear as columns. You can also enter new data and control your plot using a case table.
Table

Text Use a text box to explain your data or answer questions from your assignment.
Text

Picture Use a picture to illustrate your data. Copy the picture in its program, click in a blank part of the TinkerPlots document, then choose **Paste Picture** from the TinkerPlots **Edit** menu.

Plot Use a plot to graph your data.
Plot

Formula Editor You can use formulas to define attributes or filter out cases from the plot. Choose **TinkerPlots Help** from the **Help** menu to learn how.

Slider You can use a slider to change values for an attribute defined by a formula. Choose **TinkerPlots Help** from the **Help** menu to learn how.
Slider

Key Curriculum Press

Getting Started With *TinkerPlots*

You will use *TinkerPlots* to complete Problem 2.4. You will:

- Display data cards, a table of the data, and a plot (graph) window
- Move, label, and change the size of icons
- Locate the mean and median in a distribution and show these numerical values when needed

Problem 2.4 asks you to make a copy of the distribution of the amount of sugar found in cereals located on the top shelf in a supermarket.

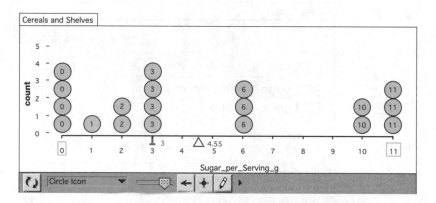

Setting Up Case Cards, Tables, and Plots; Entering Data

Begin by opening *TinkerPlots*. Drag the data **Cards** icon into your workspace.

Enter the name of the new **Attribute**.

Collection 1			
			new case 1 ◀▶

Attribute	Value	Unit	F...
sugar_per_serving			○
<new attribute>			

Enter the **Unit** of measure.

Collection 1			
			new case 1 ◀▶

Attribute	Value	Unit	F...
sugar_per_serving		g	○
<new attribute>			

Enter the data **Value** for Case 1.

Collection 1			
			new case 1 ◀▶

Attribute	Value	Unit	F...
sugar_per_serving	⊊	g	○
<new attribute>			

Click on ▶ at the top of the
card to move to Case 2.

Collection 1			
			new case 2 ◀▶

Attribute	Value	Unit	F...
sugar_per_serving		g	○
<new attribute>			

Enter the data **Value** for Case 2.

Collection 1			
		●	case 2 of 2 ◀▶

Attribute	Value	Unit	F...
sugar_per_serving	3	g	○
<new attribute>			

If you want to change the name from "Collection 1," double click on the name and then enter a name for the collection.

Rename Collection

Collection 1

Cancel   OK

Rename Collection

Servings of Cereal

Cancel   OK

Select and drag a **Plot** window into your workspace. You can stretch the window so it looks like a rectangle. You will see two icons representing the two cases you have entered. Then, select the attribute you just entered.

Servings of Cereal

case 2 of 2 ◄►

Attribute	Value	Unit	F...
sugar_per_serving	3	g	○
<new attribute>			

Servings of Cereal

Circle Icon   ▼   ⬚   ← ✛ ✎ ▶

Notice that the icons have some colors to them. Once you select an attribute, you can do actions on the plot. In this situation, the first things you want to do are label the icons with their data values and change the icons size to a larger size.

These actions are shown completed on the next page. To do the actions, you need to select the attribute "sugar_per_serving." Once you have done these actions, you can change the icons to a light blue color if you wish. To get the light blue icons, select the light blue icon on the attribute card.

Attribute	Value	Unit	F...

Click on **Label** and select
Labels Centered. You will see each
icon labeled with its number of grams
of sugar.

Set the size to **Icon Size 32**.

Select and drag **Table**; it shows the data values for the two cases
you entered. Your workspace will look something like this.

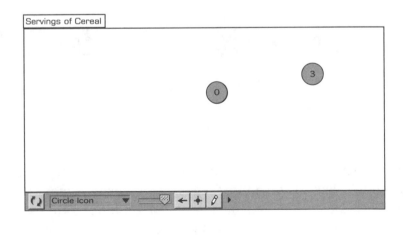

Enter the rest of the data values. You can enter them directly on the table. Each time you enter a data value, a data card is created and an icon is added to the plot. You can see Case 17 highlighted in the table and on the plot below.

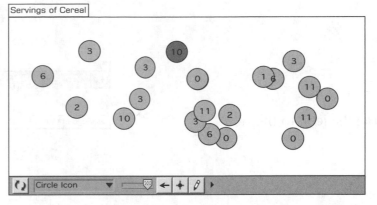

Servings of Cereal		
	sugar...	<new>
1	0	
2	3	
3	0	
4	0	
5	0	
6	1	
7	2	
8	2	
9	3	
10	3	
11	3	
12	3	
13	6	
14	6	
15	6	
16	10	
17	10	
18	11	
19	11	
20	11	

Separating Data to Make a Dot Plot; Sizing and Labeling Icons

Highlight the attribute name "sugar_per_serving" on a data card.

What do you notice about what happens to the colors of the icons? What do you think this means?

Separate the icons to make a dot plot. Grab an icon and drag it to the right until a number line appears. Then let go. You may have to drag a few times to get to a dot plot.

Start.

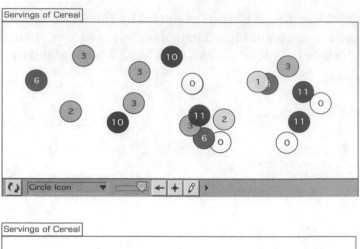

Drag the icon to the right.

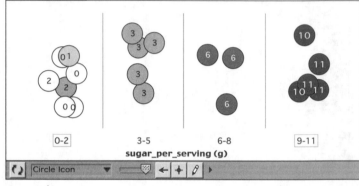

Continue to drag the icon to the right.

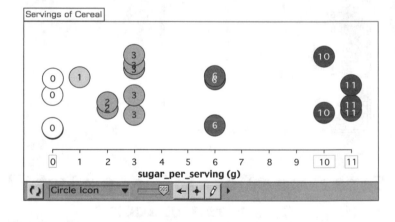

Choose **Stack** from the
menu so you have a dot plot.

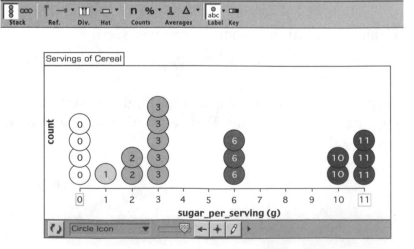

Locating the Median and the Mean; Showing Numeric Values

You can use the menu bar to mark and locate measures of center and show their numeric values. To show the mean, select the △; to show the median, select ⊥. Then you can choose **Show Numeric Value(s)**. Your *TinkerPlots* workspace will look something like this.

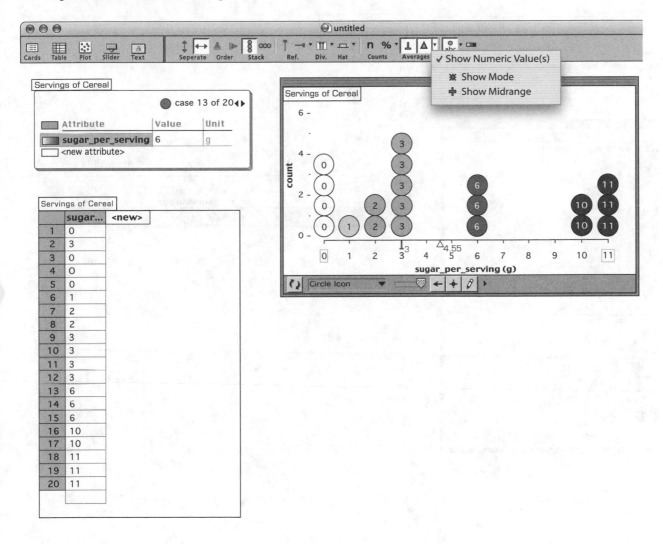

To complete the questions in Problem 2.4, you are asked to make changes to the distribution you just created.

You can do this by making changes in the table of data. You can remove a cereal with 6 grams of sugar and replace it with a cereal with 9 grams of sugar by changing one of the "6" data values to a "9" data value. See the example below where Case 13 was changed from 6 grams of sugar to 9 grams of sugar.

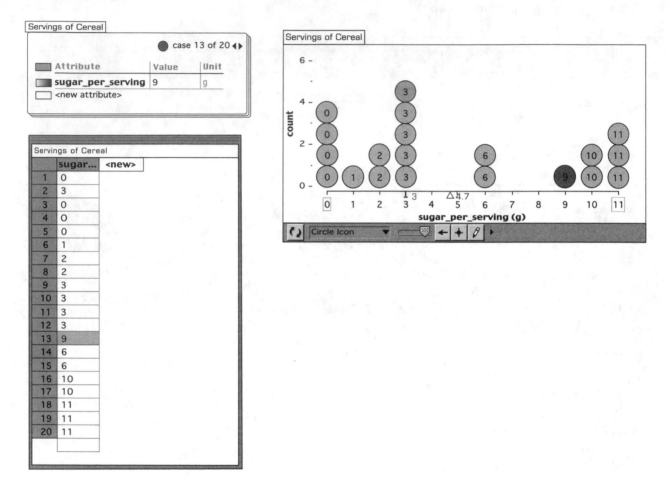

Investigation 3

Exploring With *TinkerPlots*

You will use *TinkerPlots* to complete Problems 3.3 and 3.4. You will need the data Reaction Times Using Dominant Hand for 40 Students, which is in this file: React Time DH 40 Students.tp

To complete Problems 3.3 and 3.4, you need to know more about:

- **Data Cards**

  A data card displays attribute names and values.

  There is one card for each case (40 cases).

  Some of the attributes are categorical data (Name and Gender) and some are numerical data (all other attributes).

  You scroll forward and backward by clicking on arrows at the top of the card.

- **Data Table**

  A data table is a spreadsheet-like table that shows the cases in rows with the attributes as labels for the columns.

- **Plot (Graph) Window**

  Icons, one for each case, appear in graph window.

  Icons can be all one color (e.g., blue) or can have multiple colors, depending on if they are numerical or categorical data.

- **Text Box**

  A text box displays information typed about the data set or a plot or an analysis question.

Data can be modified either on the data card (by double clicking an attribute value) or in the data table (by changing a data value).

Data appear highlighted in two ways in the plot window:

- Select (click on) the blue Attribute title to have icons appear as all one color. Then, selecting one or more icons will show them highlighted in red.

- Select (click on) a specific attribute name to have icons appear in colors that are related to the given attribute. Numerical data will show color from lighter to darker reflecting least to greatest values. Categorical data will show distinct colors for different values (e.g., many different colors when Name is selected or just two different colors when Gender is selected).

When you select a plot window, you will see several buttons on a menu bar. The buttons are named so you will know what they do.

Selecting the Attribute title bar will make the icons light blue. The case of Diana is highlighted below.

React Time DH 40 Students

● case 20 of 40 ◀▶

	Attribute	Value	Unit
	Name	Diana	
	Gender	F	
	Age	twelve	
	Fastest _ Time	0.59	sec
	Slowest _ Time	1.08	sec
	Trial _ 1	1.02	sec
	Trial _ 2	0.83	sec
	Trial _ 3	0.73	sec
	Trial _ 4	1.08	sec
	Trial _ 5	0.59	sec

React Time DH 40 Students

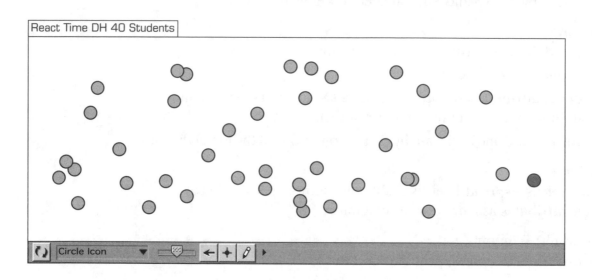

Circle Icon ▼

React Time DH 40 Students

	Name	Gender	Age	Faste...	Slowe...	Trial_1	Trial_2	Trial_3	Trial_4	Trial_5
14	Carly	F	thirteen	0.85	1.63	1.01	1.03	1.07	0.85	1.63
15	Julie	F	eleven	0.79	1.11	1.11	0.79	0.97	0.8	0.82
16	Jasmine	F	eleven	0.84	1.02	0.99	0.89	1.02	0.84	0.93
17	Gracie	F	twelve	0.85	0.95	0.86	0.95	0.91	0.85	0.9
18	Crystal	F	eleven	0.88	1	0.9	0.89	1	0.88	0.98
19	Ashlyn	F	thirteen	0.95	1.26	1.01	0.95	1.26	1.04	1.05
20	Diana	F	twelve	0.59	1.08	1.02	0.83	0.73	1.08	0.59
21	Isaiah	M	eleven	0.93	1.44	1	1.27	1.14	1.44	0.93
22	Frank	M	eleven	0.84	1.34	0.84	1.34	1.06	1.01	0.88
23	Caleb	M	eleven	0.92	1.25	1.04	1.25	0.94	0.92	1
24	Andrew	M	eleven	0.76	1.12	1.01	0.8	1.12	1.03	0.76
25	Matthew	M	thirteen	1.18	1.38	1.18	1.3	1.28	1.38	1.33
26	Rafael	M	eleven	0.63	1.07	0.85	0.7	1.07	0.63	0.78
27	Jeremy	M	twelve	0.61	1.1	0.85	0.85	1.1	0.67	0.61
28	Evan	M	eleven	0.85	1.14	0.86	1.08	1.14	1.1	1.13

Selecting Attributes;
Separating and Ordering Data

Step 1   In the plot window:
Select the bottom left button with arrows on it. This mixes
the icons up and removes any graph.

Step 2   On the data card:
Select the specific attribute, Gender. Also select the Key
button on the right of the menu bar. What do you notice
about the colors of the icons? Why do you think this is so?

Select the specific attribute, Fastest_Time. Also select the
Key button if it is not already selected. What do you notice
about the colors of the icons? Why do you think this is so?

Step 3   In the Plot Window:
Select Gender again. Select one icon and drag to the right.
What do you notice?

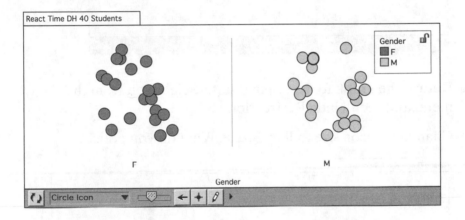

Find the Stack button on the menu and select the vertical
stack. What do you notice?

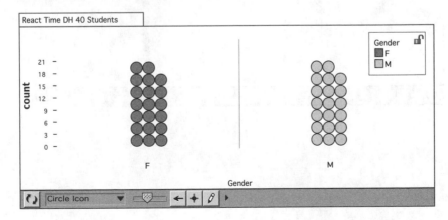

De-select **Key**. Find the **Counts** button on the menu and select **n**. What do you notice?

Stretch the graph using the right corner of the plot window. What do you notice?

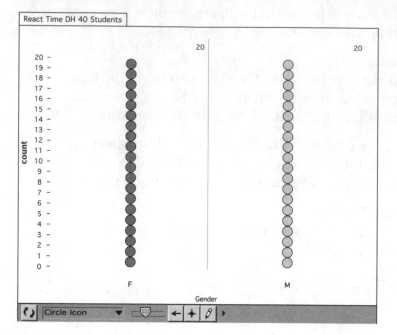

Return the graph to the original state. Select **Edit** from the menu and then Undo Resize Plot.

Change the icon size to Icon Size 8. What do you notice?

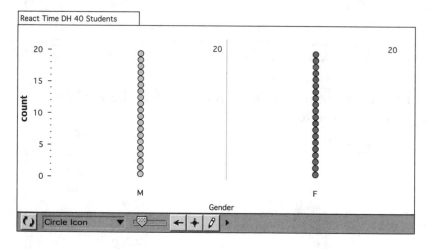

Step 4 In the Plot Window, mix up the icons.

Select Fastest_Time. Under **Plot** in the menu bar, choose options and select "Continuous style—horizontal bins." Select one icon and start to separate to the right. Stop and look, then separate some more. What do you notice?

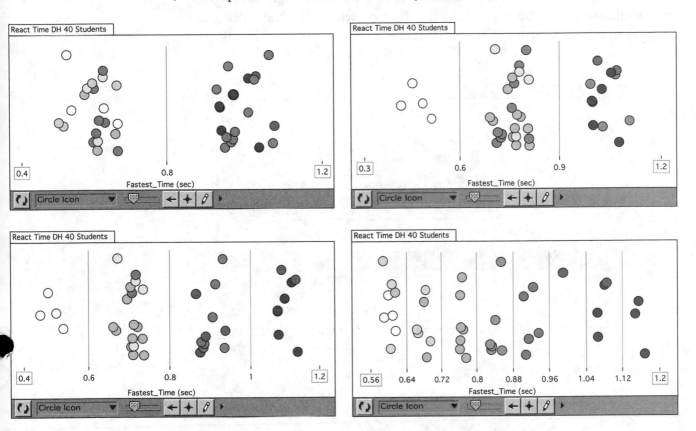

Up to how many sections does the action of separating make before the data are fully separated?

Finish separating until there are no more sections. Make a dot plot by selecting the vertical stack above the **Stack** button in the menu bar.

Making Choices About Icons

Choose an icon size that lets you see the shape of the distribution. Often, large icon sizes like 32 distort the shape of the distribution. The larger icons may make it appear that there are clusters of data when there actually are not or that there are no gaps in the distribution when there actually are. So, you need to experiment with icon sizes.

Icon Size 32

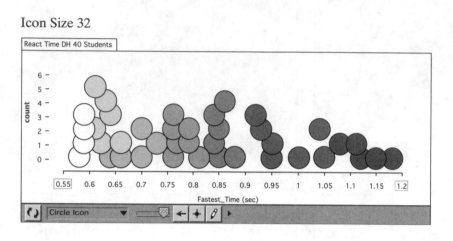

Icon Size 16

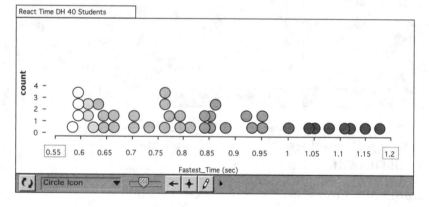

Icon Size 8

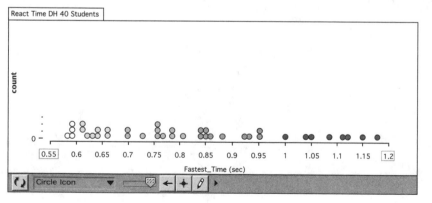

You can use larger icon sizes and still see the shape if you stretch the plot window to make it wider.

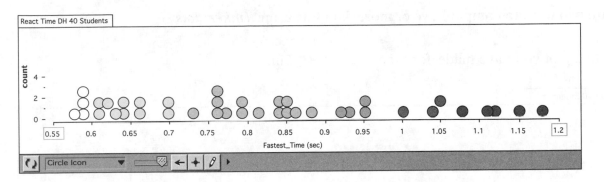

The card at the right shows that the data are now being sorted by Gender. The plot below shows the menu of choices for icon shapes and actions on icons.

You can use the menu to change the shape of the icons. You can also do actions on icons, such as Fuse or Hide.

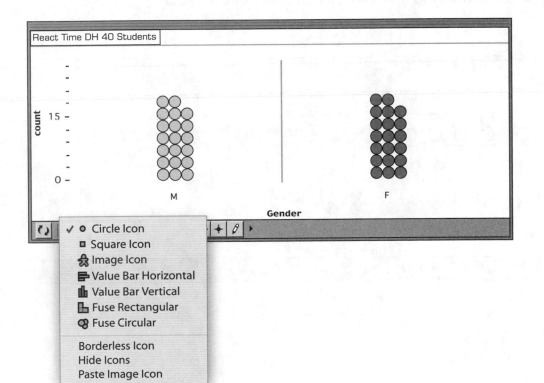

Comparing Data Using Graphs

There are two ways to compare two or more data sets using *TinkerPlots*.

Method 1
Begin with a plot you have made, for example, Fastest_Time.

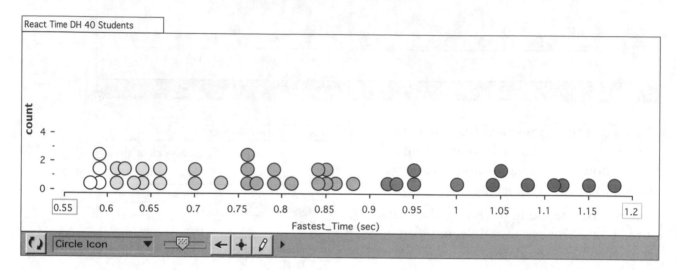

Suppose you want to compare boys' and girls' fastest times. When you select the attribute of Gender, the icons change to two colors. Select an icon and drag it vertically up to make two plots that show Fastest_Time, one for each group of students.

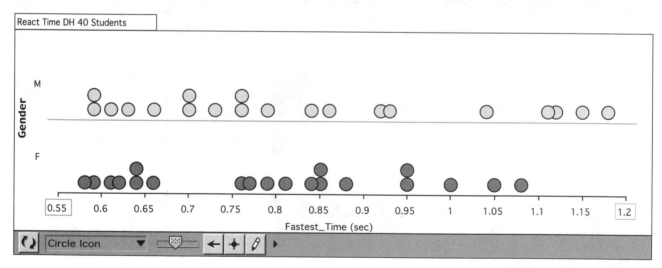

Method 2

Set up two different graphs. When you use two different graphs, you may need to make changes in the scales of one or both graphs in order to have the *same scales* on both graphs. Suppose you want to compare Fastest_Time with Slowest_Time. You would use two different graphs. However, because the scales are different, you cannot easily make comparisons.

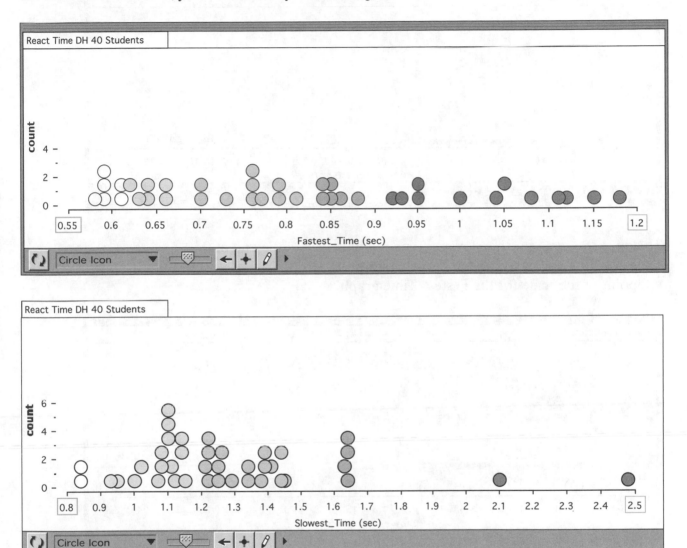

To adjust the scale for Fastest_Time, double-click on the end of the scale at 1.2. You can edit the axis by changing "1.2" to "2.5," the upper end point of the scale for the Slowest_Time graph. When you do this, you will see the lower end of the scale automatically adjusts to 0.5; this endpoint is fine.

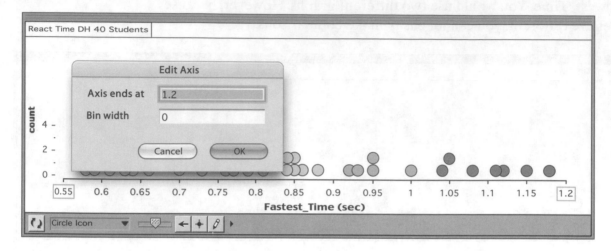

To adjust the scale for the Slowest_Time double-click on the end of the scale at 0.8. You can edit the axis by changing "0.8" to "0.5," the lower endpoint of the scale for the Fastest_Time graph.

To color all the icons identically, select the title "Attribute" on any data card. This will cause all the icons to change to a light blue color. Notice the scales that resulted from the changes just made.

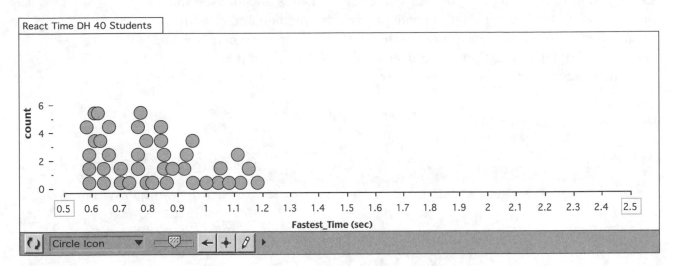

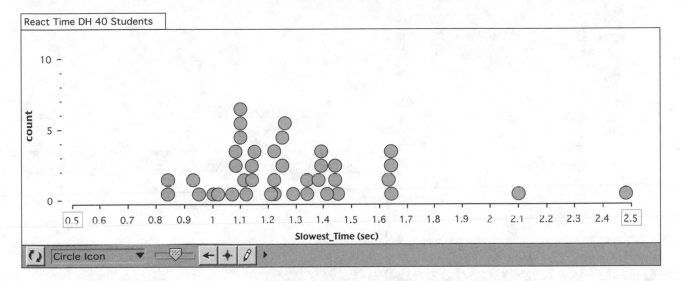

You can make adjustments to the scale on any graph you make, not just two different graphs that you want to compare. Changing the scale often helps make it easier to see the shape of the distribution.

Using Mean, Median, and Mode

Once you have made a plot, you can locate the measures of center on the plot. There are two buttons in the menu bar, one for median and one for mean. Next to these buttons is an arrowhead. It gives a menu where you can choose to show the mode and the numeric value(s) for any of these measures of center marked on a graph. You can also show the midrange, a number not used here.

Can you figure out what the midrange is?

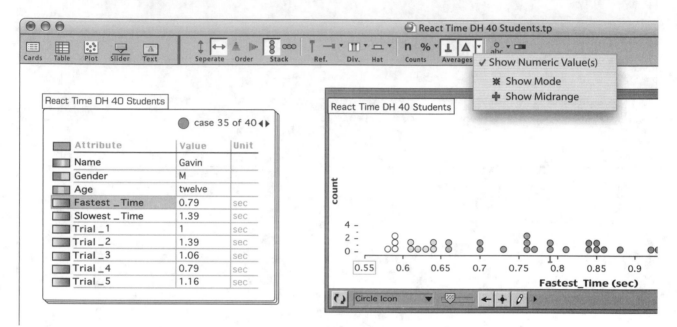

Using Reference Lines and Dividers

Drawing a reference line or dividers lets you partition a distribution so you can look at smaller sections. For example, you often want a count or percent of the number of data values at or above the mean and below the mean. You can view this information easily in two steps.

Step 1 Find the Ref. button on the menu and select the vertical reference line. Move the reference line so it is positioned at the mean value. This helps you see the data above and below the mean.

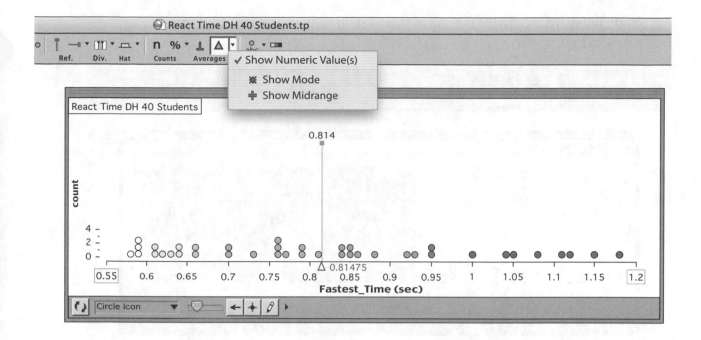

Step 2 Often, you want a count or percent of the number of data values at or above the mean and below the mean. You can add *dividers* that will help you do this. Select the Div. button from the menu. The dividers button divides the distribution into three equal intervals based on the range of the axis. The intervals are shaded alternately white and gray. Find the Counts button. You can choose to display the number of data values in an interval using **n**, the percent of data values in an interval using **%**, or both.

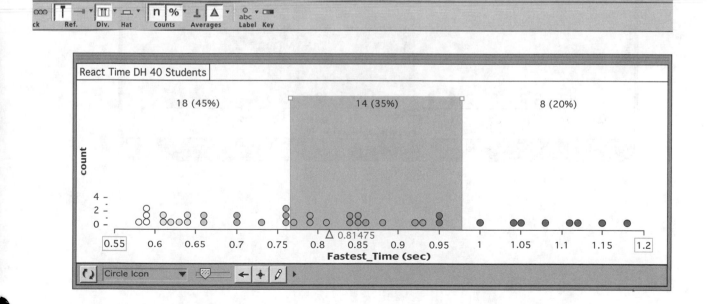

You can move the dividers to show the distribution separated into only two sections.

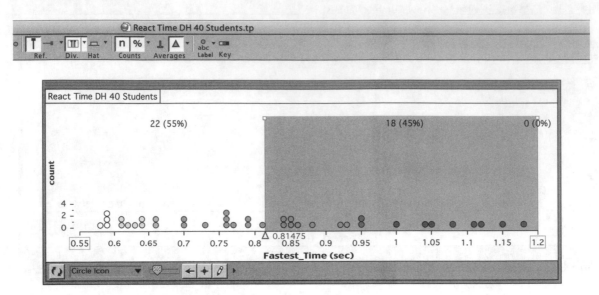

You can see the choices you have for inserting dividers by looking at the menu that is found using the arrow next to Div.

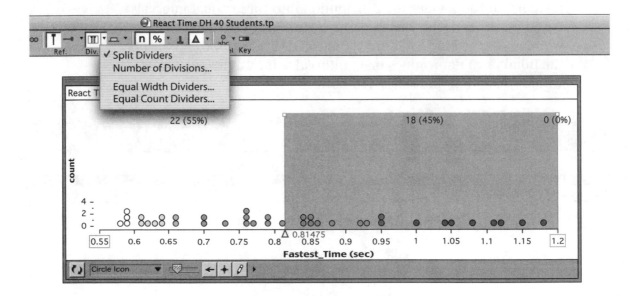

Investigation 4

Exploring Further With *TinkerPlots*

You will use *TinkerPlots* to complete Problem 4.2. You will need roller coaster data, which is in this file: Coasters S & W 9–6–04.tp.

To complete Problem 4.2, you need to know more about:

- Separating distributions horizontally and vertically
- Comparing "slices of plots" and their measures of center and range to look for relationships

Looking for Relationships: Separating Data Horizontally and Vertically

In Problem 4.2, you explore the Top_Speed of wood and steel roller coasters. You also look at speed in relation to several different attributes.

Attributes in the database:

Name of Roller Coaster Ride

Amusement Park Location

State Located

Year Opened

Maximum Drop (feet)

Maximum Height (feet)

Track Length (feet)

Top Speed reported (mi/h)

Duration of Ride (minutes)

(Sharpest) Angle of Descent

Type of Coaster (Wood or Steel)

Attribute	Value	Unit
Name	American Eagle	
Park	Six Flags Great America	
State	IL	
Year_Open	1981	
Maximum_Drop	147	ft
Maximum_Height	127	ft
Track_Length	4650	ft
Top_Speed	66	mph
Duration	2.38	min
Angle_Descent	55	degrees
Type	wood	

To compare the wood and steel roller coasters, you need to make a graph of the speeds of all the roller coasters. Then, select the attribute of Type to separate the data vertically into two groups, wood coasters and steel coasters.

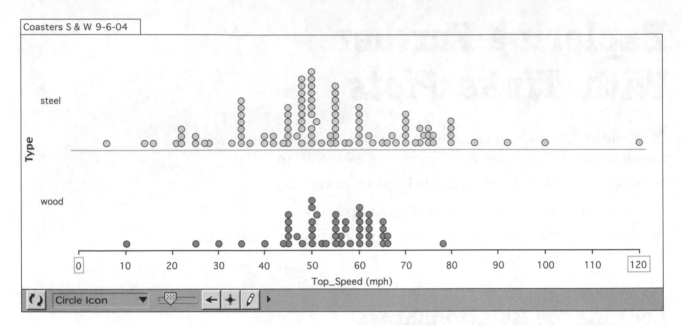

You can use these graphs and the actions you take on the graphs to help you answer the questions from Problem 4.2. For example, the graphs below use dividers to look at and compare sections for each type of coaster.

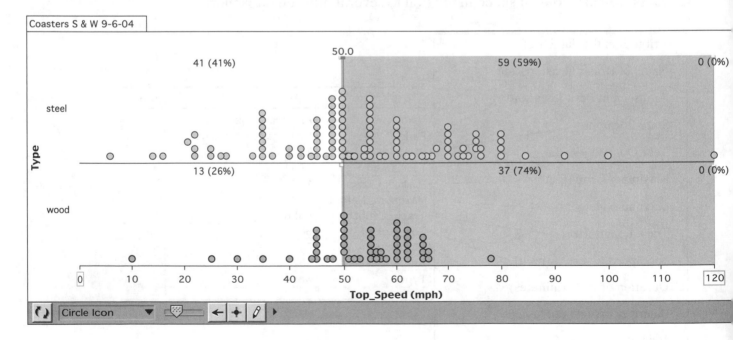

Sometimes you want to look at the relationship between two numerical variables, as in Question D of Problem 4.2. You might wonder if speed of a roller coaster has anything to do with the maximum height of a roller coaster.

Separate the roller coaster data to make a dot plot that shows the distribution of speeds. Then, select the attribute of Maximum_Height. Begin to separate the data vertically to make a partially-separated plot with several "slices" of distributions of speeds as they relate to intervals of heights.

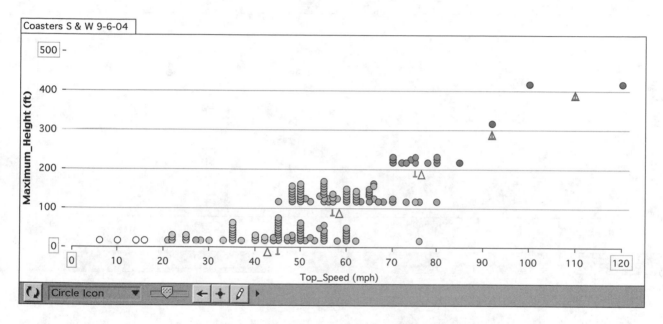

- What do you notice about the speeds in relation to the heights? Why do you think this might be true?

- What do you notice about the means and medians of the speeds in relation to the heights of the coasters? Why do you think this might be true?

When the plot is fully-separated, you will get a graph like the one shown on the next page.

Using Medians and Reference Lines With Fully-Separated Plots

When you look at relationships between two different attributes like Top_Speed and Maximum_Height, you can locate the median for each attribute and place reference lines at these two medians. This will divide the graph into four parts.

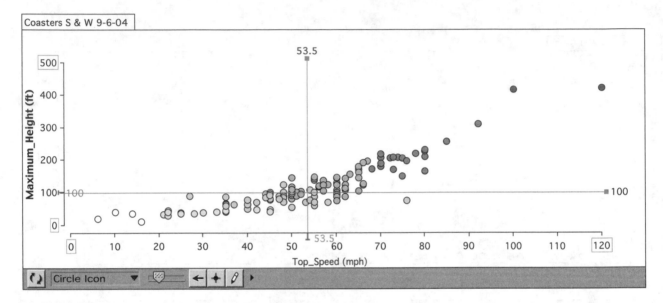

- What is true about the data located in the upper right quadrant?
- What is true about the data located in the upper left quadrant?
- What is true about the data located in the lower right quadrant?
- What is true about the data located in the lower left quadrant?

Index

INDEX

Acknowledgments

Team Credits

The people who made up the **Connected Mathematics 2** team—representing editorial, editorial services, design services, and production services—are listed below. Bold type denotes core team members.

Leora Adler, Judith Buice, Kerry Cashman, Patrick Culleton, Sheila DeFazio, Richard Heater, **Barbara Hollingdale, Jayne Holman,** Karen Holtzman, **Etta Jacobs,** Christine Lee, Carolyn Lock, Catherine Maglio, **Dotti Marshall,** Rich McMahon, Eve Melnechuk, Kristin Mingrone, Terri Mitchell, **Marsha Novak,** Irene Rubin, Donna Russo, Robin Samper, Siri Schwartzman, **Nancy Smith,** Emily Soltanoff, **Mark Tricca,** Paula Vergith, Roberta Warshaw, Helen Young

Additional Credits

Diana Bonfilio, Mairead Reddin, Michael Torocsik, nSight, Inc.

Technical Illustration

Schawk, Inc.

Cover Design

tom white.images

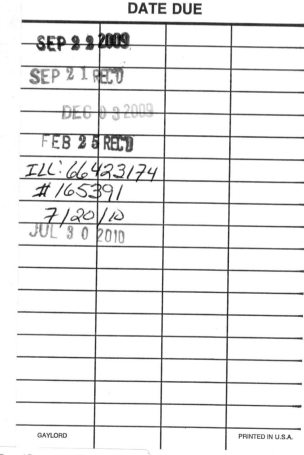